THE NOVELS
OF JOHN STEINBECK

A CRITICAL STUDY

HOWARD LEVANT

With an Introduction by Warren French

University of Missouri Press, 1974

Excerpts from the following books are reprinted by permission of
The Viking Press, Inc.: From *The Log from the Sea of Cortez* by
John Steinbeck, Copyright 1941 by John Steinbeck and Edward F.
Ricketts, Copyright 1951 by John Steinbeck, Copyright © renewed
1969 by John Steinbeck and Edward F. Ricketts, Jr. From *Cup of Gold*
by John Steinbeck, Copyright 1929, Copyright © renewed 1957 by
John Steinbeck. From *To a God Unknown* by John Steinbeck, Copy-
right 1933, Copyright © renewed 1961 by John Steinbeck. From *The
Pastures of Heaven* by John Steinbeck, Copyright 1932, Copyright ©
renewed 1960 by John Steinbeck. From *Tortilla Flat* by John Steinbeck, Copyright 1935, Copyright © renewed 1963 by John Steinbeck.
From *In Dubious Battle* by John Steinbeck, Copyright 1936, Copyright
© renewed 1964 by John Steinbeck. From *The Grapes of Wrath* by
John Steinbeck, Copyright 1939, Copyright © renewed 1967 by John
Steinbeck. From *Of Mice and Men* by John Steinbeck, Copyright
1937, Copyright © renewed 1965 by John Steinbeck. From *The Moon
Is Down* by John Steinbeck, Copyright 1942, Copyright © renewed
by Elaine Steinbeck, John Steinbeck IV, and Thom Steinbeck. From
Burning Bright by John Steinbeck, Copyright 1950 by John Steinbeck.
From *Cannery Row* by John Steinbeck, Copyright 1945 by John
Steinbeck, Copyright © renewed 1973 by Elaine Steinbeck, John
Steinbeck IV, and Thom Steinbeck. From *The Pearl* by John Steinbeck,
Copyright 1945 by John Steinbeck, Copyright © renewed 1973 by
Elaine Steinbeck, John Steinbeck IV, and Thom Steinbeck. From *The
Wayward Bus* by John Steinbeck, Copyright 1947 by John Steinbeck.
From *East of Eden* by John Steinbeck, Copyright 1952 by John Stein-
beck. From *Sweet Thursday* by John Steinbeck, Copyright 1954 by
John Steinbeck. From *The Short Reign of Pippin IV* by John Stein-
beck, Copyright 1957 by John Steinbeck. From *The Winter of Our
Discontent* by John Steinbeck, Copyright © 1961 by John Steinbeck.

Permissions for quotation from a number of other works are acknowledged at point of use.

The substance of Chapter 2 appeared as "*Tortilla Flat*: The Shape
of John Steinbeck's Career," in *PMLA* (October 1970). Reprinted by
permission of the Modern Language Association of America. The
substance of Chapter 3 appeared as "The Unity of *In Dubious
Battle*: Violence and Dehumanization," in *Modern Fiction Studies*, 11
(Spring 1965). *Modern Fiction Studies* © 1965 by Purdue Research
Foundation, West Lafayette, Ind. Reprinted by permission.

TO VIRGINIA, JONATHAN, AND MOIRA

Contents

Introduction, Warren French, ... ix

Preface, ... 1

1. The First Novels, ... 10
   Cup of Gold
   To a God Unknown
   The Pastures of Heaven

2. The First Public Success, ... 52
   Tortilla Flat

3. Panorama and Drama Unified, ... 74
   In Dubious Battle

4. The Fully Matured Art, ... 93
   The Grapes of Wrath

5. Three Play-Novelettes, ... 130
   Of Mice and Men
   The Moon Is Down
   Burning Bright

6. "Is" Thinking, ... 164
   Cannery Row

7. The Natural Parable, ... 185
   The Pearl

8. Pure Allegory, ... 207
   The Wayward Bus

9. Lapsed Allegory, ... 234
   East of Eden

10. "Hooptedoodle," 259
    Sweet Thursday

11. Jeu d'esprit, ... 273
    The Short Reign of Pippin IV

12. The End of the Road, ... 288
    The Winter of Our Discontent

Epilogue, ... 301

Selected Works by John Steinbeck, ... 303

Introduction

A Turning Point in Steinbeck Studies

"Too often Steinbeck's work has been viewed piecemeal, even when the critical intention has been a rounded view," writes Howard Levant in his preface to this book. The same comment may be made of published surveys of Steinbeck criticism.

Peter Lisca prepared the earliest of these for E. W. Tedlock, Jr., and C. V. Wicker's *Steinbeck and His Critics* (Albuquerque: University of New Mexico Press, 1957) and drew upon it for his own *The Wide World of John Steinbeck* (New Brunswick, N.J.: Rutgers University Press, 1958). He later expanded it into "A Survey of Steinbeck Criticism to 1971" for Tetsumaro Hayashi's *Steinbeck's Literary Dimension* (Metuchen, N.J.: Scarecrow Press, 1973). In the meantime I had contributed a differently organized survey to Jackson Bryer's *Fifteen Modern American Authors* (Durham, N.C.: Duke University Press, 1969), which was updated when the book was revised as *Sixteen Modern American Authors* (New York: W. W. Norton & Company, Inc.).

While there is no need to tread again the ground covered by all these essays, a differently oriented review of major criticisms is needed to point out why Levant's book is not just another study of a frequently discussed author, but a starting point for any useful future analyses of Steinbeck's fiction—why it marks a turning point from unsynchronized and often repetitive appreciations to a long-needed rigorously objective comparison of the individual success or failure of the fictions against criteria precisely formulated in advance.

Just as Levant observes that Steinbeck's work has often been viewed "piecemeal," so previous surveys of the criticism have been "after the fact" accounts that report what trends have developed rather than measure the adequacy of the criticism in the study of any single aspect of Steinbeck's art. Just as Levant in this book attempts consistently to consider the "structural adequacy" of Steinbeck's longer fictions, so I wish in this introductory essay to review major earlier criticism from the single viewpoint of determining its contribution to the problem of finding as Levant does an "intelligent and coherent sense of what structure is and can do" as the "something missing" in Steinbeck's "otherwise brilliant work."

The study of few authors has yet progressed to the point of subjecting them to this kind of "constructionist" criticism—an examination of the adequacy of their blueprints to the embodiment of their vision. We have so far had only "appreciations" of even such respected contemporaries of Steinbeck's as Katherine Anne Porter, Thornton Wilder, and Thomas Wolfe. Richard Lehan's *Theodore Dreiser: His World and His Novels* (Carbondale: Southern Illinois University Press) appeared as recently as 1969 and Sheldon Grebstein's *Hemingway's Craft* (from the same press) in 1973. Few books even yet undertake to study an author's artistry in the invaluable manner of James E. Miller, Jr.'s *The Fictional Technique of Scott Fitzgerald* (The Hague: Martinus Nijhoff, 1957, revised in 1964 as *F. Scott Fitzgerald: His Art and His Technique,* New York: New York University Press). As I shall illustrate, the paradigmatic work of this kind of "constructionist" criticism is John G. Cawelti's study of popular American Western stories, *The Six-Gun Mystique* (Bowling Green, O.: Bowling Green University Press), published in 1971.

Although Levant's book thus breaks new ground in Steinbeck studies and exemplifies a kind of criticism that has only recently begun to flourish, it is organized in the generally chronological manner of the previous book-length studies of the novelist. Such an approach is, I think, inescapable because Steinbeck's early and late novels are so different from each other that they cannot be lumped together as if they were the products of an unvarying approach to certain technical problems. The one thing that Steinbeck's admirers and detractors agree upon is that there is a marked decline in the artistry of Steinbeck's work after 1945. A major reason for the importance of Levant's study is that it provides an objective framework for analyzing the causes of a decline that has hitherto been attributed almost entirely to events in the author's private life.

Perhaps something about Steinbeck, in fact, and his particular kind of popularity is suggested by the recognition that none of the books about him have been pioneering studies like Miller's of Fitzgerald's technique or Max Westbrook's of Walter Van Tilburg Clark's mystique. Books about Steinbeck have reflected rather than established the fashionable critical stances of the years that produced them.

There was no comprehensive study of Steinbeck's fiction until Peter Lisca's *The Wide World of John Steinbeck* appeared in 1958, after Steinbeck had been publishing for nearly three decades and only a few years before he was awarded the Nobel Prize for literature after the publication of his final novel in 1961. Early critiques had been climaxed by Harry T. Moore's *John Steinbeck: A First Critical Study* (Chicago: Normandie House, 1939), which appeared only a few months after Steinbeck scored his greatest success with *The Grapes of Wrath*. As might be expected of a lifelong enthusiast for D. H. Lawrence, Moore had already begun to lose interest in Steinbeck in the late 1930s as the passionate lyricism of his early books gave way to increasingly schematized social protest. Since—as Peter Lisca points out—Moore's book concentrated on the individual merits of each novel and lacked "an easy hypothesis for subsequent reviewers and critics to follow," it has exercised little influence.

Searching for a guide among the early writers of such "get-acquainted" studies, many subsequent critics have been overawed by the strictures of fashionable Establishment critic Edmund Wilson in *The Boys in the Back Room* (San Francisco: Colt Press, 1940) and have echoed his dubious assertion that Steinbeck "animalized" human beings. In their acceptance of Wilson's interpretation they neglected Frederic I. Carpenter's wise perception, expressed in "John Steinbeck: American Dreamer" (*Southwest Review*, July

1941) and "The Philosophical Joads" (*College English,* December 1941) of the novelist as the heir of Emerson, Whitman, and William James in decrying the loss of the American dream in an irresponsible lust for possession. (A short book by Carpenter in the early 1940s might have entirely changed the course of Steinbeck's critical reputation.) Both Carpenter and Wilson, however—as well as the handful of critics that wrote about Steinbeck during World War II when publication was difficult and most critics engaged in other activities—concentrated on what Steinbeck said rather than how he said it. When criticism became a flourishing business again on our crowded campuses after World War II, Steinbeck's "decline" had already begun, and there was little interest in the novelist's "message" of the 1930s. One of the best single essays about Steinbeck, Chester Eisinger's "Jeffersonian Agrarianism in *The Grapes of Wrath*" (*University of Kansas City Review,* Winter 1947) went virtually unnoted; and if no one was interested in what Steinbeck said, there was no reason to delve into the problem of how he put his messages together.

Peter Lisca announced, however, in the preface to his book that he wished to pay attention particularly to the "relatively unexplored" matter of Steinbeck's "craftsmanship," examining the novels and short stories "for techniques employed, as well as for the content achieved by these techniques." (The last phrase indicates the acknowledged influence upon Lisca of the argument advanced in Mark Schorer's essay, "Technique as Discovery" [*Hudson Review,* Spring 1948] that "everything is technique which is not the lump of experience itself.")

"Craftsmanship" turns out to mean to Lisca principally the author's manipulation of language into a distinctive style. *The Wide World of John Steinbeck* appeared at the peaking of the influence of the "'New Criticism" that placed strong emphasis upon close reading of texts and emphasized the artist's creation of "irony." Although New Critics often talked about structure, especially the relationship of the "tenor" of a work to the "vehicle" (though the loosely related critics sometimes exactly shifted the meaning of the two terms), they rarely dealt with works longer than lyric poems or short stories that explored intensively a single, often cryptic situation that usually resulted in some kind of "epiphany." Exhaustive analysis of a whole novel or group of novels appeared an unlikely undertaking for a cult whose high priest speculated that it would take a multi-volumed work to deal adequately with a single ode of Keats's. (Ian Watt's essay on the first paragraph of Henry James's *The Ambassadors* indicated the impracticability of publishing a truly close reading of a novel of any complexity.)

Like his predecessors and contemporaries, Lisca actually says relatively little about the structure of most of the novels. He brushes aside such a long-debated question as the categorization of *The Pastures of Heaven* with the statement that it "is not, strictly speaking, a novel, partly because the several stories are too autonomous, structurally and aesthetically." Despite Lisca's initial suggestion that his study was to differ from those that had focused on Steinbeck's "social message," it consisted largely of thematic analyses.

The limitations of Lisca's book as a study of structure are indicated by this part of his account of *Of Mice and Men*:

> The highly patterned effect achieved by these incremental motifs of symbol, action, and language is the knife edge on which criticism of *Of Mice and Men* divides. . . . On one side, it is claimed that this strong patterning creates a sense of contrivance and mechanical action, and, on the other, that the patterning actually gives a meaningful design to the story, a tone of classic fate. What is obviously needed here is some objective critical tool for determining under what conditions a sense of inevitability (to use a neutral word) should be experienced as mechanical contrivance, and when it should be experienced as catharsis effected by a sense of fate. Such a tool cannot be forged within the limits of this study (p. 137).

Howard Levant has produced precisely the kind of tool that Lisca mentions in his last sentence. Why have we had to wait for it fifteen years, a period during which Steinbeck criticism has flourished?

Lisca's last sentence also suggests that, understandably,

he did not have the space for such an effort, considering all the other tasks confronting the writer of the first full-scale study of a prolific novelist. That the forging of the tool required, as in this present effort, a book about as long as his own reinforces his estimate of its extent. Yet Lisca's use of the term *pattern* raises the doubt that he envisioned the kind of constructionist criticism that Levant has produced.

From the first sentence of the quotation above, it is evident that Lisca conceives of "patterning" almost exclusively in verbal terms (in fiction even symbols and actions are created with words). His use of the term *incremental* suggests that he conceives of patterns as—in a most extreme form—a musician like Alban Berg does when he assembles his composition by using predetermined tone-blocks.

In artistic contexts, however, "patterns"—while infinitely variable in detail—can be generally conceived of in two irreconcilable groups. On one hand there are "formulas" or "rituals"—patterns that are predetermined and simply chosen by or imposed upon the artist, so that in the most extreme examples—the classical ode, or the limerick, or the liturgies of the Catholic churches—conventional elements preclude individual innovations. We often tend to think of patterns as being thus essentially conventional. But there is another kind of patterning that is most succinctly suggested by Walt Whitman's question in *Song of Myself,* "I teach straying from me, yet who can stray from me?," which follows his assertion that "The boy I love, the same becomes a man not through derived power, but in his own right,/ Wicked rather than virtuous out of conformity or fear." Whitman's implication is that although the individual is free to choose his own patterns—even if they seem to menace the common culture—behind all such diverse individual activity there is a common underlying pattern that directs all human endeavor toward the same end. It is with these underlying, usually hidden patterns that the constructionist critic is concerned. John Cawelti explains in *The Six-Gun Mystique* how they differ from conventions:

> Conventions are elements which are known to both the creator and his audience beforehand—they consist of things like fa-

vorite plots, stereotyped characters, accepted ideas, commonly known metaphors and other linguistic devices, etc. Inventions, on the other hand, are elements which are uniquely imagined by the creator such as new kinds of characters, ideas, or linguistic forms (p. 27).

Only in dealing with the problem posed by the relationship of the Joad story and the intercalary chapters in *The Grapes of Wrath* does Lisca become involved with the comprehensive structural questions concerning a story; even his analysis of this novel dwells upon the way in which details are interrelated by themes, symbols, and styles. Of *Tortilla Flat* and *Cannery Row*, he is content to observe that they are "loose and episodic." Although, in conclusion, Lisca writes that Steinbeck's "structure not only orders materials, but gives them meaning," he does not consider the possible relationship of Steinbeck's problems with structuring to the rapid decline in artistry that he recognizes in the novels that were written after 1947. Rather, he finds the causes principally—as most other critics before Levant have—in the author's personal problems. Lisca thus provides a perceptive New Critical reading of Steinbeck's novels, reinforced by invaluable comments from the author's correspondence with his publishers and agents; but *The Wide World of John Steinbeck* is really—as the brevity and largely biographical nature of the conclusion suggests—a series of brilliant, uncorrelated readings rather than the kind of diorama on which the landscape of the novelist's world unreels before us as a unified picture.

The 1960s will doubtless be remembered as the decade of "series" of author studies—inevitable monuments to a dying school of criticism—and each eventually had to include its book on John Steinbeck. As Lisca had pointed out with understandable irritation, these books—written in compliance with the rigid formats imposed by editors and publishers—often simply echoed his organization and approach.

Although my own *John Steinbeck* (New York: Twayne Publishers, 1961) was the first of these summations to appear, I would like to pass over it for the moment in order to consider in conjunction with Lisca's book the only other that he has mentioned favorably, Joseph Fontenrose's *John Steinbeck: An Introduction and Interpretation* (New York: Barnes & Noble, Inc., 1963). Though organized in the same book-by-book fashion as the others, Fontenrose's adds more new material to Lisca's than, I believe, any other work until the book in hand. A student of classical mythology, Fontenrose illuminated especially Steinbeck's use of legendary material; but this aspect of his work is not related to our present inquiry.

Fontenrose is also considerably more sensitive to patterns than Lisca. He produced what has become a standard interpretation of *The Pastures of Heaven*, and he presents detailed parallels between the narrative sequence of Malory's *Morte d'Arthur* and *Tortilla Flat*. Although he generally follows Lisca on the pattern of *The Grapes of Wrath*, he produces a dazzlingly original analysis of *Cannery Row* as a virtuoso treatment of the mythical theme of "the Logos, the Word made flesh," in which "the author is a demiurge whose Word converts chaos into cosmos." If he had followed the pattern of this chapter throughout his book, he might have produced a tightly patterned study that would relate all Steinbeck's writings to his conclusion that in these novels "biology takes the place of history, mysticism takes the place of humanity." In reviewing the book I countered this theorizing that Steinbeck lacked "a genuine theory of society" with my own—not unkindly intended—that Fontenrose lacked "a genuine theory of fiction." Years later in a gracious correspondence, he acknowledged that he had not thought much about theories of fiction and asked about my own.

I referred him principally to Northrop Frye's statement in *The Critical Path* (Bloomington: Indiana University Press, 1971) that "the modern critic's approach is . . . not allegorical but archetypal; he seeks not so much to explain a poem in terms of its external relation to history or philosophy, but to preserve its identity as a poem and see it in its total mythological context" (precisely as Fontenrose did in his analysis of *Cannery Row*). In what I consider the most important part of my response, though, I did not so much develop my own theory as explain why I felt a need for some theory was urgent today. I should like briefly to adapt this paragraph:

> I fear that many of my former instructors would be troubled and mystified by the amorality of Frye's views; but when teachers and students no longer share the same values—as they seem not to today—students are not likely to be much concerned about what instructors think; they are going to be interested only in what can be demonstrated to have some relationship to them and their problems. To put the matter in a way that some may find vulgar, we are going to have to start selling literature.

The significant way in which I think both Lisca's and Fontenrose's books are exemplary of the critical tendencies of the years of vanishing gentility that produced them is that both proceed from the felicitous assumption that an audience already interested in literature and respectful of literary criticism exists. The critic need not, therefore, consider why the audience should be interested in his work. He is free to write an appreciation. The detailed appreciations of the New Critics of the 1940s and 1950s differed greatly from the demands of Humanistic critics of the 1920s and 1930s like Harry T. Moore or Edmund Wilson for a more Dionysian or Apollonian approach to experience. At their best, the later studies like Lisca's and Fontenrose's were grounded in a close and respectful reading of the text. Both kinds of appreciation, however, arose from a confidence—though a gradually decreasing one—that the audience asked only of the critic, Did the artist say the right things well?

Perhaps my view is too grim, but I am not convinced that an audience for such appreciations any longer exists. We cannot assume that many people today love literature. I think that before we can now talk about books and authors we must redevelop an audience interested in books and authors. Appalling as the suggestion may be to those who revere literary study, we must once again sell literature to a bewildered, suspicious, and activist public.

Most of the books about Steinbeck since Fontenrose's might collectively carry the title of Lester Jay Marks's *Thematic Design in the Novels of John Steinbeck* (The Hague: Mouton, 1969), since they treat some aspects of what Marks most comprehensively describes—as I reported in *American Literary Scholarship, 1970* (Durham, N.C.: Duke University Press, 1972)—as "a system of ideas . . . beneath the surface diversities of Steinbeck's work that reside in three recurrent thematic patterns, '—man's nature as a religious creature' who must 'create a godhead to satisfy his personal need,' a biological view of man as a 'group animal' with a will and intelligence separate from those of the individuals composing it, and the 'non-teleological concept that man lives without knowledge of the cause of his existence,' yet is spurred in a search for values by the very mystery of his life." Although emphases have differed, most of the short books about Steinbeck in various series have concentrated on religious and philosophical themes.

Richard Astro's *John Steinbeck and Edward F. Ricketts: The Shaping of a Novelist* (Minneapolis: University of Minnesota Press, 1973) differs from the others in including much new biographical material and focusing upon Ricketts's influence on Steinbeck, especially on the formation of the novelist's "non-teleological philosophy," which has intrigued many critics. Like the others, however, it is primarily concerned with what Northrop Frye describes as the explanation of literary work "in terms of its external relation to history or philosophy."

The limitations of such thematic analysis are set forth by John Cawelti in *The Six-Gun Mystique*, which has implications far beyond the popular subgenre it explores. (Tendencies at work in subtle ways in complex and original creations may be most easily illuminated through their more obvious manifestations in conventional art. Furthermore, Steinbeck's fiction up to *East of Eden* emerges from the same *Weltanschauung* as the formula Western, so Cawelti's speculations are directly applicable.)

Pointing out that "the concept of theme is extremely vague, for any element of a work can serve as a theme,"

Cawelti goes on to stress that "the method of theme analysis . . . encourages us to take elements out of context and therefore to interpret not a total work, but a random collection of isolated elements," as well as that "the analysis of works as direct reflections of social and cultural themes commonly leads to a simple equation between the works of art and other kinds of experience," even though, he argues, "if anything is clear about our experience of narrative or dramatic works it is that it is not the same as our experience of life itself." Works of art, he goes on, are experienced "as something somewhat different from life itself . . . as whole structures of action, thought, and feeling" (pp. 5–6).

On the basis of these reservations about thematic analysis of works of art, Cawelti proceeds to set forth an alternative mode of analysis that can best be called "constructionist criticism":

> A good plot model should provide a basis for explaining why each event and character is present in the work, and why these events and characters are placed in the setting they occupy. If some element remains unexplained, it is clear that the organizing principles have not been adequately stated (pp. 24–25).

I had hoped in my *John Steinbeck*, especially by answering some previous criticisms, to provide a series of the kind of "adequate plot models" that Cawelti calls for. The book grew out of papers that I had written as a graduate student on *The Red Pony* and *The Grapes of Wrath* and an uncompleted one on *Cannery Row*. I would have been happiest to write a book comprised of essays on these works and those like *The Pastures of Heaven* and *East of Eden* that present similar problems of patterning, but the format of the series that I helped to launch required another comprehensive group of New Critical readings of all the major works. Further, I had not yet hit upon anything like the generally useful analytical method that Howard Levant employs here, nor had I been able to articulate my own developing concept of the aims of criticism as precisely as John Cawelti does in the quotation above. In recently revising my book, I had originally intended to try to produce a coherent group of plot models to determine whether all the elements in Steinbeck's fictions could be explained. (I would add to John Cawelti's statement the reservation that sometimes elements cannot be explained because the author's own patterning has been inadequate or confused.)

Asked to write an essay on Steinbeck for a symposium on Naturalism, however, I found that I was beginning even to have doubts about Joseph Fontenrose's assertion that Steinbeck had no "genuine theory of society." While the novelist lacked faith in any fixed political system, he had a definite concept of man's relationship to society—rather, he had two. What confuses critics is that he completely reversed his concept during the composition of *The Grapes of Wrath*. I thought it essential to try to determine just how Steinbeck saw the world before I inspected his creation of fictional worlds. My revised book seeks, therefore, to clarify Steinbeck's views of the world and the drastic difference between his early and late fiction. Instead of paralleling Howard Levant's book, as it might have, mine partially complements it; more: I have immediately benefited from having an advance knowledge of his cogent analyses of the strengths and weaknesses of the designs of Steinbeck's books. I am sure that his observations are going to be equally useful to anyone who in the future deals with Steinbeck's fictions from any specialized point of view. Certainly I cannot imagine anyone undertaking henceforth to discuss Steinbeck confidently without pondering Levant's arguments about the adequacy of Steinbeck's patterns.

I do not expect that all others will unquestioningly accept Levant's conclusions. While I generally agree with his evaluations, we differ seriously about two books, *Of Mice and Men* and *The Pearl*. I understand from the structural point of view why he takes the positions that he does; but from the viewpoint of my own current interest in the relationship of the individual to society, I find the characters in *Of Mice and Men*—which I think Levant undervalues—fascinating people, and those in *The Pearl*—which I think he overvalues —bores. I find it interesting, however, that the only books about which we disagree come at landmark stages in Steinbeck's career: *Of Mice and Men* is the latest product of his earlier pessimism; *The Pearl*, the first work in which a determined optimism reduces the characters to two-dimensional symbols. Levant's comprehensive study provides, nevertheless, a framework for understanding why we disagree, so that differences of opinion need not lead to name-calling or to the refusal to judge that makes literary scholarship seem an aimless game to many outsiders.

I do not wish to leave the impression that Howard Levant is the only critic to contribute to the constructionist study of Steinbeck's work. Two earlier efforts deserve attention in conjunction with his work, though both serve only as supplements to it.

Lawrence William Jones's *John Steinbeck as Fabulist* (Muncie, Ind.: Steinbeck Monograph Series No. 3, 1973) is an important start toward an investigation of Steinbeck's finally disastrous fascination with the fable form, based on the theories advanced in Sheldon Sack's *Fiction and the Shape of Belief* (Berkeley: University of California Press, 1964). Lamentably, Jones was accidentally killed before he could put his work into final form, but his preliminary observations have been brilliantly and sympathetically edited by Marston LaFrance. Some full study of Steinbeck's work in the light of Sacks's categorization of fictional forms remains to be accomplished.

The most useful approach to some of Steinbeck's most controversial works, *The Pastures of Heaven* and *Tortilla Flat*, is provided by Forrest L. Ingram's *Representative Short Story Cycles of the Twentieth Century* (The Hague: Mouton, 1971), which develops a new theory for understanding some of the most important fictions of the twentieth century like Sherwood Anderson's *Winesburg, Ohio*. Ingram's book concentrates, however, on Anderson, Faulkner, and Kafka and mentions Steinbeck's books only in passing. He is preparing, I am pleased to report, further studies that will deal more fully with the complex structures of some of Steinbeck's story-cycles.

Howard Levant, it should be observed in conclusion, has properly not ventured in this ground-breaking study into a consideration of "influences" upon Steinbeck's increasing problems with the structuring of his works. I should like to suggest, however, at least one that should be investigated.

In 1962 Steinbeck wrote a preface for a new edition of *Story Writing* (New York: Viking Press, Inc.), a book by his former Stanford instructor, Edith Ronald Mirrielees, in which he observes that the basic rule she gave her students was "a story to be effective had to convey something from writer to reader, and the power of its offering was the measure of its excellence." On this point of "conveying something," Professor Mirrielees was herself much less mellow than an aging Steinbeck as he recalled her teaching. "In the thinking out of most stories," she enjoins on the first page of her book, "the thing the story is about, as apart from what merely happens in it, is of the utmost importance."

As you read Howard Levant's comments, consider whether many times—especially in *East of Eden* and other later novels—"the thing the story is about" may not have overwhelmed "what happens in it," to the detriment of the story's artistry. In *The Red Pony*, which both Levant and I admire as one of Steinbeck's finest achievements, "the thing the story is about" is "what happens in it." But what this book shows, above all, is why the same thing cannot be said of some of the later works.

W.F.
Cornish Flat, N.H.
March, 1974

Preface

A sad parallel to the popularity of John Steinbeck is the consensus among critics: Steinbeck is a flawed artist. No one denies Steinbeck's brilliance—in the handling of individual scenes, the creation of memorable characters, and above all in the possession of a superb and varied colloquial style. But there is an absence of some essential quality, noticeable before 1940, and pronounced—often disastrously pronounced—after 1940.

That something is missing is not in question, but what is missing has never quite been defined.

My belief is that Steinbeck has an abundance of every gift and craft the novelist can have—except an intelligent and coherent sense of what structure is and can do. I have written this book to consider in depth the structural adequacy of Steinbeck's longer fiction. For this purpose, I accept the rather precise definitions of both structure and materials offered by Austin Warren and René Wellek:

> It would be better [in view of the difficulties in the use of such terms as form and content for literary analysis] to rechristen all of the aesthetically indifferent elements "materials," while the manner in which they acquire aesthetic efficacy may be styled "structure." This distinction is by no means a simple renaming of the old pair, content and form. It cuts right across the old boundary lines. "Materials" include elements formerly considered part of the content, and parts formerly considered formal. "Structure" as a concept includes both content and form so far as they are organized for aesthetic purposes.[1]

As a gloss on this definition, consider the established distinction "with respect to structure . . . between two over-

1. René Wellek and Austin Warren, *Theory of Literature* (New York: Harcourt, Brace & Co., 1949), p. 141. Reprinted by permission of Harcourt Brace Jovanovich, Inc.

lapping but recognizable types of fiction—the panoramic (or epic) and the dramatic (scenic or well-made)."[2]

These definitions summarize a widely accepted perspective in critical theory; that perspective illuminates the essential reason for Steinbeck's inability in most of his novels, especially over a range of novels, to reach the highest eminence. Particularly, he has a continuing difficulty in fusing a structure and specific materials into a harmonious unity.

Steinbeck was very much aware of this problem, as evidenced in private letters and notes, in his published criticism, and in the novels themselves. It is not too much to say that for Steinbeck the significantly conscious effort in writing a novel was located precisely in attempts to work out a relationship between structure and materials. Not many writers—not even Henry James—have been as self-conscious or as puzzled as Steinbeck in facing this aspect of the art of narrative. It follows that Steinbeck is not benefited markedly by his striking if occasional success in handling the relationship between structure and materials, for each try tends to be a new effort within a consistent range. Most obviously, certain identifiable technical situations recur in Steinbeck's longer fiction.

A Steinbeck novel tends to have either a panoramic or a dramatic structure. Steinbeck works at the extremes; he rarely combines panoramic and dramatic structures. Usually a panoramic structure in a Steinbeck novel is a series of episodes that are related to each other by little more than chronology. A dramatic structure in a Steinbeck novel is more tightly organized: Events and characters are bound neatly into firm relationships by a brief or highly selective time sequence and often by a moral or philosophic motif. Steinbeck uses a fairly relaxed style with a panoramic structure; his dramatic structure has a tenser, more patterned style. A typical defect in a Steinbeck novel is that its structure— whatever its type—is developed for its own sake, independent of the materials, to the extent that structure and ma-

2. *Dictionary of World Literature,* ed. Joseph T. Shipley (New York: The Philosophical Library, 1943), p. 408. Reprinted by permission of The Philosophical Library.

terials tend to pull apart. This defect is evident in a majority of Steinbeck's novels, but it is especially evident when Steinbeck relies on allegorical elements or an allegorical scheme to shore up or stiffen either type of structure. On the other hand, a Steinbeck novel is most successful when its structure is fused harmoniously with the greatest possible variety of materials. This success is rare, but it is nearly absolute when it does occur. Finally, in such novels Steinbeck mingles panoramic and dramatic structures in developing the materials.

Repeatedly Steinbeck uses a number of formal devices to intensify the ordinary effect of a structure or, more frequently, to achieve the external appearance of an operative form by means of technique when an organic structure is not inherent in particular materials. The proliferation of such devices is a measure of Steinbeck's interest in form. I note the most common:

1. the frame,
2. the repetition or the leading use of names or significant initials,
3. interchapters or general statements of intention within the novel,
4. moral fables woven into the novel,
5. paired characters that suggest moral opposites,
6. split (not double or duplicate) heroes who suggest some basic human division, as between mind and body,
7. certain thematic motifs that become allegorical abstractions when they are not realized personal, social, or moral facts: the juxtaposition of life and death, love and hate, the people and impersonal instruments of power, or the ideal good life in contrast to reality.

At best, these devices serve to intensify the effect of a structure that is developing well, but they cannot save a structure that fails to develop properly for other reasons. Hence, they are distinctly secondary aids to order.

Certain broad stylistic effects appear on occasion to help in providing a novel with an adequate structure by establishing a tone or frame of reference. Extreme examples include argot, which is used in a number of novels, and the "universal language" in *Burning Bright*. Like the formal devices just listed—and for the same reason—these stylistic effects are secondary aids to an orderly development of a Steinbeck novel.

Steinbeck worked out a general theory of value in 1940 in *Sea of Cortez*; the theory has exact relevance to the peculiarly exaggerated extension of panoramic structure that appears in many of the late novels. Steinbeck gives his theory two names, "non-teleological" and "is" thinking. Merely for convenience, I shall refer consistently to the theory as "is" thinking. I quote, then, from the "Easter Sunday sermon" in *Sea of Cortez*:

> Non-teleological thinking concerns itself primarily not with what should be, or could be, or might be, but rather with what actually "is"—attempting at most to answer the already sufficiently difficult questions *what* or *how*, instead of *why*.[3]

Steinbeck lists several practical examples which suggest that cause–effect relationships are too simplified to be true in experience, that "the truest reason for anything's being so is that it *is*," and that the various genuine reasons for anything "could include everything."[4] The effect of the theory on structure is that any presumed need for artful design in the novel is no longer valid for Steinbeck. The theory implies that characters and events have an order and a rationale as they appear in the objective world; that art cannot improve on this order and rationale; that hence the only function of the artist is to report accurately whatever he sees in the natural world. This subordination of art to observation results in an exaggeratedly objective realism, an almost wholly undirected panoramic narrative. Steinbeck's last five or six novels exemplify the resulting narrative freedom—or chaos. For example, in the later novels the narrative reach can be epic, or it can be reduced to a series of "true" observations or episodes that are sometimes incoherently free of working thematic relationships. In these novels the reader can be told that certain events have certain meanings within an allegorical system, which forces a con-

3. John Steinbeck and Edward F. Ricketts, *Sea of Cortez* (New York: The Viking Press, Inc., 1941), p. 135.
4. Ibid., p. 148.

flict between the loose method of narration and the close meaning that is imposed on the narrative. All of these elements are full grown in *East of Eden*. Significantly, they are present also in Steinbeck's earliest fiction, although much less at an extreme. The literary application of "is" thinking exaggerates several tendencies that are deeply rooted in Steinbeck's art. The critic's problem, therefore, is to trace and perhaps to explain a development rather than to study a new departure. In short, the career proceeds in a more orderly way than a first glance might suggest, for what may seem to be new starts are deeply rooted in Steinbeck's concern to achieve a harmony between structure and materials.

I propose that to study the novels from this viewpoint can permit a judicious, friendly judgment of each novel in the context of a greater appreciation of a shape to Steinbeck's long career. The unpleasant fact is that too often Steinbeck's work has been viewed piecemeal, even when the critical intention has been to achieve a rounded view. As the main result, Steinbeck's "place" among American writers has continued to be less secure—since less defined—than any of the major novelists of his age. Notoriously, a seesaw of defense or attack in particular instances is the striking characteristic of much Steinbeck criticism. I am not, to be sure, the first or the only Steinbeckian to attempt a rounded evaluation or to think that such evaluation is preferable to self-contained divisions into pro or con. I can but hope that my viewpoint has its claimed efficacy in the candid judgment of the ideal or Johnsonian reader.

Consider, now, the argument of this book.

Steinbeck begins with a developed sense of the artful in fiction. He does not write a disguised autobiography two or three times over. From the beginning, he searches for ways to achieve an ordered harmony in his art. He finds two distinct kinds of structure—panoramic and dramatic—to order his materials. Each of the first two novels is a fairly pure example of each structure. A number of aesthetic problems emerge, but Steinbeck does not solve them. Indeed, he is never able to work clear of these problems except par-

tially and (as it were) by accident when circumstances minimize or resolve them. The combination of panoramic and
dramatic structures is most evident in *In Dubious Battle*
and to a somewhat lesser extent in *The Grapes of Wrath*.
Steinbeck reaches his peak as an artist in these two novels.
Meanwhile, various events and pressures lead to a simplified
approach to structure, as in the three play-novelettes, and the
results are unfortunate. At about the same time, "is" thinking offers a promising lead. Following such different novels
as *Cannery Row* and *The Pearl* and the rather pure allegory,
The Wayward Bus (all indebted to "is" thinking, for better
or worse), Steinbeck settles on an extreme panoramic structure in *East of Eden* and the novels that follow. Frequently,
in his final years, Steinbeck turned to journalism. In this
work, as in all his work, an interest in technique was directed
toward a harmony of structure and materials.

This sketch reveals a complexity which forbids any simple
reduction of Steinbeck's career. He is serious and talented.
His extremely uneven career calls for a particularly careful
evaluation of his work; it precludes any simplistic dismissal.

Still, beyond the pattern of a constant search for an
elusive harmony between structure and materials, it does
appear that Steinbeck tends to move away from narrative
order over the range of his longer fiction. Steinbeck worked
largely by instinct, but he felt a strong need to work from a
plan.[5] Often, in practice, he deviated widely and disastrously from a cogent plan that implied the achievement of a
harmony between structure and materials; the result could
be a novel consisting of a visible structure and visible materials that are not resolved in each other. On rare occasions,
when a structure is "given," so to speak (in the sense that
The Pearl is a natural parable), Steinbeck reverses his movement away from order. Whether total or partial, this re-

---

5. Lewis Gannett, "Introduction: John Steinbeck's Way of Writing," *The Viking Portable Steinbeck* (New York: The Viking Press,
Inc., 1946), pp. vii–xxvii; Peter Lisca, *The Wide World of John Steinbeck* (New Brunswick: Rutgers University Press, 1958), pp. 39–40,
56–57, 73–79, 112, 133–34, 146–47, 184–86, 219, 231–32, 262. Excerpts
from this work are reprinted by permission of Rutgers University
Press.

versal is momentary at best, but it occurs more than once. Hence, Steinbeck's career proceeds in a series of zigzags, not in a straight line, and he does not "grow" as better or more fortunate writers do by applying the lessons of imperfect earlier work to the present. There is a slow but definite movement—much accelerated in his last years—away from order.

This situation creates a number of problems for the analytical critic of Steinbeck's longer fiction. First, the critic must be especially careful and insightful in matching criteria that are inevitably blunt (however closely terms are defined) with the actual complexities in Steinbeck's career. There is the critic's temptation to presume false similarities between novels. In fact, in its order, each novel presents a somewhat different approach, and often enough a radically different approach, to the achievement of a harmony between structure and materials. The author's search is fairly constant; the particular approaches and circumstances are not. Frequently, even apparent connections between different novels are quite misleading. Group-man occurs in several novels but the meaning of the concept shifts; the character named "Doc" recurs but changes strikingly from novel to novel; even a reuse of materials, such as class war, biological studies, or *paisano* life, does not ensure a thematic similarity between two novels. Yet the uncommonly irregular career does not permit the uncomplicated judgment that Steinbeck merely changed his mind. Certainly there is a pattern in Steinbeck's work, but it is not simple: It is Steinbeck's constant but changing search for a harmony between structure and materials. That search, in its dual directions, justifies the welter of technical devices and the differing materials and clarifies Steinbeck's tendency to move away from order in the latest novels. The one direction suggests efforts to achieve harmony externally, through new devices or materials; the other suggests despair of achieving a harmony. It is true that, at his best, when structure and materials most fully cohere, Steinbeck has produced some of the more distinguished literature of our time, in spite of the equal truth that much of his longer fiction contains enough imperfection to have removed a less gifted writer from critical attention.

So the peculiarly mixed bag that John Steinbeck presents is a special testing of the purpose of criticism: to draw just distinctions, to make correct judgments in complex instances.

A second critical difficulty relates to Steinbeck's tendency to proceed with fresh starts—there are notable exceptions —once it is clear that a certain technique or materials lead away from or do not lead directly toward a harmony between structure and materials. But the vital and constant factor is Steinbeck's continuing efforts to achieve, or at least to define, a fictive harmony.

A third consideration is that panoramic and dramatic structures occur separately or in combination in novel after novel; a specific novel under discussion may be quite different from its neighbors, depending on what kind of structure is predominant and on how adequately it functions.

Fourth, because Steinbeck tends to compose by parts, not by the whole (with some notable exceptions), and can permit himself considerable freedom of invention once the general form of the novel is established, the critic may be faced with a novel in which excellent episodes do not connect fully with other episodes or advance an otherwise strong development. In either circumstance, critical analysis is correspondingly complicated.

Finally, at times the longer fiction has been viewed rather exclusively in terms of the ideas it expresses. For example, group-man may be considered an ideological concept. No one denies the relevance of that consideration, but an analytical viewpoint must emphasize the dramatic function of the concept in its fictive context, whereas a purely ideological approach lifts out the concept, free of the novel, into a life of its own. The main point is that an analysis of Steinbeck's art necessitates a transfer from the criticism of ideas to the criticism of aesthetic values.

My general purpose is to offer an analytica. study of John Steinbeck's narrative art in its most crucial aspect over the entire range of the longer fiction. Therefore, I address the evidence of close reading to a theoretical issue, for evidence must be the sole test of theory. If the evidence supports the theory, there will be a double but related result: The reader will gain an enriched comprehension of John Steinbeck's artistic quality, and the rational process of criticism will be served.

The most sympathetic judgment cannot always be favorable if it is to be honest, not to say rational. Simple and exclusive praise is not synonymous with the exercise of critical judgment. Yet, on the testimony of a devotion of twenty years to the work of John Steinbeck, I can say that my delight and respect have increased, not withered, and my contemplation of a great artist with great flaws has been an immeasurable reward of the spirit, measured against the ruin of the years. That truth is the real substance of this book.

Because the facts of Steinbeck's development are important, I keep to the chronological order of first book publication. There are two exceptions. I examine Steinbeck's third published novel, *To a God Unknown*, following the first published novel, *Cup of Gold*. The bibliographical evidence indicates an earlier rather than a later date of composition for *To a God Unknown*, and my analysis illuminates that evidence. And I group the three play-novelettes in one chapter. Their publication dates are 1937, 1942, and 1950, but their conscious similarity in technique outweighs their chronological order.

1

The First Novels

Cup of Gold

Steinbeck remarked, seven years after the publication of *Cup of Gold*,[1] that there was not much to the novel "outside of a certain lyric quality."[2] A suitable gloss is that *Cup of Gold* reduces itself to a lyric cry because its materials and its structure are not in harmonious relationship.

This is not to say that *Cup of Gold* is a worthless novel. Especially in its context as apprentice work, it is highly ambitious. In conception it is both a philosophic novel of character and a romantic novel of adventure, and its technique suggests that Steinbeck knows how a novel can be developed.

The materials concern the life of the seventeenth-century English pirate, Sir Henry Morgan. The structure is multiple and somewhat contradictory. The novel is mainly a panoramic structure of linked episodic detail, an account of Morgan's life, but at times Steinbeck shifts to a dramatic structure to focus on a close study of Morgan's character. Many technical devices are evident, such as flashbacks, foreshadowing, interchapters, inserted brief narratives, internal monologue, a play on names, a dream sequence, a cluster of images and symbols, ironic confrontations and juxtapositions, parallels and oppositions, and a range of style that includes approximations of Welsh talk, the talk of the English gentry, the lingo of the New World half-breed, the formal talk of the Spanish grandee, and a precise observational, usually authorial language.

All these devices suggest that from the start Steinbeck

1. John Steinbeck, *Cup of Gold: A Life of Sir Henry Morgan, with Occasional Reference to History* (New York: Robert M. McBride Co., Inc., 1929). Hereafter cited as *CG*.

2. Peter Lisca, *The Wide World of John Steinbeck* (New Brunswick: Rutgers University Press, 1958), p. 26.

is ambitiously interested in technique. His apprentice novel is the reverse of the sprawling autobiographical opus that traditionally the young novelist produces. Yet, on closer study, the ambitious conception and the richness of the technical detail suggest why *Cup of Gold* is a failure as a novel. The conception is contradictory, in that a study of character and a record of adventure need to be distinguished before they can be combined; further, most of the technical detail is an effort—frequently clumsy, but at times highly successful—to provide the novel with an external narrative clarity. In essence, the materials and the structure tend to pull against each other. Steinbeck is able to suggest at least the outlines of his conception through technique, but frequently he is unable to bring the right technique into an adequate relationship with some particular novelistic problem involved in his conception.

These broad observations introduce points that require a close view of materials, structure, and technical devices. The effort is all the more worth while because *Cup of Gold* represents to a considerable extent the general pattern of Steinbeck's efforts to create adequate longer fictions.

The basic materials are obviously and highly romantic, but Steinbeck avoids in the main a vague romanticism of language and mood, in agreement with his philosophic conception of Morgan's character. What draws Steinbeck to treat Morgan thus is not the notion of the swashbuckling, rather childish, Hollywood version of the pirate hero but the far more complex idea of a gifted idealist (even a solipsist) in conflict with a world that consists only of material fact. The distinction is that Steinbeck's Morgan suggests Milton's Satan, as viewed by Romantic artists and critics, far more strongly than Hollywood's typical buccaneer.

Steinbeck's treatment of Morgan's life permits no doubt of this distinction. *Cup of Gold* is subtitled, "A Life of Sir Henry Morgan, with Occasional Reference to History." The novel is a selection of events in Morgan's life; it is in no sense a documentary novel. Much historical fact is omitted, most markedly the more brutal details of Morgan's career; several facts are greatly expanded, since they contribute to

Steinbeck's conception of Morgan's character; and much that is purely imaginary is introduced into the novel. The materials that are used, expanded, or invented suggest that Steinbeck's aim is to present a study of egoism. Steinbeck's conception of Morgan asserts that, when the power of will of an essentially mediocre man is strong enough, it can produce an ideal vision of self that becomes a total self-absorption, and thus the man becomes a monster. If such a man remains honest enough and is placed in self-revealing situations, in time he is forced to recognize his monstrous power and his mediocrity as facts, and he must deal with their implications. This grand conception can be the basis of a significant novel—possibly of a great novel.

Two unrelated technical devices cause Steinbeck to fail in the execution of the novel. The first is Steinbeck's decision to tell the story mainly from Morgan's point of view; the author must then relate the history of a confused man from within that man's confused perceptions of his aims and character. Morgan, as a consequence, does not emerge at crucial moments as a distinct person. He acts arbitrarily, spasmodically, and no clear motivation emerges. The second is the use of arbitrary shifts from panoramic scenes to dramatic detail, from sweeping events or general commentary to concrete particulars. These techniques tend to reduce fictional depth, to generalize and abstract the fictive process.

For example, instead of absorbing the background of the age into the novel—conditions in England and conditions affecting piracy in the Caribbean in the seventeenth century —Steinbeck halts the narration altogether on four occasions to present separate background essays. These "real" materials do not combine, as interchapters, with the continued record of Morgan's largely imaginary personality. The minor characters are presented no less flatly, often in a prefatory essay that indicates the moral condition each character is to represent. None except Morgan are changed by the separate blocks of action in which they participate. Too frequently, then, given the generalized movement of the novel, the abstract presentation and static roles of the minor characters, and the inverted handling of Morgan, Steinbeck is forced to explain the specific direction and meaning of the narrative in his own voice or risk a self-contained flow of events and interactions. In summary, these structural choices are the reasons why the novel's materials do not move or develop by their own nature; the narrator's voice must arrange and explain the thrust of the episodes and the significance of the minor characters.

Steinbeck worked out *Cup of Gold* intentionally and carefully, hence, these techniques cannot be accidental; in fact, they all recur in the later novels. Their constancy in his work suggests that Steinbeck has a certain blindness—not to technique, which is abundant—but to what a given technique can or cannot do.

A typical example will illustrate the nature of the failure. To explain the effect of Morgan's interview with Ysobel, Steinbeck introduces a foreshadowing scene in which Old Robert and Merlin discuss Morgan's idealism and agree that no man's idealism can endure. The scene requires a shift from Panama, where the relevant action is occurring, back to Wales, just before the novel reaches its emotional height. The shift is awkward but it is carefully worked out and clearly intended. In fact, the inserted conversation is necessary to inform the reader—as Morgan cannot—that in reality Ysobel is Morgan's bad luck.

Frequent explanations of this kind, in stopping or clogging the narrative, produce a species of fictional limbo. An emphasis on Morgan's character could result if the novel were wholly a dramatic structure, but that emphasis is not achieved. Too often Steinbeck relies on a panoramic structure. Actually, he does not seem to be completely aware of a difference between the separate kinds of structure. But so far as this novel is the ultimate evidence, Steinbeck is attracted toward a dramatic structure, a focus on Morgan's point of view.

Clearly, Morgan's is the major point of view. To present his conception of Morgan's personality, Steinbeck observes him as the young fellow in Wales, as the indentured servant in Barbados, as the most successful pirate in the Caribbean, and finally as the Lieutenant-Governor of Jamaica. This focus means that Morgan is treated in more detail than any of the minor characters, but his roles remain the materials of an episodic novel, a panoramic structure, and accordingly he is not clearly visualized or established in much psychological depth. Paradoxically, Steinbeck's focus on Morgan contributes to the impression of a rather superficial view of the man's personality. Steinbeck emphasizes an abstract moral history of the soul's pilgrimage in search of its definition rather than a concrete, episodic account of a Welsh boy's climb from obscurity to royal favor. In this paradoxical handling of Morgan's life, Steinbeck's choice of a dramatic structure contradicts but does not alter the essentially broad, panoramic nature of his materials—the episodic blocks of action in the life of a famous pirate.

All of these difficulties are the outcome of Steinbeck's admirable effort to present more than a buccaneering tale. Yet the only way to raise Morgan's career above its merely swashbuckling base, Steinbeck finds, is to use Morgan and his adventures to present a philosophic problem in character and in motivation. This ambitious and interesting purpose does not alter the panoramic quality of the materials. The final result is that Steinbeck's interpretation of character is superimposed on the materials of Morgan's career.

I shall examine these points in closer detail, in relation to the specific unfolding of events and the development of the major characterizations.

The early chapters are not devoted to scene painting or analysis of character, but to the backgrounds of Morgan's sexual idealism. Steinbeck's aim is to contrast the material and public success that Morgan achieves with his personal inability (due to his own confusion of mind) to find a suitable object for his idealism—a mortal woman to match his need. This strong theme is vitiated by its explanatory presentation, for Morgan's idealism emerges as a "behavior pattern," a mechanical, cause-and-effect sequence. At times that sequence is the only apparent element of structure. The mechanism qualifies the impact of the character's willful motivation.

The crux is evident in particular details. Morgan does not attach any love to his weak father, Old Robert, but he does have an implicit respect for his practical, strong-minded mother, Elizabeth. Elizabeth is also the name of the young peasant girl he yearns for sexually from a distance, whence he idealizes her. The painfully sharp conflict between sexual reality and sexual idealism is figured precisely in a night vision. As Morgan prepares to run away from Wales to a life of buccaneering in the New World, he stops to admire the peasant girl through her cottage window, as in a vision, but then he whistles to her:

> Elizabeth opened the door and stood framed against the inside light. The fire was behind her. Henry could see the black outline of her figure through her dress. He saw the fine curve of her legs and the swell of her hips. A wild shame filled him, for her and for himself.[3]

The real, sensual girl blots out—literally—the night's idealism, and Morgan runs away, in part to avoid a recognition of the real–ideal division in his mind, for despair lies that way.

This theme is dropped or displaced by the details of Morgan's adventures. The structure shifts from dramatic to panoramic, and the materials shift from an exploration of Morgan's inner life to an episodic account of the adventures of a young man set loose in the world. Steinbeck does not seem to be aware of the shift. Certainly he does not justify it.

Essentially, the novel begins again. Morgan walks in an ecstasy of expectation to Cardiff, where he is tricked by a worldly-wise supposed friend, a sailor named Tim, into agreeing to sail to the New World as an indentured servant. Implicitly, Morgan's shock at discovering that he is a slave in the New World parallels his shock at discovering that sexuality denies idealism; explicitly, on the level of narrative action, these shocks are reflected only indirectly or by their result: Morgan is determined to master the evil, reductive factuality that he has discovered in the world. To begin

3. *CG*, p. 33.

with, he masters his master, James Flower, by pretending to become his friend. Suggestively named, Flower is an ineffective esthete, the owner of a plantation in Barbados. As a link, his dreamy mind is much like Old Robert's mind; as a contrast, Morgan cultivates a cold mind, a slave manager's mind. He runs Flower's plantation with a fearful efficiency. Once he discovers that most slaves will obey a stern, remote master, he schools himself in the icy authority that suits such a master. He is realistic, even brutal; he is no longer idealistic and dreamy. Just here, the earlier themes reappear, free-floating through these materials. Possibly, it is suggested, Morgan's enduring wish to be a pirate is a false goal; the true goal may be his impractical achievement of a sexual ideal. His memories of Elizabeth become increasingly romantic—or false. On the narrative surface, he draws practical hints on military tactics from Flower's old classical books, he persuades Flower to buy a ship which he names "Elizabeth," and he learns to master—to sail and to navigate —"Elizabeth." Clearly, this increasing mastery of the world is identified with all that is evil in the world. The very process dehumanizes Morgan and inverts his former idealism. The proof is a purely sexual relationship with his mulatto mistress:

> Henry thought of her as a delicate machine perfectly made for pleasure, a sexual contraption.[4]

This brilliantly machined image differs from Morgan's "pure" memory of Elizabeth, but without gain, for the ideal has become sentimental.

These oppositions may be taken either as "moments" of experience in the life of a young man or as the objective symbols of Morgan's painfully divided sensibility; there is no middle ground. Clearly enough, the episodic account has symbolic overtones. Themes, details, and images concentrate a dramatic structure, a "scenic" study of Morgan's character in thematic relation to the conflict between the real and ideal. As elements in the narrative, these details become too easily the materials of a panoramic structure, a not quite

4. *CG*, p. 89.

external record of a young man's adventures in the world. In short, this part of the novel is neither a completely realistic narrative nor a completely symbolic construct. Hence, the oppositions continue in their unresolved tension.

The handling of the next stage in Morgan's career is further evidence of the irresolution at the heart of Steinbeck's narrative method.

Now the utterly realistic Morgan becomes a pirate. He is successful because he transforms a romantic trade into a coldly rational operation, a business venture. To emphasize this primary fact, Steinbeck hurries over the materials, compressing ten years of Morgan's life and some of his most exciting adventures into a few pages. The collapse of time returns the narrative flow to a dramatic structure, to a focus on Morgan's character. He is a manager, hence an isolated man. Success depends on discipline, which demands a figure of authority. Morgan plays that role. But suddenly, for no stated reason, he wants a friend and he wants to be loved. To fulfill these needs, he forces a friendship with a young, carefree, witty pirate named Coeur de Gris, and he insists on a plan to capture Panama, "the cup of gold," with the sole and private motive of winning the love of a transposed Helen of Troy whom the buccaneers call La Santa Roja.

As these ideas and turns of plot develop, *Cup of Gold* becomes an increasingly arbitrary system of symbolic, even allegorical, assertion. Correspondingly, its development grows less realistic.

If narrative clarity is obscured, there is nothing but clarity in Steinbeck's thematic scheme, which can be stated as a series of propositions: The life of reason equates with the practice of business or management; that life is external and desiccating. Man's inner, irrational need for friendship and love is opposed to his external, rationalized drives to be successful, to control power and wealth, to master other men through terror or intellectual superiority. These are themes or presumptions that Steinbeck will stay with throughout his career. But how to state them adequately in *Cup of Gold*?

Technique asserts, it does not embody, a set of themes. The initial problems remain. Steinbeck does not attempt to

solve them. Instead, in a maneuver as typical as the introduction of a character in a prefatory essay, Steinbeck introduces a new element, the symbolic La Santa Roja. This
move is not a solution but a complication of the existing
narrative problems.

The use of symbol and image in *Cup of Gold* throws a
piercing, enduring light on Steinbeck's concept of narrative
form. Therefore, direct analysis of the novel must give way
at this point to a full consideration of what Steinbeck does
with symbol and image.

The full, golden moon is a primary symbol and the central, intentional control of the novel's structure. It is, first,
the title of the novel. The author uses it to unify character
and theme. Several of Merlin's comments identify Morgan's romanticism with the moth's desire to reach the moon;
Panama is called "the cup of gold," signifying the pull of
the richest city in the New World for the ordinary moth-
man or the presence of La Santa Roja for the extraordinary
moth-man—for Morgan. But the symbol loses force in these
mechanical counterpoints. Because their widely separated
values do not build an organic or equated unity, their pooled
qualities tend to be decorative rather than organizational.[5]
The earth symbol is less ambitious, or less divided, so it is
realized more persuasively in its significant parallel with the
moon symbol. The distinction is that a precise observational
quality informs Old Robert's love of the earth and of roses,
the mulatto's worship of nature gods, and the descriptions
of the jungle near Panama. These violent or mysterious realities of nature are a powerful qualification of Morgan's
egoistic romanticism. Their modest, self-contained integrity
contrasts markedly with the strained, artificial functions
of the moon symbol.

The most successful symbolism is in the correlation of
piracy with Morgan's special kind of idealism. Piracy, for

---

5. Harry Thornton Moore, *The Novels of John Steinbeck* (Chicago:
Normandie House, 1939), pp. 12–13. Moore lists many other meanings
or motifs; his intention is not mine, but his listings tend to support
my view, since they cover much ground and are not organically
combined or equated. Excerpts from this work are reprinted by permission of the author.

Morgan, is a species of intellectual adventure, not a release of the lusts and passions of ordinary men. Therefore, Morgan refuses to adopt the free manners and customs of the typical pirate captain. His men presume that his intellectual superiority is the reason for his control. In fact, Morgan wants to avoid the contamination of emotional release. He is the coldly rational businessman. In a literal sense, he molds piracy to match the businesslike, realistic surface of his mind. Nevertheless, as a pirate, he applies the metaphor of "capture" to every human relationship. So when he hears rumors of a fabulous woman, La Santa Roja, whose Christian name, Ysobel, is the Spanish for Elizabeth, his reaction is to plan a capture of her admiring love through the capture of Panama, where she lives. The earlier symbolic pattern is repeated: Ysobel is an image of pure sexuality to Morgan's men, but their captain imagines or hopes that she is the fulfillment—as she is the release—of his old pattern of sexual idealism.[6] And the disillusion is repeated. Morgan's simple idea of "capture" is plainly inadequate; he suffers a real and a symbolic fall when he encounters Ysobel.

In summary, then, Steinbeck's symbols and images can be less than functionally adequate. The less ambitious operate best, evidently because they are least subject to strain or manipulation.

There is a recovery: Some of the best pages in *Cup of Gold* comprise the narrative of the capture of Panama, for Steinbeck is a driving storyteller. Here, however, is a characteristic inconsistency. The reader has been prepared exhaustively for an exploration of Morgan's character; the switch to a suspenseful narrative presents merely the greatest of Morgan's conquests. But this is interlude, not conclusion. The narrative drive ceases, with a shift from panoramic to dramatic structure, once Panama is captured. Now the focus is on Morgan's personality, as read by Ysobel.

6. Steinbeck places imagery associating Ysobel with Helen on the same level of importance as the mechanical trick of the play on the name, Elizabeth–Ysobel. There seems to be a minor failure here in sorting out one symbolic quality from another or perhaps in placing all literary devices on the same level.

Morgan's first interview with Ysobel establishes that she is not a goddess, not the Helen of the New World, but a thoroughly evil woman. She has been raised to greatness by the intensity of her knowledge of evil and her drive to experience new kinds of evil. On her part she expects Morgan to be a ruffian, not a romantic idealist. From the height of her knowledge of evil she regards Morgan as a childish fellow.

This revelation is sudden. More turns follow. We are told that Morgan has pretended to be a strong man, that in fact he is only a mediocre fellow, as feeble and childish as Old Robert or James Flower. Ysobel is the means to the revelation of these truths, and there is authorial help. She contrasts the assured power of her only lover—an absolutely evil man who is her ideal—with Morgan's ineffectual bluster in his efforts to "capture" her. She tells Morgan that her lover was caught and hanged, but Morgan has won successes and honors; her lover beat her, but Morgan tries to win her with fine words or empty, brutal gestures. In essence, Ysobel's lover had been what Morgan pretends to be; his strength was a total rejection of the social order. Morgan lives and has always lived (we are told) by the conventional standards of material success and money; he is weak.

The credibility of this revelation is weakened by its suddenness and by Steinbeck's presenting Ysobel as a metaphysical condition rather than a realized human being. The artifice is extreme, since Ysobel is not allowed to function beyond the ambiguous implications of her symbolic name. Above all, we are *told* the sudden truth; we do not *see* it develop.

The author's intention is clear. He uses various structures and materials to contrast the fact that Morgan's pull to piracy represents a desire for a success that society will recognize with the retained idealism that he is unable to find in the material world. Unhappily, piracy—his chosen avenue for success—would seem destined to lead him far from sexual idealism. The savage, popularly held notion of piracy does equate, however, with Ysobel's knowledge of evil and her rejection of society. Her insight into Morgan's character combines the two halves of his life: Ysobel seems to Morgan beforehand to be the sexual ideal, but in the proof she is a mechanical entity much like the mulatto girl. This operative pattern may be artificial, but it is neat. Here as elsewhere, Steinbeck puts more emphasis—faith—on mechanical pattern than on an organic form.

With all due consistency, the final episode in *Cup of Gold* is a mechanical, not an organic, necessity. Its sole justification is that it is needed to fill out the pattern of Morgan's life.

We see Morgan, after Ysobel's rejection, living as Lieutenant-Governor of Jamaica. He has been pardoned and is now the worthy husband of still another Elizabeth, his stuffy uncle's daughter (he is tricked into the marriage). In his new role, Judge Morgan condemns old pirate friends to death to preserve his public status. Finally, as he lies dying in a state bed, a fever-born image of the ideal Elizabeth appears to him, and he realizes the futility of his lifelong search.

These final, swiftly panoramic scenes demonstrate that Morgan plays the public hypocrite, once he is convinced of his inner hypocrisy. They relate early Morgan to later Morgan, businesslike Morgan to hypocrite Morgan, and they prove the accuracy of Ysobel's insight. The knitting-up of the novel displays a skillful technique. The only missing element is any comprehension of why Morgan is as he is. Hence, the novel's core is hollow.

Certainly, then, *Cup of Gold* is an interesting failure, at times a superb panoramic narrative, at times a full realization of minute particulars. The failure results from the fact that the various styles, the several actions, and the bright characterizations cannot disguise a pervasive structural uncertainty. Structure appears in the novel in response to shifting particulars, not as organic form, and the various materials—the analytical biography and the adventure tale —are never firmly sorted out. *Cup of Gold* gives the impression of having been composed in bits and pieces, as a seemingly fretful improvisation; actually, it was carefully thought out and repeatedly revised.[7] Without benefit of hindsight, it is an unusually exciting first novel—the presentation of a rich, unorganized talent that gave promise of a bright future for its author. But hindsight will observe the merely intentional linking of Morgan's romanticisms and his essential mediocrity, for Steinbeck cannot seem to implement that developed abstraction as a harmony of structure and materials. Ominously for his future as a writer, the wealth of technique is a chaotic scattering throughout the novel, not the instrument of a harmonious unity of the unusually various materials.

Steinbeck never escapes that kind of imbalance, but he knows that it exists, and he attempts various solutions over a period of almost forty years.

To a God Unknown

To a God Unknown[8] was published in 1933, one year after the publication of *The Pastures of Heaven*, but good bibliographical evidence and excellent critical reasons suggest that *To a God Unknown* may be considered the immediate successor to *Cup of Gold*.

The bibliographical evidence advanced by Harry Thornton Moore in his pioneer study and extended by Peter Lisca in his recent critical biography indicates that *To a God Unknown* has an earlier rather than a later place in Steinbeck's development as a novelist. According to Moore and Lisca, Steinbeck had been thinking of *To a God Unknown* as early as 1929, the publication date of *Cup of Gold. To a God Unknown* had existed in two versions that predate the third or published version. The earliest draft, *The Green Lady*, is of indeterminate date, but is known to have been offered without success to several publishers. The second version, *To an Unknown God*, was completed by Steinbeck

7. Lisca, p. 26. Evidently *Cup of Gold* was rewritten six times over a period of several years.

8. John Steinbeck, *To a God Unknown* (New York: Robert O. Ballou, 1933). Hereafter cited as *TGU*.

and was being offered to publishers early in 1931, before Steinbeck began *The Pastures of Heaven*. Steinbeck withdrew this draft in August 1931, in order to revise it completely and finally. The work of revision continued into early 1933, whereupon the novel was published.[9] Peter Lisca remarks: "No other Steinbeck novel except *East of Eden* has been in progress so long or undergone such extensive reworking."[10]

Even without this evidence, it might seem that *To a God Unknown* is related more closely to *Cup of Gold* than to *The Pastures of Heaven*. Different as their materials are, *To a God Unknown* and *Cup of Gold* share an important technical similarity; both novels attempt to mingle dramatic and panoramic structures. The later novel demonstrates, however, a more thorough harmony between its structure and its materials.

To a God Unknown is a history of the agricultural settlement of California, from the point of view of the novel's hero, Joseph Wayne, a quasi-believer in animism, and a priest or god of fertility in nature. That is, while the materials concerning the history of the settlement threaten to demand a panoramic structure, the point of view, located in the specific history and outlook of Joseph Wayne, assures the necessity of a dramatic structure. Steinbeck's real progress in mastery of technique can be observed in the resultant mingling of structures. To pursue that progress, far more than to reinforce the supporting bibliographical evidence, I shall analyze *To a God Unknown* at this point, one step out of its order of publication.

From a closer and more strictly aesthetic view, the two novels differ rather sharply in a very suggestive way. *Cup of Gold* fails because Steinbeck is unable to do more with his materials than to suggest through a mingled structure what he sees implied in them. *To a God Unknown* fails because Steinbeck undertakes a task that is all but impossible to achieve, especially in the relationship between structure and materials. The difficulty does not lie in Steinbeck's

9. Moore, pp. 30–31; Lisca, pp. 39–41.
10. Lisca, p. 41.

handling of a wealth of technical detail of the kind in *Cup of Gold* nor, as in *Cup of Gold*, in resolving rather obvious cross-purposes between materials and structure. The difficulty lies mainly, as it does in part throughout *Cup of Gold*, in Steinbeck's conception of the central character. The earlier drafts demonstrate, however, that Steinbeck progressed steadily and with increasing clarity toward a profound understanding of the relationship between materials and structure. Moore records that Steinbeck's first version, taken from a play that a friend had written, contains a forty-year hiatus. In the second half of that first version,

> the leading character, Andy, was almost insanely in love with a California forest. He was misunderstood by his prosaic wife, who read evil into his strange, almost aesthetic love for his daughter, whom he identified in some way with the forest-spirit. At the end of the book the forest was ablaze, and Andy walked sacrificially into it.[11]

The hiatus disappeared when Steinbeck reworked the manuscript into its present form, at a distance from its origin as a play. He gave the work unity by collapsing the first half of the first version into a brief frame scene and by locating the major part of the action in a California valley during a few years in the lives of a related set of characters. Indeed, in the final version, Joseph Wayne, who corresponds to Andy, has no sexual problems and no daughter. Still, these changes are not enough, for they do not confront the problem of making nature worship credible.

Steinbeck's conception of Joseph Wayne presents the prime difficulty. Joseph's lucidity is qualified by his double and essentially unarticulated role—a step up, nevertheless, from Henry Morgan. Joseph is a worshiper of nature, as suggested by events and by the responses of minor characters, but his ultimate role as a priest or god of nature emerges only at the conclusion. The novel is, therefore, a long preparation for an action that is withheld until the last moment. This withholding of identity encourages the belief that Joseph's worship of nature is a curious personal stance, a minor aberration, until the ending asserts its greater claim.

11. Moore, p. 30.

The authorial indecision that presents Joseph, until the last possible moment, as a confused mystic rather than a convinced priest or god profoundly affects the credible presentation of nature worship.

A religion is an institution with a priest class and a god requiring worship; mystical experience is a private, often noncommunicable apprehension of divinity. Steinbeck accords nature worship the status of a definite religious attitude with at least an implied institutional basis, but he has Joseph search continually for belief in his mystical experiences and for the very right to worship nature. These opposites are not resolved. On its own terms, the novel should be the history of a cult, not a continual search (as it is for Joseph) for a validation of mysticism; and Joseph should be a forthright priest or god, not (as he is) an anxious worshiper uncertain of his right to worship.

Joseph's double role is rooted in Steinbeck's evident wish to present an objective narrative, to have the novel "tell itself" with as little authorial direction as possible. A close study of Joseph's characterization and function will focus the resulting difficulties in particular details.

The opening scene establishes Joseph's role as a priest. His patriarchal father, John, agrees that Joseph's intended move in 1903 from the Wayne farm "near Pittsford in Vermont" to the fertile, virgin land in California is necessary.[12] With a blessing, John makes Joseph, the third son, the leader of the Wayne family and a priest. Joseph is so blessed because, like John, he is a worshiper of life or of fertility in nature. It is implied that this worship has a long history in the Wayne family.

The credibility of this initial material depends on John's saintly manner and on the reader's willingness to respond to the idea of a primitive, direct apprehension of divinity in nature. For example, John does not use the symbolic forehead blessing but places Joseph's hand on his genitals for the old blessing of the fertility cult.

These materials require a dramatic structure, a concentration on the identity of Joseph's role and person. If that is

12. *TGU*, pp. 4–5.

Steinbeck's aim, it is blunted considerably, since Joseph's awareness of his role as priest is muted in much of the rest of the novel and emerges explicitly only at the conclusion, when Joseph kills himself in self-sacrifice to end a long drouth. But the drouth, not his conviction of his role, seems to be the force that brings Joseph to resume his priesthood or godhood. Even then, shortly before his suicide, he openly confesses his role only to his Indian servant and friend, Juanito, who, being a primitive, can understand Joseph's claim to the identity and person of the priest or god:

> Listen, Juanito, first there was the land, and then I came to watch over the land; and now the land is nearly dead. Only this rock and I remain. I am the land.[13]

Steinbeck may intend Joseph's long silence to suggest a conflict of attitudes toward nature worship before presenting at last a proof of its validity in "the marketplace of ideas." The structural difficulty is that Steinbeck sacrifices formal coherence in order to establish the intellectual basis of the novel. Further study of Joseph's characterization reveals the mainly unfortunate results of Steinbeck's decision.

Joseph's silence, it appears, is motivated by his fear of condemnation, so much so that his rationalistic fear seems more powerful at times than his profound identity with the land. This trait of character inhibits the scope and method of the narrative, since an essentially mystical content can be rendered only by suggestion. Hence, the novel contains a wealth of episodic detail within a panoramic structure, but that wealth is in conflict with the evident need for a dramatic structure, a focus on Joseph, since the novel is properly a history of Joseph and a record of his impact on other people. Steinbeck cannot resolve the structural problem presented by the fact that Joseph's self-awareness is limited although it is the essential content of the novel. As a partial solution, Steinbeck chooses to test, explore, and validate Joseph's history and personality by the responses of the people around him. This choice increases the impression of

13. *TGU*, p. 296.

Joseph's customary fearful passivity without clarifying the point of view.

It is easy to understand how Steinbeck backed into an impossible series of checks and balances. To establish the validity of nature worship is as important as to create a credible, self-defined hero. We can admire Steinbeck's willingness to accomplish the first necessity by letting the hero himself doubt the validity of his faith through much of the novel. That doubt may seem incredible, given the opening scene, and bravery is foolish if its results are unfortunate, as they are here. In any case, Joseph is characterized by an uncertainty that qualifies his being the lucid center of a dramatic structure. Having a series of minor characters evaluate Joseph's implicit claim to priesthood or godhood exaggerates but does not resolve the narrative crux.

The essence of the problem is that, having created Joseph and postulated his unique situation, Steinbeck proceeds to construct *To a God Unknown* as a series of detached, isolated scenes, not as a unified, thoroughly organic whole. Significantly, this is the situation—less intensified by the odd materials and the absolute need for a dramatic structure—in *Cup of Gold*.

On the positive side, the confrontations between Joseph and the various minor characters are masterful in themselves. If they do not touch the central issue of presenting Joseph's multiple self-awareness as an organic whole, at least, as in *Cup of Gold*, they comprise a connected series of responses to Joseph. They therefore provide a sense of an unfolding narrative —undirected as it is toward an ultimate goal—which tends to restate rather than to develop the novel's intellectual outlines. In a very restricted sense, as Lisca has pointed out, the novel may be considered a study of character so far as the minor characters suggest a range of possible approaches to "the unknown god" through their responses to Joseph.[14] This valid point does not alter the incoherent relationship between structure and materials.

14. Lisca, pp. 48–50.

Joseph is the hero of the novel, not "the unknown god," and the indirect presentation of Joseph, coupled with his own doubts of his role and faith, creates a narrative situation in which the materials are repeated in parallels—served up by each minor character—rather than developed progressively toward some definite conclusion.

Consider the responses of the minor characters to Joseph.

John's creation of a leader and a priest in Joseph counterweighs the several negative responses of Joseph's three brothers, Burton, Thomas, and Benjy, of Father Angelo, the Catholic priest, of the nameless old man by the sea, and of Thomas's wife, Rama. Burton, the oldest brother, is a strict Protestant, a 98 per cent celibate, a sick man; his function is to reject Joseph completely. This is climaxed by his killing an oak tree that he knows Joseph worships as the soul of John, their dead father. Burton's motive is that he cannot admit the claims of any faith but his own. Yet his attempt to destroy Joseph's link with John is a willful denial of life; it is prefigured in his tiny share of vital force. Thomas is not intelligent enough to realize that Joseph has a significant role. He is not quite an animal, but his instincts go outward to animals; a completely healthy creature, he worships nothing. Benjy rejects Joseph in that he is a sensual man, a minor Don Juan, void of any mental or spiritual dimensions. As an ultimate figure of ignorance, Benjy is stabbed in the back while making love to Juanito's wife.

The common element in these rejections is some kind of ignorance of the divine vitality. Burton has no vital spark to speak of; Thomas's vitality pours outward to nonhuman life; Benjy's vitality is expressed irresponsibly to human life. Of these three negatives, Joseph is in closest natural sympathy with the semianimal, Thomas.

The rejections are structured carefully to cover the entire range of ordinary human behavior. But because the brothers do not function in their own right, they threaten constantly to become metaphysical qualities like Ysobel. And because Steinbeck gives them so much consideration, we can be misled into believing the brothers are important in themselves. Benjy especially is presented in far more detail than would be necessary to outline an attractive rascal. In short, Steinbeck finds the brothers interesting, so he makes more of them than structural considerations alone might warrant. In this, as in the larger matter of Joseph's character, Steinbeck creates for immediate effects and loses control of the total structure.

The other minor characters are kept more firmly in hand, but similar problems of judgment are evident. On a trip, Joseph and Thomas find an old man by the sea. The old man worships nature by instinct, simply to be "happy." Arbitrarily made wholly unaware of his own role for the moment, Joseph hopes to discover the old man's reason for worshipping nature. The old man has no secrets; he is ignorant; he does not need to understand why he performs his rituals, which are consequently void of meaning. His function in the structural pattern is to deny Joseph's need for intellectual certainty, since his contented ignorance permits symbols to substitute for a direct apprehension of "the unknown god." Thomas's response to the old man's rituals —"It seems a trap, a kind of little trap"—implies that mere experience does not signify undersatnding, and Joseph learns from Thomas's insight rather than from the old man's rituals.[15] We may conclude, also, that the old man is more ignorant and more dangerous to Joseph than his brothers are. Again, in making this point, Steinbeck fractures the structural pattern. Thomas's role here violates his basic definition as a natural man. He does not play the holy innocent, given insight, anywhere else in the novel. Clearly, Steinbeck does not care greatly for structural integrity when it conflicts with a point he needs to make.

Rama is equally a negative force. She is a type of the curious Eve, quite free of religious sensibility. Her curiosity takes a practical turn, and on the night that Joseph's wife is killed, Rama bursts into Joseph's room and rapes him. This strange event is intended to be purely symbolic. Rama wishes to test Joseph's personal divinity out of curiosity; when she is certain that he is a man, she rejects his role, on the strength of her practical logic. Rama's rational denial is intentionally

15. *TGU*, p. 274.

grotesque, and the failure of her reasoning power to divine Joseph's genuine role is as extreme as the grotesque ignorance of the old man.

But the ground is covered. As the three brothers suggest a range of ordinary response to Joseph, so Rama and the old man suggest the response of reason and of instinct. In each paradigmatic case, the inability of these people to comprehend nature worship transfers to Joseph and defines his isolation.

Father Angelo is a more fully developed figure. He combines instinct and reason within the ordinary range of knowledge accumulated in the course of the history of the Church. He understands what nature worship is and what Joseph represents, but he is not a nature worshiper, and his understanding protects the Church. Fairly early in the novel, Father Angelo warns Joseph:

> When his ceremony [of starting a fiesta] was finished, Joseph walked to the tree and poured a little wine on its bark, and he heard the priest's voice speaking softly beside him: "This is not a good thing to do, my son. . . . Be careful of the groves, my son. Jesus is a better saviour than a hamadryad." And his smile became tender, for Father Angelo was a wise as well as a learned man.[16]

There is considerable ambiguity in Father Angelo's tenderness. He implies the Church can absorb many beliefs although it must stamp out any belief it cannot absorb. This initial and interesting tension vanishes, to return only in a changed shape at the end of the novel when the drouth is at its worst. Then Joseph attempts to unite his faith with that of the Church by asking Father Angelo to pray for rain. The priest refuses, and Joseph goes to his rock shrine to sacrifice himself to bring the rain. Because there is no transition of any consequence between Father Angelo's initial implied threat and Joseph's ultimate plea, the necessary parallel between the two men is not fully articulated. Rather it is strained by Steinbeck's development of a limited and confusing irony at the close of the novel. Once Father Angelo is alone, after refusing Joseph's plea, we see that he

16. *TGU*, pp. 157–58.

respects Joseph's role and the validity of nature worship too much for the good of his soul:

> He was shaken by the force of the man. He looked up at one of his pictures, a descent from the cross, and he thought, "Thank God this man has no message. Thank God he has no will to be remembered, to be believed in." And, in sudden heresy, "else there might be a new Christ here in the West." Father Angelo got up then, and went into the church. And he prayed for Joseph's soul before the high altar, and he prayed forgiveness for his own heresy, and then, before he went away, he prayed that the rain might come quickly and save the dying land.[17]

Joseph's enduring uncertainty that he is right qualifies the impact of Father Angelo's recognition, which, in any case, is timed to coincide roughly with Joseph's death. Steinbeck is far more interested in ironic parallels than in articulating the relationship between the two men—or their positions— and this interest limits the structural importance of Father Angelo's point of view. Significantly, Joseph is both denied and supported by Father Angelo's stances. The opportunity to clarify Joseph's personality and his roles is sacrificed to the momentary irony. The error is more serious than Steinbeck's too-developed interest in Benjy or Thomas's sudden role as a holy innocent, since it undoes a potentially major structural element. Steinbeck's lack of sustained interest in such matters is indicated by his failure to develop Father Angelo's role more carefully or even to keep him more constantly in view. Certainly there is no doubt that Father Angelo and Joseph are natural antagonists and might, if placed in closer relationships, illuminate each other's position. Very likely the substitution of irony for illumination depends on Steinbeck's initial decision to present Joseph, in much of the novel, as a confused seeker. The priest or god of nature could oppose Father Angelo; all the seeker can produce is irony. Here, then, as in much of Steinbeck's work, one is left with a vision of what might have been in Steinbeck's mind: the vision is solid enough to suggest a far greater novel than we have.

17. *TGU*, p. 310.

The suggestion in Father Angelo's sudden recognition of Joseph as a god opens the novel to extraordinary insights. The dramatic difficulty is that the recognition is a flash rather than a developed part of a structure. Joseph's own personality is too vague to carry much of the weight of such insight, and Father Angelo is not carried through the novel in a major role. Also, we understand—as a final irony—that Joseph is dead or dying when the priest experiences the flash of recognition. Hence, it is possible that Steinbeck perceived the paralleling of Father Angelo and Joseph much as we do—as a sudden recognition, unprepared essentially by previous materials and structural developments. That *To a God Unknown* has a largely panoramic structure, with part succeeding part rather than developing of organic necessity, lends credit to this possible conclusion.

What Steinbeck can accomplish with luck and a necessary minimum of preparation is suggested by his handling of a final negative force. The natives in the town are a group, a negative force, subject to irony. The irony is that the natives are Joseph's potential followers if he declares himself a god, or at least a body of willing friends if he declares his priesthood. Joseph does neither even in the crisis of the drouth. On the last page of the novel, therefore, Father Angelo sees the natives in the streets engaging in what amounts to a fertility rite as the rain comes down; yet, being undirected, the instinctual rites turn into mere animal sexuality, which the priest recognizes.

> The priest knew . . . they would be wearing the skins of animals, although they didn't know why they wore them. The pounding rhythm grew louder and more insistent, and the chanting voices shrill and hysterical. "They'll be taking off their clothes," the priest whispered, "and they'll roll in the mud. They'll be rutting like pigs in the mud."[18]

The irony is functional. Sexual intercourse may be a fertility rite, but Father Angelo defines the nature of the orgy by comparing the natives to pigs. They have no leader or public myth to give their rites a properly religious import. As they decline into animals, so they might have risen to grace as

18. *TGU*, pp. 324–25.

followers of a god or priest of nature. Father Angelo suggests the lost chance, of which Joseph is never aware:

> They wanted the rain so, poor children. I'll preach against them on Sunday. I'll give everybody a little penance.[19]

The ironic consequence of Joseph's ignorance of his actual role as either god or priest balances the irony of an orgy the Church can accept as a momentary (hence a lesser) evil. Irony operates in this instance in relation to a structural intention and in harmony with the materials.

To a God Unknown is a more profound and a more fully realized novel than *Cup of Gold*. The two novels differ considerably in their materials but share a number of points of technique. Their different kinds and degrees of failure stem from the same basic misunderstanding of what a structure is and can do. This similarity is significant, not the difference in the range of materials.

Steinbeck's narration is roundabout in both novels. The reader does much of the work of creation. The more complex or ambitious the novel, the more there is for the reader to complete. *To a God Unknown* demands more work of this sort because it is more complex and ambitious than *Cup of Gold*. The hero in *Cup of Gold* can seem to be superficially motivated or visualized, while the hero in *To a God Unknown* is carefully made vague. Or new topics in *Cup of Gold* serve to attempt to conceal structural difficulties, while in *To a God Unknown* these difficulties are ensured by Steinbeck's decision to present a series of responses to Joseph, not Joseph himself, and to keep Joseph as vague a character as possible. In both novels the apparent concentration on a hero seems to demand a dramatic structure, but the structure is mainly panoramic, perhaps to help Steinbeck to avoid the clarity of presentation which a dramatic structure invites. In both novels the wealth of technical devices tends to impose an order that is not implicit in the materials and that substitutes for the achievement of an organic harmony between structure and materials. For all of these reasons, the denser, more important novel ex-

19. *TGU*, p. 325.

hibits the more extreme structural imperfection. Steinbeck thinks of structure as mechanical rather than organic—determined rather than necessary—and, seemingly uncertain regarding the proper use of structure, he settles for mingled forms that are mainly panoramic in relation to materials that demand a dramatic structure. When the materials do require a panoramic structure, as in *The Pastures of Heaven*, Steinbeck is clearly more at ease, and he produces work of significantly higher quality. But even as obviously panoramic a novel as *The Pastures of Heaven* is not altogether free of structural uncertainty.

The Pastures of Heaven

Steinbeck's high ambitions continue in *The Pastures of Heaven*.[20] Besides, the novel is a very good one. However, Steinbeck's stated intention (which has been preserved) can be distinguished from his accomplishment. Not that intention matters in itself; frequently, writers have altered a plan in the heat of composition. That is not the point in the present instance. The rather sharp conflict in one area between the intention and the result is highly revealing of Steinbeck's difficulties in achieving a harmony between structure and materials.

Steinbeck's full statement of his intentions, written before the composition of *The Pastures of Heaven*, is as follows:

> There is, about twelve miles from Monterey, a valley in the hills called Corral de Tierra. Because I am using its people I have named it Las Pasturas del Cielo. The valley was for years known as the happy valley because of the unique harmony which existed among its twenty families. About ten years ago a new family moved in on one of the ranches. They were ordinary people, ill educated but honest and as kindly as any. In fact, in their whole history I cannot find that they have committed a really malicious act nor an act which was not dictated by honorable expedience or out and out altruism. But about the M——s there was a flavor of evil. Everyone

20. John Steinbeck, *The Pastures of Heaven* (New York: Brewer, Warren & Putnam, 1932). Hereafter cited as *PH*.

they came in contact with was injured. Every place they went dissension sprang up. There have been two murders, a suicide, many quarrels and a great deal of unhappiness in the Pastures of Heaven, and all of these things can be traced to the influence of the M——s. So much is true. I am using the following method. The manuscript is made up of stories each one complete in itself, having its rise, climax and ending. Each story deals with a family or individual. They are tied together only by the common locality and by the contact with the M——s. I am trying to show this peculiar evil cloud which follows the M——s.[21]

Steinbeck keeps to this plan, except that the Munroes (the M——s) do not at all constitute the center of reference that Steinbeck had in mind.

The aim of this chapter is to determine why the Munroe family does not have the central, organic function that Steinbeck intended and to indicate what happens to the structure of the novel as a consequence of the author's relative failure to use the family as a unifying device.

The locale of *The Pastures of Heaven* is a California valley. The time is around 1925. The materials are the lives of individuals whose common factor is their living, more than is usual, in worlds of their own imaginations or fears. These people are forced by various circumstances to recognize and to conform to the larger, stronger, and often hostile pressures of a society that represents the "real" world. The structure of the novel is as complex as these materials would suggest. Excluding several frame chapters, the novel consists of nine episodes—private and different experiences—that tend to be developed as panoramic structures. The quite separate framework consists of the frame chapters at the opening and close of the novel and of frequent references to the Munroe family. This framework seems intended to supply the novel with a dramatic structure of sorts. In this it conflicts with the panoramic structure that is characteristic of the nine episodes. Therefore, we need to examine the relationship between the framework and the central part of the novel. The best approach is to analyze, first, the function of the Munroe family.

21. Lisca, pp. 56–57.

The presence of the Munroes in the initial framework chapters and in the central chapters indicates that Steinbeck follows the letter of his intention—to supply the materials, the nine episodes, with an established and constant point of view through the medium of the Munroe family. The nine episodes are random and wide-ranging slices of life, most of them interesting in themselves. Free of any dramatic or ideological framework, they can only suggest the totality of life in The Pastures of Heaven. Steinbeck's apparent attitude is that the episodes fall into a dramatic structure when they are read within a framework of ironic values established by the mere presence—no more—of the Munroe family. That is, Steinbeck seems to want the effect of both a panoramic and a dramatic structure, and this intention recalls the multiple structural aims of the first two novels. But the intention operates in *The Pastures of Heaven* on a much more sophisticated and complex level than in its predecessors. This indicates Steinbeck's growth as an artist. His intention recalls strikingly the technique of *The Turn of the Screw*, in that the innocence of the central figure or figures (the governess, the Munroes) permits the reader to notice a pattern of irony that is not visible to anyone within the novel. Weighing the comparison, we can see where Steinbeck fails. Henry James makes a positive virtue of the limited point of view of the governess, but, as his letter suggests, Steinbeck writes out of merely a simple, unqualified certainty that the Munroes *will* unify the novel. They do not. In effect, the novel is left to "tell itself," much like *To a God Unknown*—a generalization, admittedly—but we need to know why the Munroe family does not fulfill the unifying function that Steinbeck has in mind.

Study of the framework provides part of the answer. This framework is a series of ironic contrasts between good, primitive, or "natural" behavior and bad, civilized, or "unnatural" behavior.[22] The contrasts have the disadvantage of

---

22. Frederic I. Carpenter, "John Steinbeck, American Dreamer," *Southwest Review*, 21 (Summer 1941), 458–59. Carpenter offers an interestingly parallel statement from a point of view that is quite different from mine.

tending to exist (although delightfully) for themselves and to reveal their limited reference all too quickly. The irony begins, to be sure, as a means of establishing a point of view. We see, in a brief lead-in scene, "sometime around 1776," the year of American independence, a brutal Spanish corporal with a squad of cavalry in the act of tracking down twenty runaway Indians who have been forced into common labor and into the salvation offered by the Church.[23] The corporal finds the Indians "in attitudes of abandon," enjoying sexual freedom; he chains them, and, on the return trip, he finds "a long valley floored with green pasturage," a valley so beautiful that he is moved to speak of the place as "the green pastures of Heaven to which our Lord leadeth us."[24] The ironic contrast points to the line of chained, subdued Indians (they are being led back to work and salvation, certainly not to green pastures) and, in a wider scope —much later in time—to the corporal's own imprisonment by his companions. A deepening irony is his beginning to rot away from pox he acquired from an Indian woman; his vow to return to the "sweet" valley will be unfulfilled. The reader is safely left to draw the moral conclusion that any valley is or means what men make of it. These initial ironies are completed in the last chapter, by the innocent comments of the bus passengers who look down on The Pastures of Heaven from the heights of the roadway, in their relative freedom, and see—after we have been informed of a catalogue of human misery—only the peacefully sweet land.

In this way Steinbeck establishes that the locale of the novel is not heaven, only the usual post-Edenic exile. The ironic verbal byplay tends to make the contrast less than damning; it is firmly established as merely ironic. The notion that Steinbeck is only playing a word-game becomes more pronounced as the novel proceeds and the ironies become less controlled and more limited to their own context. We learn that the ironic battle on the Battle farm, in The Pastures of Heaven, had continued for two generations and that it is a battle with a metaphysical evil which the opening frame locates on the ironically named farm in the ironically

23. *PH*, p. 1.　　　　24. *PH*, pp. 1–2.

named town. Such play with words tends to control the development of characters and events.[25] The Battles are made
much of for ironic purposes, quite aside from their possible
function in the framework. Steinbeck indulges in so many
witty verbal antics that a reader may easily miss the point
that a metaphysical evil is present and, therefore, may miss
the function of these initial chapters. But the witty phrases
that Steinbeck uses to outline the characters of the various
original inhabitants of the Battle farm should speak for themselves. George Battle, who first settled the land in 1863,
appears in two matched notations that mark the quality of
his youth and age by their phrasing:

> George Battle looked about for a good investment in a woman.

> George Battle was old at fifty, bent with work, pleasureless
> and dour. His eyes never left the ground he worked with so
> patiently. His hands were hard and black and covered with
> little crevices, like the pads of a bear.[26]

The details are realized brilliantly—and that realization of
detail is the flaw of the passages in their relation to the total
structure. The notations do not refer of necessity to the
metaphysical evil or to the framework. By much straining
of implication, we can understand that George Battle brings
evil into the land through his unnatural life and that John,
his only son, embodies the consequences of George's life;
but none of this is clearly at hand. The brilliant and witty
description is founded on the man, not on what the man sig-
nifies. Here, then, as in earlier work, Steinbeck commits the
basic error of presenting materials that are not fused with
an intended structure. Steinbeck's characterization of John
Battle evidences this error. John appears in two matched notations, like his father. In the first he goes off, while his
father is living, "missionarying in a caravan," and in the
second, more detailed notation, he returns to claim the farm.
The passage deserves extended quotation:

25. One detail is concealed. We could not know, without going
to Steinbeck's letters, that the name of the real valley has been
changed to a more directly ironic name. Of course, the irony in the
name is clear enough as it is.

26. *PH*, pp. 1, 8–9.

John's life was devoted to a struggle with devils. . . . The farm slipped back to nature, but the devils grew stronger and more important. . . . One day in the deepening twilight John crept carefully upon a lilac bush in his own yard. He knew the bush sheltered a secret gathering of fiends. When he was so close that they could not escape, he jumped to his feet and lunged toward the lilac, flailing his stick and screaming. Aroused by the slashing blows, a snake rattled sleepily and raised its flat, hard head. John dropped his stick and shuddered, for the dry sharp warning of a snake is a terrifying sound. He fell upon his knees and prayed for a moment. Suddenly he shouted, "This is the damned serpent. Out, devil," and sprang forward with clutching fingers. The snake struck him three times in the throat. . . . He struggled very little, and died in a few minutes.[27]

In itself, the passage is brilliant. Nevertheless, except dimly by a strained implication, it does not relate to the intended framework. Steinbeck is too intent on having a bit of fun with a quite mad religious fanatic to consider the necessity of establishing the framework. Abstractly, and far below the surface, the framework is realized in the degeneration from George to John; unlike his father, John is entirely out of nature. But this insight is hidden. The idiotic, carefully rendered death is far more visible than its potential function.

These objections pertain equally to the functioning of the Munroe family. Steinbeck treats all of them as figures of fun, as cruder versions of Babbitt. They are a "normal" American family, civilized only in the sense that they are wholly materialistic. Each family member wants some tangible image that may signify an appropriate bourgeois status. Mrs. Munroe wants a solidly furnished house. The daughter, Mae, at nineteen wants only a good marriage. The son, Jimmie, at seventeen thoroughly accepts the values and standards of science in its popular sense. Bert, the father, firmly believes in the identification of free will and free enterprise. Fantastic accidents have prevented success —money—from blessing him. Steinbeck is very funny in outlining these people, even though he uses the essay method of characterization that is common in *Cup of Gold*. But

27. *PH*, pp. 9–10.

the comical essays fail to establish the function of the Munroes as "carriers" of the metaphysical evil; actually, they
distract attention from that identification. Only Bert's bad
luck is a reasonably visible connection—and it is not promi-
nently in view—with the metaphysical evil the Battles left
on their farm. In short, in dealing with the Munroes as in
dealing with the Battles, Steinbeck is far more interested in
exposing ironies than in establishing a structure. The reader
is left to deduce (if he can) the role of the Munroe family.
The clearest link is Bert's insight, after he has bought the
farm, since even his comic manner does not conceal the insight completely:

> I've had a lot of bad luck. . . . And what do I do? First
> thing out of the box, I buy a place that's supposed to be
> under a curse. Well, I just happened to think, maybe my
> curse and the farm's curse got to fighting and killed each
> other off. I'm dead certain they've gone, anyway.[28]

In reality, as suggested through the succeeding episodes,
the two curses merge, strengthen, and turn outward to the
community. But Bert's responsibility remains too far beneath the surface of irony and of broad comedy to refer with
clear visibility to the curse.

There is no doubt that Steinbeck intended this quite indirect, or dimly suggested, manner of indicating the function
of the Munroe family. His letter points out that the bad influence of the M——s was never visible. We have seen, in
both of Steinbeck's earlier novels, but particularly in *To a
God Unknown*, that he is all too capable of indirection
where structure is concerned.

Yet, the extreme indirection that argues the Munroe family is not capable of supporting a metaphysical evil within
their comical human limitations is complicated beyond
reason by the presence in the family of one tragic person
who is definitely not a Babbitt. The youngest son, Manfred,
has an adenoidal condition that (as yet unknown to anyone)
has arrested the development of his brain. Why Manfred
is included in the family is not clear. He is only mentioned;

---

28. *PH*, pp. 24–25.

nothing is made of him. Possibly, in some unarticulated allegorical scheme he might be intended to illustrate the flaws and uncertainties that even a "normal" American family cannot escape. As the novel exists, Manfred is only a tangible instance of loose ends in the framework. He is more than nonfunctional; he is machinery with no visible function. By existing, therefore, Manfred negates even the intended or theoretical function of the framework on its own terms.

These observations suggest that Steinbeck's overt aims in *The Pastures of Heaven* are badly confused, in spite of his cogent letter. Primarily, the structural difficulties indicate the nature and extent of that confusion.

Having established these points, we must consider now whether any other factor lends to the novel a degree of structural firmness in harmony with the materials in the nine episodes. As a unit, these episodes are somewhat more unified than a series of interchangeable stories because all of them concern a recognition—the pressure of social norms reveals to each character an evil side of his nature. Thus, each episode concerns the development of a different character in relation to a common theme. Yet, an essentially exterior "solution" is imposed at the climaxes of eight of the nine episodes by reference to the metaphysical evil and to the Munroes as unwitting but effective carriers of the evil. These "solutions" simplify the previous development of the materials because each operates as a *deus ex machina*. None follows adequately from events or from characterization because each is rather simplified in itself and because the intended function of the Munroes is obscured in the framework chapters.

The second episode, the story of the idiot boy, Tularecito, will serve as a typical example of Steinbeck's procedure. Tularecito is given a tragic division of talents. On the one hand, although his brain is underdeveloped, he is huge, strong, gentle, with the gift of drawing animals on a blackboard and of carving them in sandstone. On the other hand, his strongest feeling is a sense of extreme loneliness, an almost total isolation from other people—from normal humanity. A social complication occurs when Tularecito is required to attend school. His guardian acts as a chorus throughout this episode; he states the truth that social pressures, like those which produce the school law, are not necessarily good:

> This Little Frog should not be going to school. He can work: he can do marvelous things with his hands, but he cannot learn to do the simple little things of the school. He is not crazy; he is one of those whom God has not quite finished.[29]

Tularecito is not an idiot, but a deviate. His difficulties are typical, not peculiar; shocking, not curious; for he is the individual, the image of ourselves, set in a group that forces him to conform to standards he cannot acquire.

Steinbeck drops this universalism, relatively, to emphasize Tularecito's loneliness. The rather gushing teacher, Miss Morgan, describes gnomes and other fairy-tale creatures to her class; she believes that children should have rich imaginations. Tularecito is the only student who is affected because he recognizes himself in the description of the gnomes. He feels that if he digs far enough he will find "his people," and he begins to dig in Bert's orchard. Bert covers the hole; Tularecito sees Bert, clubs him with his shovel, and in due course is committed to an asylum for the criminally insane.

The real content of the episode—Tularecito's character and the general problem of isolation—is forgotten in the process of fitting the episode into the easy ironies—present mainly at the conclusion—that are associated with the framework. The conclusion is exciting enough, as holes and clubbings must be, but the violence does not conceal entirely the shift in the logic of the prior development of the materials. Instead, the conclusion has the practical effect of forcing Tularecito, as a character in a situation, to exist apart from the framework and thus apart from the violent climax.[30] Because the essential story has no organic link

29. *PH*, p. 64.

30. *Of Mice and Men* offers a significant parallel. Our interest in Lennie's predicament survives his violent death, perhaps in part because the violent conclusion is not relevant entirely to the predicament—as seems to be the case here, on a smaller scale.

with the machinery of the framework—although that machinery is intended to unify the episodes into one organic structure—the story is mainly a panoramic structure by default.

The other episodes, except for the fourth and sixth, follow the same pattern; their climaxes do not have an organic link with the preceding development of the materials. Even brief outlines of those episodes indicate the validity of this judgment. "Shark" Wicks is greedy to the extent of pretending to be rich. When he discovers financial value in his daughter's virginity he ceases to be human. The episode develops as a study of Wicks's inhumanity. His unmasking, after Jimmie speaks to his daughter, as a poor man unable to pay a fine, sacrifices the theme of inhumanity for an easy contrast between the actual (poor) man and the self-created, false image of the rich man. Mrs. Van Deventer kills her deranged daughter when she finds Bert talking to her, but this violent solution is really a means of avoiding the deeper irony—more clearly related to the materials—that Mrs. Van Deventer is as insane as her daughter. The Lopez sisters view themselves as perfectly honest women in a business world. They see nothing immoral in giving their favors to any man who buys three of their enchiladas until they are condemned as prostitutes by the community as the result of a practical joke that in all innocence Bert cannot help playing. This easily ironic solution avoids a deeper, more difficult exploration of the juxtaposition of commercial and human systems of value, which is the logic of the materials. In fact, this episode takes so huge a logical leap to reach its imposed ironic solution by reference to the framework that the sisters can appear to be morons.[31] The sixth episode

31. Moore, p. 30. Moore records that this episode was in the manuscript, "The Green Lady," but was recast for its use here. It is of interest that at least one episode predates the framework and the Munroe family, especially since the poor "fit" of the episode is typical rather than otherwise.

Richard Astro's recent study corrects some of Moore's data, particularly by setting back the first drafts that Steinbeck worked on to 1927 (from 1929, as Moore has suggested), and by establishing that "The Green Lady" certainly existed as an incomplete set of drafts, by Webster F. Street, for a three-act play. See Richard Astro, *John*

differs somewhat in its structure, but for the worse, since it is based on a sentimental cliché rather than on characterization. As an account of Molly Morgan's ambiguous feelings toward her kindly but drunken father, the episode provides a melodramatic contrast of the nice daughter and the worthless father. Steinbeck employs linked, complex flashbacks, but the well-made plot in which Bert objectifies Molly's own guilt is the first unqualified example in Steinbeck's work of a narrative that requires a wholly sentimental response.

Since these episodes have conclusions that are pasted on the materials rather than developed from them, the imposed framework separates from the materials. The separate episodes exist as more or less isolated stories—and very good stories. Because the stories develop in large part without reference to the framework, which operates only at the conclusion (frequently in the last paragraphs), the stories are not distorted to any great extent. They are essentially panoramic structures, essentially untouched by the framework.

The three concluding episodes are more nearly organic unities. It is probably significant that Steinbeck added these episodes in the late stages of the composition of the novel.[32] Still, they reveal, to some extent, the gap between a convincing development of the materials and an overly easy solution through the framework. That gap, however, is much less damaging than in the earlier episodes.

In the seventh episode, Raymond Banks's insensitivity to death is the central theme, suggested chiefly by his custom of visiting the warden of a prison, a boyhood friend, whenever there is to be an execution. There is no easy ironic contrast between normal and abnormal behavior, as in previous episodes. Instead, Banks is presented as a supernormally dull person who is able to feel the emotions of ordinary people only through their reactions to an event as extreme as violent death. In this oddity, Banks is as isolated as Tularecito. The episode hinges structurally on the contrast

Steinbeck and Edward F. Ricketts: The Shaping of a Novelist (Minneapolis: The University of Minnesota Press, 1973), pp. 81–83.

32. Moore, p. 30.

between Banks's simplicity and the community's horror. Bert's function is to make Banks aware of the community's secret opinion of him. Bert does this by nagging Banks for an invitation to an execution, which he gets, but in the end he refuses to attend.

In the eighth episode, Pat Humbert is presented as an isolated man, like Tularecito and Banks, cut off from life by a fostered sense of duty to care for his sickly, despotic parents. After they die, Pat tries at thirty to begin his life. He shuts the house, moves into the barn, and joins civic groups that use him "unmercifully."[33] Pat is so acutely aware of his isolation and so intent on associating it with the farmhouse that he does not observe that a rose bush, which he had let grow wild for ten years, has covered the house and made it beautiful. One day, he overhears Mae Munroe say, as she passes by, that the house must be as lovely inside as it is outside; her remark inspires Pat to refurbish his life. He opens the house secretly and, as secretly, rebuilds the interior. He feels that he can woo Mae with the beauty of the house. The link is symbolic. The ugly man with ugly memories feels that he can seem beautiful if his property—a material exterior—is made beautiful. As soon as the house is ready to be seen, Pat learns by accident from Bert Munroe that Mae is to marry Bill Whiteside. We deduce that materialism has been a false god to Pat. The effective use of symbol for structural purposes is a new element in Steinbeck's work. It contrasts sharply with his mechanistic use of Freudian symbols in *To a God Unknown*. Moreover, the analysis of Pat's involuted character governs the development of the episode. That analysis is far more credible than the rather abstract operation of the curse, which indeed has only a tangential reference to the events.

The ninth episode depends, like the eighth, rather fully on characterization for its significance. The episode is a history of three generations of the Whiteside family. The controlling metaphor is the lust of Richard, the founder from New England, to establish an enduring family and his inability to mold nature as he wishes. His only child,

33. *PH*, p. 228.

John, is a saintly man, not the empire builder he desires. John's only child, Bill, brusquely leaves the land for a business in town. The communication between generations is almost nil. Now this generational irony of characterization is abandoned for a heavily symbolic focus on the magnificent ancestral house, the visual "sign" of the original Whiteside hopes for a dynasty. This focus is intended to draw the framework of the curse and the Munroes into the episode. Bert is responsible for the accidental burning of the Whiteside house. However, the fire does not equate with the generational irony; further, it occurs after the final breakdown of the relationship between John and Bill. The major theme of the father–son impasse is fully developed; the fire has almost no effect on the clarity of that theme. Hence, the machinery of the framework is invoked to minimal effect.

The high artistic value of these three episodes depends on the restrictive effect of the framework on their internal development. The remarkable fourth episode is the strongest and most thorough, so it is useful to study that episode in some detail.

The fourth episode is an account of the transformation of Junius Maltby from a natural man to an artificial man in response to the conformist pressures of a society that Mrs. Munroe represents and personifies. Maltby lives with his son, Robbie, in a dream world built on the essays and novels of Robert Louis Stevenson. Maltby's life exemplifies the innocence of a child and he is loved by everyone. His recognition of social demands—reality—crushes his world. Robbie appears at school with no shoes and ragged clothes, and Mrs. Munroe prevails on her husband (a newly elected member of the school board) to do something about this apparently neglected child. The community must agree to aid the Maltbys, a matter complicated by the fact that Maltby has been envied for his freedom for many years. A gift of "a few little shirts and a pair of overalls and some shoes" is arranged.[34] Miss Morgan tries to save Robbie from the shame of charity, without success. The ironic contrast be-

34. *PH*, p. 136.

tween Mrs. Munroe and Miss Morgan has a clear structural function. Miss Morgan is our point of view. We see through her eyes and judge by her implied feelings. She has visited the Maltby farm, where Junius spends his days playing imaginative games with Robbie and his friends, and she has noticed that everyone around Junius is happy. But she is unable to state such intangible values to counter Mrs. Munroe's practical social concern. The basic tension in the episode is the conflict between Miss Morgan's moral insight and her social concern. (We have seen, in his earlier work, that Steinbeck is prone to shape conflicts indirectly, thereby separating structure from materials, or to force mechanical parallels without regard for credibility. Happily, in this instance, the paralleled conflict is inherent in the materials, and its indirection is a natural kind of hesitation, for Miss Morgan's conflict is analogous to Maltby's recognition that social demands do matter.) Even when Miss Morgan meets the unhappy but conforming Maltby with Robbie at the conclusion of the episode and near Christmas, she is unable to speak to them from her heart:

> They were dressed in cheap new clothes, and both of them walked as though their feet were sore. Miss Morgan looked closely at the little boy. . . . His face was sullen and unhappy. . . . She looked up quickly. It was Junius shorn of his beard. She hadn't realized that he was so old. . . . On his face there was a look of deep puzzlement. . . . "You see," he explained simply. "I didn't know I was doing an injury to the boy. . . . You can see that he shouldn't be brought up in poverty. You can see that, can't you. I didn't know what people were saying about us."[35]

In addition to the other materials, this confrontation suggests that the episode has several connecting layers, that it involves Miss Morgan and the Maltbys in a profound contrast of social values, not merely in a superficial irony. The role that Mrs. Munroe plays represents far more than the rather abstract workings of the curse, for she is the embodiment of a heartless meddling and of an emphasis on materialistic social values. Her function is to represent evil that

35. *PH*, pp. 138–39.

wears the trappings of social approval while it tramples on private happiness. The metaphysical evil, the curse, with its thin, artificial texture, is left far behind. The fact is that no one—least of all Junius Maltby—can deny the correctness of Mrs. Munroe's social concern. Even the essential goodness of John Whiteside cannot save Junius Maltby from a self-recognition that is false because it denies the genuine happiness of his previous, socially nonconforming life.

The structure is in harmony with these materials. It is a dramatic structure, focused on Junius Maltby through the controlled point of view that Miss Morgan provides. The symbols of freedom and of social coercion—the run-down Maltby farm, the neat pile of clothes presented to Robbie— are natural and never forced. Miss Morgan's ambiguous feelings are represented with particular force and with restrained irony. For example, at their final meeting, when Junius tells Miss Morgan that he is going away to renew his old life as an accountant although he has not worked for twenty years, she is unable to reassure him, to say that his life has been good, despite her sudden awareness of his real virtue. She is unable to speak because she accepts in part the assumptions of an official, social charity that denies Junius's virtue. Her complicity cancels her perception.

The concentrated excellence of this episode, the complex, thoroughly articulated, but organic relationship of structure to materials, suggest everything that is right in the best of Steinbeck's first three novels. His handling of the Munroes offers an entirely opposite view of his art. Most important, the Munroes simply do not have the central, organizing function that Steinbeck intended, but this is not due altogether to any lack of authorial skill. The Munroes seem to be exactly what Steinbeck intends them to be—innocent, commonplace, the last people anyone would expect to transmit evil. They are given no aura of importance. They initiate nothing. They stumble upon problems that exist and unknowingly they bring those problems to a head. But in concentrating on the ironic disparity between what they are and what they effect, Steinbeck permits the trivial and the accidental to govern his conception of the Munroes. For example, Tularecito could have dug in anyone's orchard. The fact that he digs in Bert's orchard is too overtly accidental to have much convincing fictional significance. Steinbeck insists on stressing precisely the personal insignificance and triviality of the Munroes and of their actions. They are never involved in the lives of others to the extent that their responsibility for the evil they transmit is evident to anyone in the novel. Further, Steinbeck avoids any association of the Munroes with the demonic or even with the mildly sinister. They are absolutely normal people. As a consequence, any importance in the role that Steinbeck assigns to the Munroes tends to evaporate. His propensity for emphasizing irony is responsible for denying the Munroes the reality or significance that even a thin character in a novel should have. Explicitly, then, the Munroes and the curse they transmit do not unify the novel in any sense of a dramatic structure. They are too dimly characterized to be convincing agents of anything; they are merely ironic, self-contained figures.

Clearly, Steinbeck's aim in characterizing the Munroes as he does is to domesticate our sense of evil. He fails in this aim because domestication cannot be identified merely with the ironic or the trivial or with an essentially whimsical conception of character. It is, therefore, to be expected that the Munroes are much less interesting than most of their victims. They are not presented in the depth or with the understanding that Steinbeck devotes to the other characters. Often, too, they are imposed on an episode that must be manipulated to permit a concluding reference to them.

Most damaging, the presence of the Munroes compromises the operating structure of the novel in that they are represented as carrying an abstract metaphysical evil into the community. Basically, however, the episodes concern social or psychological problems—not metaphysical problems. The nature of each story permits an external, mechanical "solution" to a developed exploration of a social or psychological problem. Where the framework is largely ignored or where the Munroes suggest social attitudes rather than metaphysical evil, there is an exception. Most often, the framework is pasted as an exterior form upon an essentially panoramic development of materials. Harry Thornton Moore compresses these observations into an insight by suggesting that *The Pastures of Heaven* "is really a group of loosely connected stories that are given a suggestion of unity by an artificial frame."[36] I prefer to point in more detail, and perhaps with more heat, to the structural damage effected by that artificial frame. The damage prevents Steinbeck's first extraordinary novel from being a very great novel; it is merely a very good novel. Further, it is all too clear, using hindsight, that Steinbeck does not outgrow the notion that an imposed framework will produce narrative order nor discover how to avoid the consequent manipulation of structure. Perhaps it is significant that Moore's book ends with a study of *The Grapes of Wrath*—before (as I think) Steinbeck came to accept structural imperfection.

Yet, "the suggestion of unity" in *The Pastures of Heaven* is not a result of the manifestly inoperative structure that Steinbeck intends the novel to have. Rather, the central point of reference is the muted, recurring theme of social pressure. The loose, panoramic structure suits the loosely related episodes. At best, there is a suggestion of a dramatic structure, but it remains just out of eyesight.[37]

Steinbeck uses the essentials of this suggestive relationship between structure and materials in such work as *Tortilla Flat* and *Cannery Row*, but the somewhat improvised development of these novels, so like *The Pastures of Heaven* in that respect, implies accident, not a fully developed sense of a craft.

A writer who works out relationships between structure and materials by accident is likely to have a rather uncertain career. Failure will be as likely as success. *Cup of Gold* and *To a God Unknown* do not exhaust the possibilities of failure. The element of accident does not make, either, for

36. Moore, p. 18.
37. *The Pastures of Heaven* seems related or possibly indebted, in a general fashion, to the form that one finds in Sherwood Anderson's *Winesburg, Ohio*. For a suggestive hint, see Moore, p. 92.

an immediately visible pattern in a career. The pattern is there but it may not be overt. Each new effort can seem to be a new start, slightly indebted—if at all—to earlier work. But if Steinbeck's original plan for *The Pastures of Heaven* had been more visible, had dominated the materials, he probably would have created a novel very like some of his least successful efforts—a novel controlled excessively by external devices that relate to an abstract, rather gimmicky idea. The line between success and failure can be that thin if accident rules.

The Pastures of Heaven is an extremely important novel, then, in relation to Steinbeck's career, since it throws considerable light on the best and worst aspects of his sense of craft. In isolation, considered purely for itself, however, *The Pastures of Heaven* is a charming set of episodes, a further illumination of Sherwood Anderson's country of the mind and of Anderson's craft. Steinbeck is lucky for the time being in his debts and accidents.

2

The First Public Success

Tortilla Flat

To understand more fully why one of the most promising of recent American novelists did not develop into a major figure, we must examine *Tortilla Flat*[1] closely and in the round, for it is crucially significant in the record of John Steinbeck's artistic development.

Tortilla Flat poses three major considerations. First, it is an artistic success in that it evidences a high degree of harmony between structure and materials—far more so than in any work Steinbeck had written earlier; but Steinbeck had external reason to ignore this fact. Second, *Tortilla Flat* is flawed in its conclusion by the imposition of an arbitrary, predetermined order on the events; Steinbeck cultivates this tendency in the future. Third, Steinbeck's first big-selling contact with a mass, adoring audience was caused by the same *Tortilla Flat*; Steinbeck's future view of his work and his relationship to his audience was influenced strongly by what he considered a dismaying success. Now, I suggest, to examine together these various aspects of *Tortilla Flat* will illuminate perhaps the most crucial turning point in Steinbeck's development.

The first major consideration is the artistic success. Several of Steinbeck's early novels have complex histories of overlapping periods of composition. This is not true of *Tortilla Flat*. The bibliographical evidence is that it follows *The Pastures of Heaven* immediately in date of composition and in date of publication.[2] A strictly literary comparison strengthens the implied connection between the two novels. Both are conceived as collections of episodes. Both have a

1. John Steinbeck, *Tortilla Flat* (New York: Covici, Friede, Inc., 1935). Hereafter cited as *TF*.
2. Peter Lisca, *The Wide World of John Steinbeck* (New Brunswick: Rutgers University Press, 1958), pp. 72–73.

highly visible structural machinery—the Munroe family and the curse in *The Pastures of Heaven*, the Malory parallel in *Tortilla Flat*—that Steinbeck is willing to leave as an implication. Both novels take place in a definite geographical setting—the farming community named "The Pastures of Heaven" and the hill above Monterey where the *paisanos* live. Each novel deals with a specific group of persons. The farmers and the country aristocracy are familiar enough, but, to the outsider, the *paisanos* are considerably more exotic—"a mixture of Spanish, Indian, Mexican, and assorted Caucasian bloods."[3] Finally, it can be said that while the style of *Tortilla Flat* is mainly an approximation of Spanish diction and the style of *The Pastures of Heaven* is mainly Steinbeck's observational diction (except in the episode concerning the Lopez sisters, in which the style common to *Tortilla Flat* is used), both styles have a lucidity, other considerations being equal, that indicates usually that Steinbeck is doing his best work.[4] So these two novels share an essential similarity in structural machinery, in the groups of characters, and in the truth of the two styles, and this likeness distinguishes them relatively from Steinbeck's first two novels. But there is a striking difference between the structural importance and effect of the Munroes and the curse on the one hand and the Malory parallel on the other. The difference reveals a great deal about Steinbeck's intentions and abilities.

There is no doubt of Steinbeck's intentions regarding the important function of the Malory parallel. Steinbeck insisted repeatedly, before and since its publication, that *Tortilla Flat* is "openly based" on the structure of *Morte d'Arthur*.[5] Despite this insistence, my study of Malory's romance confirms Peter Lisca's view that the parallel operates

3. *TF*, p. 11.
4. The sisters are, of course, *paisanos*. See Henry Thornton Moore, *The Novels of John Steinbeck* (Chicago: Normandie House, 1939), p. 20.
5. Lisca, pp. 76–79; Joseph Fontenrose, *John Steinbeck: An Introduction and Interpretation* (New York: Barnes & Noble, Inc., 1963), pp. 36–41. Excerpts from this work are reprinted by permission of Holt, Rinehart and Winston, Inc.

only in minor and external details and, hence, does not perform its intended function of unifying *Tortilla Flat*.[6] This fault was evident to Steinbeck from the beginning of the marketing of the manuscript. Various publishers objected to what they felt was a lack of form in the novel, and Steinbeck felt compelled to write a detailed letter to his literary agents to explain what he had intended to achieve by way of a structure:

> The form is that of the Malory version, the coming of Arthur and the mystic quality of owning a house, the forming of the round table, the adventures of the knights and finally, the mystic adventures of Danny. However, I seem not to have made any of this clear. The main issue was to present a little known and, to me delightful people. Is not this cycle story or theme enough? Perhaps it is not enough because I have not made it clear enough. Now, if it is not enough, then I must make it clearer. What do you think of putting in an interlocutor, who between each incident interprets the incident, morally, aesthetically, historically, but in the manner of the paisanos themselves. . . . I don't intend to make the parallel of the Round Table more clear, but simply to show that a cycle is there. You will remember that the association forms, flowers and dies.[7]

Happily, the novel does not have an interlocutor. Considered more seriously, this explanation reveals Steinbeck's difficulty in linking chosen materials—the *paisanos*, "a little known and, to me delightful people"—with an appropriate structure. We can observe Steinbeck's humble and nearly absolute uncertainty with a terrible clarity.[8] The two

6. Joseph Henry Jackson accepts too uncritically Steinbeck's assertion that a clear and operative parallel exists between *Morte d'Arthur* and *Tortilla Flat*. See p. viii of Jackson's Introduction to *The Short Novels of John Steinbeck* (New York: The Viking Press, Inc., 1953). Joseph Fontenrose provides a labored reading to demonstrate that "Malory's Arthur story did in fact determine the narrative sequence and pervade the whole content" (p. 36). "Based on" is probably a larger claim than "pervade," and Fontenrose's method will serve any cause. Indeed, Fontenrose's ingenuity is so strained in Steinbeck's defense as to demonstrate the nearly invisible operative quality of the asserted parallel for any possible "common reader."

7. Lisca, p. 76.

8. The context of the letter indicates that Steinbeck is speaking of the version of *Tortilla Flat* that was published eventually. The

concluding sentences reveal that structure ought to get in the way of materials as little as possible and, to that end, should function on a primitive level. Surely the rhythm of "a cycle" is as extreme a simplification of structure as one can imagine. It is true that *Tortilla Flat* has a cyclic rhythm, but the resulting type of structure is too universal to be identified readily as a debt to Malory, at least in as close a parallel as Steinbeck's opening sentence would indicate.

If it appears that the Malory parallel does not function as effectively as Steinbeck had intended, nevertheless the result aids rather than harms his aim to achieve some degree of harmony between structure and materials. The letter and the novel indicate that, whatever his intentions, Steinbeck indeed placed greater emphasis on the general idea of a cycle than on the external, intended parallel to *Morte d'-Arthur*. The consequence is fortunate. *Tortilla Flat* suffers far less from its ties to an external, intended parallel than *The Pastures of Heaven*. Stated more positively, Steinbeck appears willing to develop *Tortilla Flat* as an organic whole, bound only lightly to its parallel with *Morte d'Arthur*. His letter suggests that he arrived at this willingness at least in part by accident. I suggest an alternate possibility: that he grew more willing with *Tortilla Flat* than with *The Pastures of Heaven* to let a novel follow its own bent.[9] This possibility is supported by the excellence of the individual episodes and by the style, which suggests Steinbeck's experience and probable confidence in a growing ability to manage brief episodes with authority. Of course, neither explanation is adequate. The first suggests that all we need to know is that basic technical matters confused Steinbeck; the second does not explain why several of the later novels resemble the rigid constructions that Steinbeck hoped to

significant point is that Steinbeck appears to have little insight into the relationships between structure and materials even, in this instance, when the act of creation is essentially complete.

9. E. M. Forster, *Aspects of the Novel* (New York: Harcourt, Brace & Co., 1927), pp. 140–44. Forster points out that on occasion a work in hand will develop its own logic, sometimes in spite of the novelist's plan. Excerpts from this work are reprinted by permission of Harcourt Brace Jovanovich, Inc.

achieve, according to his recorded plans, in *The Pastures of Heaven* and in *Tortilla Flat*, in spite of his mature experience and recorded confidence in his medium. Despite the inadequacy of explanations in this instance, they do emphasize the central point that *Tortilla Flat* exhibits far more functional harmony between structure and materials than any of Steinbeck's previous novels. Close examination of the actual construction confirms this view.

Tortilla Flat is mainly a panoramic structure—a group of episodes—that can appear to have the unity of a dramatic structure to the extent that a cyclic rhythm and a common theme are evident to the reader. I believe the cyclic rhythm is evident in terms of the common theme that Steinbeck announces in the Preface to the novel; "The paisanos are clean of commercialism, free of the complicated systems of American business, and, having nothing that can be stolen, exploited, or mortgaged, that system has not attacked them very vigorously."[10] The contrast between *paisanos* and "systems of American business" allows Steinbeck to control the arrangement and development of the episodes in the novel from a central point of view. That is, each episode is a moral parable in which a *paisano* is tempted by the things of this world "of American business," but survives in the end with his soul intact.

The particular applications of this common theme can be followed in detail. The novel begins with an economic fact: Danny's ownership of two houses left to him by his grandfather. The episode concerns Danny's weight of ownership until he is able to get rid of his excess property by "renting" one house to his friends. The structure of the episode depends on a comic reversal, on the fact that "rent" in *paisano* economics is a way of saying "live in for nothing." The reversal or inversion of ordinary economic and social terms is common to every episode, but the method is presented explicitly here, at the beginning. To emphasize the point, Pilon, one of Danny's more introspective friends, announces the prevailing attitude of the *paisano* toward responsibility in the normal world, the economic and social

10. *TF*, p. 11.

world "of American business": "I am getting into debt to him," he thought bitterly. "My freedom will be cut off."[11] The *paisano* is irresponsible in the sense that his personal freedom is the only possession that he really treasures, and since freedom is necessarily destroyed by possessions and by the assumptions "of American business," it is expressed most frequently in specifics as an economic freedom.

The social code that follows from this economic definition of freedom is that society is useful in so far as it provides the *paisano* with enough to eat and drink, but social value itself exists only vis-à-vis personal economic freedom. There is no virtue in having to earn what is literally a living, and therefore *paisanos* work to avoid work in order to enjoy a free life. In agreement with this social paradox, wine is especially prized—it is more important than food—because it has pleasant social effects.

The burden of rationalizing this way of life is left to Pilon. He is the philosopher in *paisano* society. He states any immediate choice in its universal sense, but always from the bias of personal economic freedom. Thus, early in the novel, when he inspects Danny's house, Pilon states a clear definition of the good social life as the *paisano* sees it:

> While Danny went to Monterey to have the water turned on, Pilon wandered into the weed-tangled back yard. Fruit trees were there, bony and black with age, and gnarled and broken from neglect. A few tent-like chicken coops lay among the weeds. A pile of rusty barrel hoops, a heap of ashes, and a sodden mattress. Pilon looked over the fence into Mrs. Morales' chicken yard, and after a moment of consideration he opened a few small holes in the fence for the hens. "They will like to make nests in the tall weeds," he thought kindly. He considered how he could make a figure-four trap in case the roosters came in too and bothered the hens and kept them from the nests. "We will live happily," he thought again. Danny came back indignant from Monterey. "That company wants a deposit," he said. "Deposit?" "Yes. They want three dollars before they will turn on the water." "Three dollars," Pilon said severely, "is three gallons of wine. And when that is gone, we will borrow a bucket of water from Mrs. Morales, next door." "But we haven't three dollars for wine." "I know,"

11. *TF*, p. 30.

> Pilon said. "Maybe we can borrow a little wine from Mrs. Morales."[12]

Pilon rejects the ironically described Eden on earth for an Eden in the neighbor's home. Even the small jobs that God assigned to Adam for reasons of health are too much for Pilon.

All of this suggests that *paisanos* know by instinct how to distinguish a legitimate or real claim from an unreasonable or unreal claim on the individual. If it requires any work that can be refused, the desire to have money is as unreal a claim as the water company's demand for a deposit. But if Danny and his friends *find* money or valuables the event is real—a tangible miracle that promotes the continuation of the good life. Steinbeck's complicated and even sophisticated application of this principle in specific episodes is at once a justification of the cyclic development of the novel as a panoramic structure and the central factor that unifies the materials within a common theme.

A major complication is that, on occasion, even a *paisano* can be tempted or corrupted by things of this world. Steinbeck places such temptations and corruptions within a comic frame, implying that the essential innocence of the *paisano* survives every assault. For example, Sweets Ramirez gains much social status in Tortilla Flat from receiving a gift of a vacuum cleaner from Danny. The cleaner has no motor, and Sweets has no electricity in her house, but she continues to run the machine over her floor to impress her neighbors. Her simplicity occasions a rather sophisticated parody of the normal standards of value; her possible conversion to those standards is not the point of focus.

The *paisanos* are undeniably a colorful people, and *Tortilla Flat* has been read often enough merely as a potpourri of exotic local color. If it were no more than that, it probably would not communicate the insights and the pleasure that it does. In reality, Steinbeck's linking a colorful people to a basically serious view of social and economic values tends to humanize the idea and to domesticate the

12. *TF*, p. 29.

people. Irony is the natural mode of this double process, and therefore the details of its management are relevant to an understanding of the harmonious relationship between structure and materials.

Irony in *Tortilla Flat*, disarming as it is in its comic guise, nevertheless asks a controlled series of basic questions concerning the best and most valuable ways of achieving the good life—within a series of episodes. It would be misleading to conclude that *Tortilla Flat* is a work of philosophy or that Steinbeck intended the novel to be a philosophy. Instead, as a work of art, it is a far more dangerous attack on normal attitudes than much philosophy can hope to be.

It will be useful to analyze more closely what these points involve by studying a complete, typical episode, such as the one that continues through Chapters IV, V, and VI. The three chapters bear the following titles:

IV. How Jesus Maria Corcoran, a good man, became an unwilling vehicle of evil.
V. How Saint Francis turned the tide and put a gentle punishment on Pilon and Pablo and Jesus Maria.
VI. How three sinful men, through contrition, attained peace. How Danny's friends swore comradeship.

The titles are modeled generally after Malory's, but they operate in the novel as comic inversions of their apparent meaning. (This quite limited practical use of *Morte d'Arthur* contradicts clearly Steinbeck's inflated claims for the theoretical function of the parallel.) First, then, the grandiosity of the titles is in sharp contrast with the chronicles of small beer that follow. The precise method of this comedy of inversion is indicated by a consideration of the actual events in the three chapters. Mrs. Morales is thought to be rich because she has $200 in the bank. She is Danny's neighbor, and Danny courts her. In order to bring her some gift besides his charming manners, Danny asks for rent from Pilon and Pablo. Ironically, they have been discussing evil tendencies in women; they are forced to produce some money to finance Danny's pursuit of this woman. They discover Jesus Maria drunk in a ditch, and he tells them of selling a salvaged rowboat for $7 and of spending most of this money on Arabella Gross. All has not gone to satisfy Arabella's pleasures; Jesus Maria still has $3 in his pockets. Thereupon Pilon and Pablo rent "the use of their house to Jesus for fifteen dollars a month," with $3 down—but they spend the $2 they finally get on wine for Danny and Mrs. Morales.[13] This incident concludes Chapter IV. The action in Chapter V is simply that Pilon and Pablo get drunk on the wine at their house, and a candle that Pablo had bought to give to Saint Francis is lit, burns down, and sets the house on fire. Chapter VI contains two parallel actions. Mrs. Morales loses interest in Danny because he owns only one house. Yet, among the friends the atmosphere of a happy male group—now including Jesus Maria—is restored and strengthened by Jesus Maria's sudden pledge to Danny.

Even this brief summary indicates several differences, beyond simple inversion, between the chapter titles and the events themselves. The rather simple, mechanical contrast is transcended almost immediately, since the real subject of the episode is an exploration of the meaning of friendship within an economic frame of reference. What matters is friendship, and, in the nature of *paisano* society, it is restricted wholly to men. Women are either meanly or cheerfully predatory, incapable of friendship, and certainly not part of the Round Table motif of "a band of brothers." Further, in *paisano* society women tend to corrupt men if their relationship to men is other than sexual. Mrs. Morales is interested in Danny's wealth, as Danny is interested in hers, so it is proper that Mrs. Morales should drop Danny when he loses economic status. Puns emphasize the point. Mrs. Morales is a moral woman of business, and no doubt Steinbeck intended the pun. The pun on the name Arabella Gross, who is the reverse of Mrs. Morales, seems as intentional. Arabella's pleasures are merely gross, or purely physical. These puns become witty insights into human nature as we realize that Arabella Gross is like Mrs. Morales in being attracted to any man who suits her. Jesus Maria's name is as suitable, for, like Christ, Jesus Maria assumes a duty toward humanity so far as Danny represents humanity. The

13. *TF*, p. 63.

artificial quality of the puns and allegorical names is subsumed by the controlled, ironic wit that, consequently, justifies the artifice. For example, the salvation of friendship
is dependent on "a gentle punishment," which is the burning of Danny's excess house. That loss reduces Danny's
economic status sharply, thus returning him to essential humanity—almost bare of worldly goods—in the guise of his
friends' love for him.

The exploration of the meaning of friendship is controlled
in another regard. Steinbeck avoids any taint of sentimentality in the notion of friendship. The economic duties of
friendship are resisted by all of the men. We see this in the
passage that follows Jesus Maria's pledge, "It shall be our
burden and our duty to see that there is always food in the
house for Danny."

> Pilon and Pablo looked up in alarm, but the thing was said;
> a beautiful and generous thing. No man would with impunity
> destroy it. Even Jesus Maria understood, after it was said,
> the magnitude of his statement. They could only hope that
> Danny would forget it. "For," Pilon mused to himself, "if
> this promise were enforced, it would be worse than rent. It
> would be slavery." "We swear it, Danny!" he said. They sat
> about the stove with tears in their eyes, and their love for
> one another was almost unbearable.[14]

Pilon's summary of resistance to the economic aspect of the
pledge prevents any slide into sentimentality. And so far
as it is economic, the pledge is not kept; so far as it implies
the beautiful ideal of friendship—the round table, the band
of brothers—it is kept. Pilon understands and expresses the
ironic division between the pure intention and the practical
effect, but the division is felt by all of the men and their
knowledge prevents Danny from testing the pledge. The
identity of understanding between the men is the solid basis
for their friendship and the essence of their identity as
paisanos. And so this episode ends.

The ironic tension that permits the functioning of the
witty insight is a consequence of a fully controlled handling
of materials. The resulting authorial control promotes a

14. *TF*, p. 90.

harmony between structure and materials. The structure is not isolated nor is it used to force meanings into the materials, and the materials are not allowed to become an end in themselves. Because of this essential control, large themes and secondary aids to order, such as a general statement of intent, a significant use of names, a stylized diction, the pairing of Danny and Pilon that Mme Claude-Edmonde Magny has noticed, and the theme of the good life—all contribute to Steinbeck's total conception of the novel.[15] There are excellent results in characterization as well. The *paisanos* appear all too humanly paradoxical because of the complex and flexible control that determines their actions. Hence, the chance that Steinbeck will merely exploit exotic materials is not realized. He keeps the episode from dropping into allegory by permitting his characters to confront a complex problem and to give complex responses to it, the whole being subject to irony.

Since this episode is typical of the four or five central episodes in *Tortilla Flat*, the novel can be examined as a unit from the perspective that has been established.

Tortilla Flat has a serious intention that fuses with its celebration of friendship. That is, the novel has a moral aim that rests on a theological base. The *paisano* concept of friendship stems from a source that is older and more profound than the Round Table. The *paisanos* are children of Mother Church. They recognize the basic Christian distinction between temporal and eternal things and translate it into a specific distinction between the temporal value of money and the eternal value of friendship. This specific distinction governs the development of every episode. Again and again some threat to friendship (and, thus, to the good life) is established in some detail. In the end, however narrow the margin, the eternal value—friendship—is sustained in the minds and hearts of the endangered *paisanos*. The

15. Claude-Edmonde Magny, "Steinbeck, or the Limits of the Impersonal Novel," in E. W. Tedlock, Jr., and C. V. Wicker, eds., *Steinbeck and His Critics* (Albuquerque: University of New Mexico Press, 1957), p. 227.

significant result is that a moral weight of theological content dignifies episodes that otherwise would be merely witty or merely ironic and dignifies a people that in other respects are merely colorful.

Proceeding through the novel, we can discover the effect of this essentially theological content. The Pirate is not robbed; instead, he is saved and drawn into the circle of friends (Chs. VII, XII); a search for hidden treasure turns into an act of friendship (Ch. VIII); an attempt at seduction by giving rich presents turns into a moral fable (Ch. IX); we see "How the Friends solaced a corporal and in return received a lesson in paternal ethics" (Ch. X); a brutal seduction turns into a friendly act (Ch. XI); the Friends keep a helpless lady in food by robbery (Ch. XII); and, finally, we see how various acts of love, when thwarted, can turn to evil (Ch. XIV).

The three final chapters (XV–XVII) do not fit this scheme. Primarily they prepare for the death of Danny. The weakness of Steinbeck's self-alleged debt to *Morte d'Arthur* is indicated clearly by the appendix which these final chapters constitute. They are detached from the harmonious relationship between structure and materials that characterizes the rest of the novel. Indeed, these chapters are excellent confirmation of E. M. Forster's contention that "nearly all novels are feeble at the end . . . because the plot requires to be wound up," and, it may be added, here the "plot" is seriously in conflict with the otherwise organic development of the novel.[16]

The conflict is apparent immediately in the title of Chapter XV: "How Danny brooded and became mad. How the devil in the shape of Torrelli assaulted Danny's House." Danny's madness does not derive from earlier events. It is a sudden turn of "plot," pasted onto rather than integrated into the economic theme and the moral content of the novel. Danny's madness is Steinbeck's means of winding up the novel. Probably something of this sort is required in view of the rather "open" structure, the essentially limitless ma-

16. Forster, pp. 144–45.

terials, and the cyclic development that have been examined. That consideration does not qualify the fact that Steinbeck's choice of a conclusion is far more detached from the preceding two thirds of the novel than it need be.

Steinbeck does seem to recognize the need to fuse the conclusion with the rest of the novel, since he clearly attempts to accomplish that fusion. The theme of Danny's madness is associated with the economic theme, as in the following sentences, early in Chapter XV: "Always the weight of the house was upon him; always the responsibility to his friends. Danny began to mope on the front porch, so that his friends thought him ill."[17] The difficulty is that Danny's sense of responsibility is a new development, not foreshadowed or linked to any circumstance introduced previously into the novel. It is clearly an external device aimed at concluding the novel. It is true that Steinbeck engages in heroic efforts to associate Danny's madness with the economic theme, as the preceding quotation suggests. Nevertheless, Danny does not feel the weight of ownership and of responsibility to his friends until these pressures become a means of concluding. The strain is all too evident in itself, so the two lines of development, the economic theme and the theme of Danny's madness, are associated rather than fused, although succeeding events presume their fusion. The actual separation of these themes produces the uncomfortable strain of the conclusion.

Thus, for example, halfway through Chapter XV, Danny disappears suddenly because of the weight of his relative wealth. Pilon is given insight into the moral truth of Danny's madness and foreshadows the concluding events: "Danny is crazy, and he is in danger. Some terrible thing will happen to him if we do not save him."[18] Steinbeck presents in isolation the economic reason for Danny's disappearance and Pilon's moral explanation; the two reasons exist separately. This division continues. "Truly the good life lay in ruins" because of Danny's practical jokes on his friends, but the destruction of the good life is equated with economic freedom from Danny's (now demented?) point of view: "The

17. *TF*, p. 259.   18. *TF*, p. 265.

house was in a state of siege. All about it raged Danny, and Danny was having a wonderful time."[19]

Danny's next bid for economic freedom is the extreme measure of selling the house to the storekeeper, Torrelli, although Danny's intentions are qualified. He is drunk when he signs away the house. As a further qualification, Danny's sudden aging, evidenced by his appearance and behavior, undercuts the sense of moral calm at the conclusion of the chapter—Danny's sudden, defeated return to his friends, after they attack Torrelli and burn Danny's note of sale. The implication is that when Danny's bid for economic freedom fails, the moral basis for living fails as well, and Danny can grow old. But the two kinds of failure remain separate; they are announced, not integrated into each other. The division is evident once again in that Danny's friends plan a party in an attempt to save the good life along with Danny, but the feverishness of their practical effort indicates its moral futility. The party is successful, but it ends with Danny's death. (Observe, by the way, that Steinbeck uses the device of an ultimate party in a number of succeeding novels. The symbolic content varies, depending on circumstances. The ease with which Steinbeck detaches the device from its present context emphasizes the largely formal conclusion of *Tortilla Flat*.)

By this point, *Tortilla Flat* is removed rather considerably from a primary focus on the economic theme and the moral content. Everything is subordinated to the new theme of Danny's madness. The friends go to work at Chin Kee's to earn money for the party, although we have seen that Danny's friends are inherently shiftless (or, rather, free). In any case, the motivating reason for the party is qualified by a moral insight, Pablo's vision of a portent of evil, "a big black bird, as big as a man," over Danny's bed.[20] This folklore or magical motif rules out the relevance of the economic theme, the need to work. Hence, the concluding pages of Chapter XVI are written in an apocalyptical style, appropriate to the description of the feverish party and to Danny's frenzy. The following passage is typical:

19. *TF*, p. 270.   20. *TF*, p. 294.

Where Danny went, a magnificent madness followed. It is passionately averred in Tortilla Flat that Danny alone drank three gallons of wine. It must be remembered, however, that Danny is now a god. In a few years it may be thirty gallons. In twenty years it may be plainly remembered that the clouds flamed and spelled DANNY in tremendous letters; that the moon dripped blood; that the wolf of the world bayed prophetically from the mountains of the Milky Way.[21]

While this consciously exaggerated folklore motif tends to save *Tortilla Flat* from a dreadfully serious tone, it so completely severs the economic theme from the theme of Danny's madness that there is no chance of a fusion in the remainder of the novel. Human and divine affairs can be fused, of course, but Steinbeck's total focus is on Danny's comic or marvelous transformation into a god.

Curiously enough, *Tortilla Flat* and *To a God Unknown* close with a transformation from the human to the divine. It is instructive to compare the two endings with this point in mind.

Both novels are unsuccessful as they end, but the reasons are quite different. *To a God Unknown* fails because Steinbeck is unwilling to deal directly with the characterization of a priest or god of nature, so the transformation is stated but never motivated. *Tortilla Flat* fails because Danny's transformational dip into fantasy is completely arbitrary. We are told that Danny goes mad and that he dies in a fall over a cliff during a "fight" with "The Enemy," but there is little in Danny's previous, established character that justifies the transformation. Evidently, in composing these final chapters, Steinbeck did not trouble greatly about a harmonious relationship between the structure and the materials within the complete novel. Putting the matter more sternly, Steinbeck commits the elementary error of winding up the novel by reshaping character to fit plot. Avoiding a definition of character is as unpleasant as the arbitrary imposition of character, alas.

This observation is not necessarily a condemnation of *Tortilla Flat*. Danny's comic transformation is surely de-

21. *TF*, pp. 298–99.

lightful in itself. The issue is that here Steinbeck sacrifices harmony to delight the reader momentarily. Steinbeck has a propensity in other novels to compose a set of momentary effects, finely engineered and fairly isolated from each other; this characteristic suggests that his willingness to fragment a novel is less an accident than a constant factor.

Tone is a related issue because it helps to suggest the attitude the reader is intended to take toward the final episode. The tone is thoroughly arch in its repeated insistence that any idea of transformation must be overwhelmingly funny in the context of *Tortilla Flat*. Danny is not a heroic warrior but a drunken *paisano,* the party is not a heroic event but a drunken brawl, Danny's friends are not a heroic group of followers but quite unheroic *paisanos,* and so on. The consequence of Steinbeck's certainty that the basic contrast must be annihilatingly funny is an almost total failure of harmony between structure and materials. Responsibility lies, in large part, in his failure to consider that the contrast is unsupported and, indeed, contradicted by much of the tone and logic of previous episodes. Yet his certainty is indicated by his eagerness to break into events in his own voice, after Danny's death.

Granting that the unsupported contrast between Danny and his friends and the death of King Arthur is not as comic as Steinbeck intends it to be, even a perfect harmony probably could not provide a sweepingly comic effect; the contrast is much too plainly a needed device to close out the novel. Still worse, Steinbeck inflates the importance of a technical necessity by emphasizing a comedy of pure contrast—in the absurdity of a *paisano* version of the death of King Arthur—beyond the comic invention or business that contrast can be made to support.

Steinbeck is more successful in Chapter XVII in establishing the contrast between Danny's low estate and his splendid military funeral. The reasons are clear. Here the contrast is muted rather than emphasized; it is detailed rather than loaded with more significance than it can bear; and it relates to the novel's primary, carefully established thesis: the opposition between economic slavery and human freedom. One detail will serve as an example of the whole. Danny's genuinely sorrowing friends feel out of place at the magnificent funeral; they observe the military ceremonies from a distance. As compared to the funeral scenes, the return to the motif of the Round Table in the concluding pages of the chapter, when the friends decide to burn Danny's house, is strikingly artificial in conception and in tone. The inflated tone of Chapter XVI is conceivable only as burlesque in its context, but in Chapter XVII the theme of economic slavery versus human freedom is too lofty to be undercut as deeply as Steinbeck seems to intend.

A concluding judgment can be positive, in the main. Despite Steinbeck's too easily satisfied sense of the comic in the concluding chapters, *Tortilla Flat* is, on the whole, a very successful novel. Its first two thirds form an organic whole, which indicates Steinbeck's artful awareness that a panoramic structure—a series of episodes—can have the unity of an entirely dramatic structure if the writer has the skill or luck to fuse a single theme with significant content. The fusion of the economic theme and the moral content is an artistic triumph of the first order. The isolation of the last third of the novel is a consequence of the imposition of a predetermined structure upon unwilling materials—pragmatic rather than architectural, unconscious rather than self-conscious. Steinbeck's tendency is to compose details rather than a whole; when the major part of the novel is excellent, as in *Tortilla Flat*, the resulting difficulties are all too evident, but the reader has been rewarded enough to forgive (perhaps).

But not forever, and not past a certain proportion of success to failure. Steinbeck's insistence that the key to the structure of *Tortilla Flat* is the alleged debt to *Morte d'Arthur*, especially in view of the actual isolation of the final chapters, is an important index to the depth of his weakness for a predetermined structure that is imposed on materials to advance a "system" of parallels. In time, as he develops his opinions still more firmly, the several parallels harden into "systems" of allegorical correspondence. Finally, in most of the late novels, there emerges an extreme simplification of the total relationship between structure and materials. On the whole, these developments are unfortunate. Since they appear to derive from Steinbeck's fondness for a predetermined structure, which is clearly evident in the concluding chapters of *Tortilla Flat*, there is justification in devoting considerable attention to what, in *Tortilla Flat*, is a relatively minor flaw.

The final major consideration is the probable impact of the popular success of *Tortilla Flat* on Steinbeck's later career. It can be said that a closely documented and a possibly contributing reason for Steinbeck's emphasis on a weakness rather than on a strength in many of the later novels is suggested by his peculiarly ambiguous view of *Tortilla Flat*. The conclusions to be drawn from the public history of *Tortilla Flat* are tentative and suggestive, yet the evidence is important enough to merit consideration, in view of the issue of Steinbeck's practice of novelistic technique. It seems reasonable to move now from objective criticism, or analysis of the novel in itself, to the more troubled area of autobiography, or Steinbeck's private view (so far as it is recorded) of what *Tortilla Flat* is and is not.

Immediately after its publication, Steinbeck apparently felt that in *Tortilla Flat* he had solved the problem of attaining a harmony between structure and materials. As we have seen, this is true, in the main, though not because of Steinbeck's efforts to set up a controlling structural parallel to *Morte d'Arthur*.[22] If Steinbeck's was a mistaken view of the actual structure of *Tortilla Flat*, as my preceding analysis demonstrates, the fact that *Tortilla Flat* became a best seller on grounds extraneous to Steinbeck's intentions was anything but helpful in clarifying his view of what he had written. Indeed, the public response seems to have confused the issue further for Steinbeck. A mass audience was enchanted by the materials of *Tortilla Flat* and totally oblivious to the alleged Malory parallel. It would seem that Steinbeck, in view of the public's acceptance of the novel, permitted himself to think of *Tortilla Flat* as the work that he had planned, since it was easy enough to blame the mass audience for

22. Lisca, pp. 74–76.

failing to perceive the alleged parallel.[23] Worse followed. In the Foreword to the Modern Library edition of *Tortilla Flat*, written in 1937, two years after the first publication of the novel, Steinbeck reported angrily that a mass audience had vulgarized his intentions—that although he acknowledged the benefits from large book sales and the sale of the movie rights, there were adverse results. Not only had the mass audience mistaken his intent, but tourists had made their way in droves to the scene of *Tortilla Flat* to observe the amusing life of the *paisanos* and perhaps to search for the secret of the gaiety and vitality of that life. In view of the damage their presence had worked, Steinbeck vowed that he would write no more about *paisano* life.[24] Clearly, this extraordinary protest and vow indicate Steinbeck's bitter certainty that he had been misread. Still more significantly, Steinbeck's implication is that if *Tortilla Flat* had been appreciated less superficially or had reached an audience with the cultural background to recognize the Malory parallel, *Tortilla Flat* would have been received as far more than merely an entertainment. Joseph Warren Beach has observed rightly that, in making this protest and vow, Steinbeck had lost his grip momentarily on the distinction between art and life[25] I suggest that Steinbeck had lost even more. The public response permitted him to value the Malory parallel beyond its merits and obscured the conditions of the operative harmony between the novel's structure and its materials.

Slowly and more generally, Steinbeck's articulated view of artistic honesty emerges out of this fuss, and, very likely, this crisis affected his artistic development. In a significantly revealing letter to his literary agents concerning his withdrawal of a manuscript entitled *L'Affaire Lettuceburg*, an early version of *The Grapes of Wrath*, Steinbeck spelled out the long-term effect of the public response to *Tortilla Flat*. In the letter he associated poverty and good writing on the

23. Lewis Gannett, "Introduction: John Steinbeck's Way of Writing," *The Viking Portable Steinbeck* (New York: The Viking Press, Inc,. 1946), p. xiv.

24. *Tortilla Flat* (New York: Modern Library, 1937), pp. i–iii.

25. Joseph Warren Beach, *American Fiction, 1920–1940* (New York: The Macmillan Company, 1941), p. 319.

one hand and financial success and bad writing on the other.[26] The expressed presumption is that the good novel does not find the faceless mass audience that Steinbeck had reached, all too unexpectedly, with *Tortilla Flat*.

Certainly this ramified experience is not an aspect of Steinbeck's private life alone; it also concerns his public artistic life. It suggests that a mass audience blinded him to the real virtues of *Tortilla Flat*, especially to the fact that, in large part, *Tortilla Flat* attains an organic harmony as the result of a far more complex play of novelistic elements than any element implied in the intended structural parallel to *Morte d'Arthur*.

Steinbeck is seldom very sure in later works of when or how he has attained a harmony between structure and materials or, more simply, of whether he is constructing good work or bad work. It seems that his mature practice is to associate good work with controlled work—with a rigid, external, thoroughly planned structure, comparable to the alleged structural debt to Malory in *Tortilla Flat*, itself a more elaborate, sophisticated version of control devices of association or parallel in the first three novels. This viewpoint is evident particularly in his repeated efforts to construct novels that owe their coherence and the harmony of their parts to an external organizing device. One thinks of the play-novelettes and of the frankly allegorical novels that became so frequent in Steinbeck's later career. A wealth of data suggests that Steinbeck's intentions are very pure, even experimental, in the construction of such novels. It is worth indulging irony to observe that most of these novels made Steinbeck a good deal of money, and that at least one of them, *Burning Bright*, is miserably written.

The novels that follow immediately after *Tortilla Flat* are among Steinbeck's finest works. The contradiction is the result of a time lag. It is clear, on the basis of a spread of dates, that Steinbeck needed a number of years to absorb fully the significance of the unexpected public response to *Tortilla Flat*. Personal outrage (expressed in the Modern Library edition's Foreword) is one result; the effect of that

26. Gannett, pp. xxi–xxiv.

outrage on succeeding work is another and is, I think, delayed until about 1940. Dates of publication and biographical evidence support this view. *In Dubious Battle* had been completed three months before the publication of *Tortilla Flat*, so its creation would not have been affected by the popular success of its predecessor.[27] Second, during the middle thirties, Steinbeck grew aware of the social and economic implications of the Depression; important materials suitable for fiction seemed to lie there. Evidently, too, the resulting momentum of creation delayed his considering deeply the significance of the popular success of *Tortilla Flat* —in the sense of its affecting his immediate work—until after the publication of *The Grapes of Wrath*.[28] Moreover, the popular success of these novels seems to have been tempered, for Steinbeck, by their socially meaningful—and, in some quarters, unpopular—materials.[29] Nothing in Steinbeck's view of *Tortilla Flat* provides distance or protection from a confusing sense of merely popular success. Third, *Of Mice and Men*, published in January 1937, enjoyed a much greater popular success than *Tortilla Flat*, but Steinbeck maintained some distance from that success through his awareness of the experimental, technical aspect of that novel. The result is clear in Steinbeck's reference to *Of Mice and Men* in his letter concerning *L'Affaire Lettuceburg*: "Mice was a thin, brittle book, and an experiment but at least it was an honest experiment."[30] Steinbeck had not taken that tough-minded attitude toward *Tortilla Flat*. Ap-

27. Lisca, p. 108.

28. Gannett and Lisca establish the basic time sequence. Steinbeck was working on a biographical sketch of a Communist district organizer in 1934, as well as on the second draft of *In Dubious Battle*; in 1936 Steinbeck wrote several articles about California's labor problems; he collected new materials concerning migrant workers from the middle of 1937, completed *The Grapes of Wrath*—it exhausted him—late in 1938, and, after publication in April 1939, its enormous success created public demands on Steinbeck that made writing impossible for some time.

29. Freeman Champney, "John Steinbeck, Californian," *The Antioch Review*, 7:3 (Fall 1947), 345–62. Martin Staples Shockley, "The Reception of *The Grapes of Wrath* in Oklahoma," *American Literature*, 15 (January 1954), 351–61.

30. Gannett, p. xxiii.

parently having no defense against its popularity, Steinbeck went so far as to disown the novel after its publication: "Curious that this second-rate book, written for relaxation, should cause this fuss. People are actually taking it seriously."[31] This rejection is difficult to account for, I think, except in the way I have suggested. Faced with the same critical problem, Peter Lisca has suggested that Steinbeck lied about the extent of the debt to Malory to impress some publisher.[32] No evidence supports this view, and Steinbeck's rigid honesty in other connections works against it. All of the evidence of which I am aware leads to the opposite conclusion, that Steinbeck thought well enough of *Tortilla Flat* to defend it—before its popular success—and continued to think well of the intended parallel to *Morte d' Arthur*.[33]

Any conclusion, then, must be ambiguous. *Tortilla Flat* is excellent work in the main; it achieves a high degree of harmony between structure and materials; and it is a significant technical accomplishment. Obviously, on the basis of this promising novel, great things lay ahead. However, Steinbeck apparently felt that *Tortilla Flat* was only another experiment in the line of the first three novels rather than a quite different work compromised only by an unjustified popular success. On that basis, if the conclusions I have suggested are drawn correctly from the evidence I have offered, Steinbeck's contemplation of his intention in *Tortilla Flat*, in combination with its popular success, promoted unfortunate consequences, especially after about 1940. From that perspective, *Tortilla Flat* had a rather sinister ultimate effect on Steinbeck's career.

31. Gannett, p. xiv.   32. Lisca, p. 78.
33. Lisca, pp. 78–79.

3

Panorama and Drama Unified

In Dubious Battle

Tortilla Flat points the difficulty Steinbeck has in form-
ing a harmonious relationship between structure and materials as well as his success in improvising that organic
harmony against the thrust of his plan for the novel. His
long-range commitment is to a rigidly externalized structure,
which he often imposed on materials. In the short run the
novel's organic unity is most evident. We may speculate that
Tortilla Flat exemplified the proper technique, the times offered the essential materials, and, intent on fusing the two,
Steinbeck created one of his most important novels.

The mixture can seem to be "as before," but there is the
difference that Steinbeck takes great care to fuse opposites
that tend to separate in the early as in the late novels. For
example, he likes to use a panoramic structure in ways that
seem more appropriate to a dramatic structure. These structural opposites are consistently fused in *In Dubious Battle*,[1]
and they become a unity and a tight as well as a suitable
fit to the materials. Close analysis illuminates the extent of
Steinbeck's artistry and of his conscious, sustained management of his opposites.

To begin with, *In Dubious Battle* comprises a specific
and a general narrative. Jim Nolan's education in violence
fuses with the general narrative of a strike of apple pickers
in the Torgas Valley in the early 1930s. Explicitly, the novel
raises a number of immediate and suspenseful questions:
Will the strike be won? What will happen to Jim, Mac, Doc,
London, Lisa? Implicitly, these questions involve a judgment
of whether idealistic aims can be squared with power tactics.
The ideological basis permits considerable depth of motivation in the central figures, especially Jim Nolan.

1. John Steinbeck, *In Dubious Battle* (New York: Covici, Friede,
1936). Hereafter cited as *IDB*.

Steinbeck's initial problem is to outline Jim's history up to the time that he enters the novel. At one stroke Steinbeck accomplishes two purposes. *In Dubious Battle* begins with an individual—Jim—not with an abstract event. Also, the objective, dramatic quality of the novel becomes evident when Jim talks about himself as a step in his joining the Communist party, for this explication presents, in disguise, some necessary background material. A controlled series of images sets the tone and sharpens the meaning of Jim's awareness that he had been "dead" and now is partly "alive." Thus, the first lines of the novel: "At last it was evening. The lights in the street outside came on, and the neon restaurant sign on the corner jerked on and off, exploding its hard red light in the air."[2] The sign conveys the ugly, mechanical "illumination" Jim has experienced. Telling of his family, Jim begins: "My mother had light blue eyes. I remember they looked like white stones."[3] Eyes like stones connote a living death; this suggestion reappears in an image uniting eye and death references in a machine image: "My mother was quieter even than before. She moved kind of like a machine, and she hardly ever said anything. Her eyes got a kind of dead look, too."[4] This sequence illuminates the inner sense of Jim's background—his father is a drunken, fighting man, his sister runs away to become a prostitute, his mother suffers and dies silently—and deepens the implications of Jim's introduction to Joy, an old Party man, whose life suggests the useless violence of Jim's father: " 'This is Joy,' said Mac. 'Joy is a veteran, aren't you, Joy?' 'Damn right,' said Joy. His eyes flared up, then almost instantly the light went out of them again."[5] This sequence indicates Jim's own passage from death to life, from "dead" eyes to "his eyes flared up." Jim is aware of his symbolic passage, for he describes his "conversion" to the Party as a "coming alive." The effect of this connected imagery is to strip Jim of his dead past and to establish him as a *tabula rasa*.

Mac is the mature Party man who is responsible for Jim's

2. *IDB*, p. 9. 3. *IDB*, p. 21.
4. *IDB*, p. 22. 5. *IDB*, p. 24.

education: "I'll train you, and then you can train new men. Kind of like teaching hunting dogs by running them with the old boys, see?"[6] Here the imagery suggests a friendly concern that connotes life; its reverse is the deadness of Jim's previous life.

There is no apparent authorial manipulation nor any imposed system of allegorical parallels. The structure is dramatic; the presentation is objective. Already this distinguishes *In Dubious Battle* from much of Steinbeck's earlier (and later) fiction. The treatment is not accidental, for once the primary values are presented within the framework of a symbolic passage from death to life, Steinbeck provides relevant, supporting events in the objective world. On their way to organize a strike, riding the rails, Mac and Jim meet men like themselves who attempt to treat them cruelly. Jim's education begins, then, when the evil he observes in these men suggests to him that all men are capable of evil and, therefore, need to be manipulated to achieve the goal of the good life. So, through the practical example, Jim deduces the conflict between ends and means and accepts the validity of the paradox that good may result from evil. Steinbeck avoids any abstract statement of these propositions; everything is realized drama.

The fruit pickers are a collection of people who "travel with" their "natural leaders," London and Dakin.[7] To implement a strike, Mac must destroy the almost pure democracy of the fruit pickers and substitute a rigid organization with himself at its head. Mac forms his organization by gaining the confidence of the men and by forcing them to recognize their genuine unity. A chance situation provides Mac with an opportunity and prefigures the development of the novel. London's daughter, Lisa, is in labor. Mac offers himself as an experienced midwife—a lie—and takes command of the situation. He puts all of the men to boiling water and collecting white rags. After Mac delivers the child successfully, the chances of the strike being "born" appear excellent. As the birth is an organic figure of the strike, so the strike's moral ambiguity is prefigured in the birth.

6. *IDB*, p. 36.   7. *IDB*, pp. 58–59, 66, 88.

Mac's aim in helping Lisa is tactical, a kind of humanitarian expediency. Mac explains to Jim: "We've got to use whatever material comes to us. That was a lucky break. We simply had to take it. 'Course it was nice to help the girl, but hell, even if it killed her, we've got to use everything."[8] Jim accepts this rule of ends and means. It works; it corresponds to what he has learned on the rails and in the camp. The weak point in Mac's reasoning is concealed, or it is not figured in events this early in the novel. The evident facts are that Mac does manipulate the men on the train, does help Lisa, and he knows that men feel a joyful unity as they work in common for a good cause. Yet Mac has to work within a large margin of chance. He understands enough psychology to play on groups and individuals and enough medicine to know that antiseptics are useful, but he does not know if he can sway London, safely deliver Lisa's baby, or form the men into a group. He must pretend to be in total control when he knows he is not; he must use magic, science, or whatever lies at hand to bridge the gap between his knowledge and his ignorance. So the implications of the birth operate as an analogue of the larger tension between ends and means. The enormous chances that Mac must take and the thin logic that justifies those chances suggest that Mac will fail to connect ends and means at some point. The immediate fact is that, once he has the men in his power, Mac can promote a strike; on a deeper level, it is certain the strike cannot produce good.

Jim remains the lyrical voice, the innocent. Jim is open to corruption by Mac's knowing use of tactics because he does not realize they may absorb principle. Mac can distinguish between what is right and what has to be done; Jim admires Mac too deeply and is too green to make that distinction.

Steinbeck's focus on Jim's responses affects his concern with a moral fable, a study of good and evil, for the immediate quality of the materials as Jim encounters them seems to encourage Steinbeck to root the moral concern in the specific conflict between ends and means within the context

8. *IDB*, p. 66.

of the strike.[9] The artistic problem is to maintain and extend the correspondence between Jim's corruption and the history of the strike and thus to develop the insight that the correspondence is complex rather than simple. The "good" intentions that inspire Jim and fuel the strike are as genuine as the "evil" that results from a subordination of principle to tactics. Also, the long view, or the discrimination of these opposites, calls for a dramatic structure. The short view, the precise detail of organizing and of running a strike, demands a panoramic structure. We need to consider how Steinbeck combines or fuses these two structures in harmony with the materials.

The novel's general organization supports these particular requirements. The first nine chapters present the economic conditions, which are the solidly realized background of Jim's education. The indictment of buccaneering capitalism is credible in its specification, which is assumed to be the entire context of individual experience. On the other hand, the ambiguous quality of the strike is evident by the end of Chapter Eight, when Mac tells Jim that the strikers cannot win and, in any case, the Party's real aim is to train the men through bitter experience to become willing spearheads of the ultimate revolution. This unscrupulous long-term purpose negates the ostensibly humanitarian short-term purpose to improve working conditions and raise wages. Still, the direct and indirect force the owners use against the strikers tends to justify ambiguous strike tactics, and the nature of the tactics complicates what could have been a simple moral choice.

Steinbeck's conception of group-man is an important as-

9. Very likely, Steinbeck's long study of the relevant materials has much to do with the specification and density of the context; the urgency of the times encouraged something more than a propagandistic approach to the materials. For summaries of the background, see Henry Thornton Moore, *The Novels of John Steinbeck* (Chicago: Normandie House, 1939), p. 41, and Peter Lisca, *The Wide World of John Steinbeck* (New Brunswick: Rutgers University Press, 1958), pp. 109–13. The entire approach contrasts sharply with the rather more artificial association of structure and materials in Steinbeck's earlier novels. Consider, for example, the slight relationship of the

pect of this grim development of the novel. Group-man is a collection of individuals, created in periods of great tension to function with enormous strength as a single organism. Group-man is defined by analogy with a group of animal cells. The qualifying fact is that group-man is a creature of violence; it is formed by and produces violence. Limited as a weapon, it is nevertheless the only effective weapon the strikers have. Obviously, being so qualified, group-man is involved in the ambiguities of the strike and contributes to them.

This concept is developed as a metaphor. The fruit pickers are the raw materials of the cell. The Party men are the "senses," leading group-man into significant action to the extent that personified violence can be led. Jim is one of these "senses." His education and the history of the strike tend to be subsumed in the need to force the creation of group-man and to maintain its existence. As the strike continues and the force encircling the strike increases, Jim comes to accept the notion of violence as an end in itself. This is Jim's ultimate corruption, as we shall see, and, in this, his personal development corresponds to the development of the strike. Group-man threatens to become an abstraction, and Steinbeck avoids this threat, in part, by maintaining a specific flow of practical details concerning the tactics of strikes and of strikebreaking. So the metaphor holds its brilliance.

Following the birth of Lisa's baby, however, the immediate need is for Mac to convince London and Dakin that a strike is necessary. Jim is kept in events when he finds the clinching argument:

> "Where you going when we get the apples picked, Mr. Dakin?" "Cotton," said Dakin. "Well, the ranches over there are bigger, even. If we take a cut here, the cotton people will cut deeper." Mac smiled encouragement and praise. "You know damn well they will," he seconded.[10]

Munroe family to events in *The Pastures of Heaven* vis-à-vis Jim's necessary relation to the strike.

10. *IDB*, p. 88.

Jim's argument reflects Mac's knowledge of tactics and marks Jim's change from pupil to practitioner. This change is made specific in Mac's later praise:

> "That was a smart thing, Jim. She was beginning to drag when you brought in that thing about that cotton. That was a smart thing." "I want to help," Jim cried. "God, Mac, this thing is singing all over me. I don't want to sleep. I want to go right on helping."[11]

Furthermore, Mac suggests that Jim's insights are superior to his; that as he, Mac, is a workhorse, Jim is a revolutionist of genius. The distinction strengthens the dramatic quality of the novel in that the two men are given explicitly different personalities. These distinctions keep the history of the strike from collapsing into a set of abstract ideas. Men rather than ideas govern the history of the strike. Thus, Jim's personality determines the use of group-man, not the "objective" force of Marxian "laws." Now "coming alive" means to Jim becoming an expert in power tactics, and while this realization is lyrical as an ideal ("This thing is singing all over me"), the process demands inhuman responses ("I don't want to sleep"). Therefore, from this point on, so far as it is Jim's history, the novel is concentrated on two parallel developments in Jim's education: his loss of humanity and, correspondingly, his growing self-confidence in his ability to lead group-man. The parallel history of the strike consists of increasingly frantic and violent efforts by the leaders— that is, Jim as a leader—to form group-man, to keep it alive, and to lead it. Jim succeeds in his efforts, but he fails to see that group-man is a force that uses and destroys his sense of his own humanity. Here the technical problem is to permit the reader to see what group-man is and does while keeping that insight from the leading characters.

Steinbeck manages this difficult problem with extraordinary skill by using a controlled allegorical figure, Dan, to spell out the nature of group-man (for the reader) early in the novel.[12] Jim works with Dan in the orchard while he and Mac are attempting to create the strike, and Dan's fall

11. *IDB*, p. 90.
12. Much later, Doc Burton invents the term *group-man* in an

through a rotten ladder is the specific event that forces the strike into being.[13] Dan, therefore, has an organic reason to be in the novel, apart from his artificial role, which is to personify History. Steinbeck makes even this artifice as plausible and organic as he can. Dan is an old, old man who has experienced many strikes, all of them unsuccessful. His experience lends distance and historic content to the extended struggle between worker and owner. Dan is essentially a pre-Marxian worker, in view of his innocent memories and a humility or lack of faith that has experienced group-man as "that big guy" who springs into life at the onset of trouble but is too unstable for the prolonged fight.[14] Ironically, Mac is mistaken in fearing that Jim may be "converted to hopelessness" by History.[15] Jim can only learn from History that group-man must be led by a strong hand. So arrogant a presumption of strength of will is a measure of Jim's corruption; Dan's penultimate function is to play off Jim's Promethean certainty.

Dan's view of group-man is not contradicted or supported at once, but Jim's certainty becomes increasingly ambiguous as we learn more of group-man. The details of Joy's death and its consequences indicate the strength and weakness of group-man. Joy arrives on a train with a group of men recruited in the city to serve, without their knowledge, as strikebreakers. When he attempts to exhort the men to reject their role as strikebreakers, Joy is shot to death by an unidentified townsman. The train engine is a symbol of the mechanical force which is capable of moving and destroying the unstable force that is group-man. The charged writing in these passages invites the reading I propose:

> The engine panted rhythmically, like a great, tired animal. London cupped his hands around his mouth. . . . His voice

argument with Mac about its true nature. But its nature is suggested explicitly at this early point.

13. Steinbeck plays on *birth* and *born* in connecting the birth of Lisa's baby and the initial possibility of a strike. It does not strain Freudian imagery to observe that Dan's "fall" is equated with the "birth" of the strike as a real thing; but Steinbeck does very well, I think, to suggest this rather mechanical parallel very lightly.

14. *IDB*, p. 73.   15. *IDB*, p. 79.

was cut off by a shriek of steam. A jet of white leaped from the side of the engine, drowning London's voice, blotting out every sound but its own swishing scream.[16]

The violence of Joy's death at this moment causes the first "birth" of group-man, and for the time its power is greater than mechanical power:

Suddenly the steam stopped. . . . A strange, heavy movement started among the men. . . . The guards aimed with their guns, but the line [of striking men] moved on, unheeding, unseeing . . . the boxcar doors were belching silent men who moved slowly in. The ends of the long line curled and circled slowly around the center of the dead man, like sheep around a nucleus. . . . The guards were frightened; riots they could stop; but this slow, silent movement of men with the wide eyes of sleepwalkers terrified them.[17]

These passages indicate the strength and weakness of group-man. Its strength is in the surprise and force of its biological formation in contrast with the artifices (engines, guns) of mechanical power and in the consequent terror it inspires. Its limitations are involved in its strength. Men need the stress of violent emotion ("blood") to become group-man; the "organism" is sheeplike; its power depends on surprise, mass, and a kind of moral recognition by those who oppose it. Group-man is limited also by its physical needs. After Joy's funeral, news arrives that food has been obtained; group-man dissolves into an aggregation of hungry men. Since the "organism" uses up huge amounts of energy, its liftime is limited and it is dependent on satisfaction of its biological needs. Even worse, as Mac and London confess to Jim, group-man is too unpredictable, too morally ambiguous to be directed effectively by anyone; their judgments echo Dan's experienced pessimism.

In spite of the evidence against the chance of a deliberate use of group-man, Jim remains confident that he can create and use it. This conviction is a measure of his will to power through violence.

Dramatic contrast is evident in the different points of

16. *IDB*, p. 167.   17. *IDB*, pp. 168–69.

view. Jim's conviction is balanced against Doc Burton's fear that group-man is a nonhuman beast with no moral dimension and that it can be used, therefore, as an indiscriminate means to any end. Doc's fear is based on moral values; it is thus superior to Dan's blind pessimism. Doc's point of view is qualified by a flaw in his nature and by the developing conditions of the strike. He suffers bitterly from his scientific detachment. He is unable to join with men or to form any deeply human contacts. His emotional deadness is indicated by the identifying tag, "his sad eyes," which qualifies the impact of his nay-saying by repeating the death–life imagery at the opening of the novel.[18] The implication is that Doc may be condemning what he cannot share. Finally, Doc's ambiguous attitude toward group-man lies in his characteristically distrusting hope that group-man may be some kind of a new, living God.[19]

Mac's point of view is also contrasted with Doc's—and implicitly with Jim's—on an equally ambiguous basis. Mac's love of individuals conflicts with a willingness to use people for the ideal aim of gaining the good life through a revolution. Mac is a humanitarian under Party discipline. He can say to Jim: "Don't you go liking people, Jim. We can't waste time liking people."[20] Mac can idealize men with equal force and validity.

Jim, Mac, and Doc suggest a balanced series of responses to group-man and to the necessities of the strike. Because Doc is permitted the most eloquent language, the dialectical victory may seem to be his. But to think so is to substitute correct doctrine for Steinbeck's interest in dramatic conflict and to ignore the qualifications of Doc's point of view along with his presence in the strike camp. In fact, the dialectical quarrel between Mac and Doc parallels their differing roles. Mac is a good man whose opportunistic tactics are justified in large part by the deliberate tactics of the owners. Doc's good intentions are paralyzed by his analytical mind, and paradox results. Doc accepts the Calvinistic position that

18. *IDB*, pp. 129, 130, 141, 147, 199, 258.
19. *IDB*, pp. 260–61.   20. *IDB*, p. 121.

social change is pointless because evil is inherent in men, but he does what he can to help men and to ensure social improvement. Doc is the objective scientist, but he finds his distance from men painful. Doc stays distant, but his benevolence is evident to everyone and he is loved by the men he cares for. These complexities or contradictions encourage dramatic conflict rather than doctrinal certainties. Jim's certainty strengthens this pattern, since it does not imply a synthesis. Jim is another sort of creature, a man who comes to love violence and power. His differences from Mac and Doc contribute to the depth and intensity of the dramatic conflict.

I do not imply that Steinbeck fails to resolve the novel. The interfused final stages of the strike and of Jim's education provide a resolution of great force, which derives in large part from the context we have been examining.

Mac's idea that everything has its "use," in view of the needs of the strike—or the revolution—is qualified when he refuses to "use" Jim, first, out of love for him and, later, out of respect for Jim's special talents as a leader. But a change occurs halfway through the novel when Mac confesses to Jim that he is "so scared the strike'll crack," and adds, "I feel like it's mine."[21] Mac's humanly credible feelings contrast with Jim's certainty. Jim suggests a historic parallel from Herodotus for the use of violence: He not only takes over leadership, he directs the strike toward violence.

The change is clarified by Jim's visit to Dan. Their conversation defines the function of leadership in the context of group-man:

> [Dan's] eyes grew soft and childlike. "I'll lead 'em," he said gently. "All the hundreds o' years that's what the workin' stiffs needed, a leader. I'll lead 'em through to the light. All they got to do is just what I say. I'll say, 'You lazy bastards get over there!' an' by Christ, they'll git, 'cause I won't have no lazy bastards. When I speak, they got to jump, right now." And then he smiled with affection. "The poor damn rats," he said. "They never had nobody to tell 'em what to do. They never had no real leader." "That's right," Jim agreed. "Well, you'll see some changes now," Dan exclaimed. "You

21. *IDB*, pp. 192–93.

tell 'em I said so. Tell 'em I'm workin' out a plan. I'll be up and around in a couple of days. Tell 'em just to have patience till I get up an' lead 'em." "Sure I'll tell 'em," said Jim.[22]

The technical function of this passage is similar to the Elizabethan device of the play within the play. A single scene or episode seems to be detached from the main action, but in fact it clarifies or foreshadows the main action indirectly and in an exaggerated fashion. So, indirectly, Steinbeck provides a foreshadowing of the strike's development into pure violence under Jim's leadership. Dan's feverishly exaggerated projection of the private will is less dangerous than Jim's actual authoritarian rule which operates silently, behind the scenes, and therefore appears to be selfless.

Still, in this extraordinary novel, Dan becomes more than the semiallegorical voice of History. He is drawn into an organic relationship with Jim's education and the progress of the strike through the suggestion that both he and Jim are sick with gangrene. The implication is that Dan's imaginary rule and Jim's actual direction of the strike into violence are not separated into dream and fact but are, similarly, consequences of fever. Significantly, Jim absorbs much of Mac's function after he has been removed from direct action by a bullet wound, and Jim's faith in violence increases proportionately as the wound infects. Neither Mac, London, nor Jim can be aware that Jim has gangrene because Jim could not influence events or remain on the scene if his illness were recognized. Credibility is dealt with by the suggestion of a symbolic relationship between Jim and Dan. Dan's physical decline is observed in a close detail that could not be justified on its own merits. And by this point, Doc has been removed.

Jim's attitude toward violence conflicts now with Mac's. Mac will do anything for the cause, but he reacts against violence while Jim welcomes it. This distinction is repeated throughout the second half of the novel, but it is put most forcefully at first appearance, when Mac has to smash the face of a boy found planning to snipe at the strikers' camp:

22. *IDB*, p. 282.

"I hope they don't catch anybody else; I couldn't do it again."
"You'd have to do it again," said Jim. Mac looked at him with
something of fear in his eyes. "You're getting beyond me,
Jim. I'm getting scared of you. I've seen men like you before. . . . I know you're right. Cold thought to fight madness.
I know all that. God Almighty, Jim, it's not human. I'm scared
of you."[23]

The novel can develop in terms of Jim's inhuman logic because in theory Mac accepts Jim's faith in violence. The
distinction is that Mac remains human in practice, since he
is more removed from a worship of violence than Jim.

The dramatic question at this point is to what extent "cold
thought" is valid in practice. The answer is supplied by an
action—by Jim's control of group-man in its final appearance in the novel. The discouraged strikers are jolted into
group-man by the "blood" of a violent fight between London
and a potential leader and possible spy named Burke. London does not know how to use this newly-formed group-
man until Jim gestures toward a roadblock the strikers had
refused to attack earlier. Now the roadblock is smashed
easily. "Cold thought" is represented by Jim's working out
of sight, through the apparent leadership of London, for
Jim wants the reality rather than the appearance of power.
But "cold thought" is an illusory control. Jim and Mac are
nearly attacked when the men come back from the roadblock, and only the speedy disintegration of group-man
saves them. Jim is permitted a recognition of the horror of
what he has directed when he reports to Mac: "It was like
all of them disappeared, and it was just one big—animal,
going down the road."[24]

Even when it becomes clear that the battle is lost as well
as dubious, Jim and Mac are caught too deeply to wish to
escape from the consequences, which they perceive. Their
initial, humanitarian purpose is lost in the violence which
subsumes the strike. The final stage of Jim's education corresponds to the final stage of the strike, for in each, means
determine ends and tactics swallow up principle.

23. *IDB*, p. 280.   24. *IDB*, p. 322.

The ambiguity of "use" is explicitly the literary tool Steinbeck depends on to suggest these points in dramatic terms. The strike becomes increasingly a struggle to gain power; thus it demands the use of many persons. Only Mac, Doc, and Jim choose to be used. The rest is manipulation; even considered choices are not free of ambiguity. Doc is in the camp for multiple reasons; his humanitarianism and his scientific wish to observe group-man in action are too divergent to be resolved. Mac is realist enough to admit the truth of power: "Everybody hates us; our own side and the enemy. And if we won, Jim, if we put it over, our own side would kill us."[25] Jim chooses his role because at first he wishes to come alive, but his inhuman desire to "use" power reaches a peak just before his death when he offers to pull off his bandage "and get a flow of blood" to provide the shock that group-man needs to get itself "born."[26] Jim leaves the novel in this ultimate impersonalization, his face "transfigured" so that "a furious light of energy seemed to shine from it."[27] He manages to lose himself so completely, to be so "used," that very little of the human is left; perhaps it is not bearing down too hard on the metaphor to suggest that Jim's "transfigured" face is godlike because it is not human.

Steinbeck does not depend only on this climax of ambiguity. Jim's final education is clarified from several points of view. Doc and Lisa state ambiguous and qualified opinions that refer to Jim's education and to the development of the strike. Doc's ultimate reality is original sin:

> "Man has met and defeated every obstacle, every enemy except one. He cannot win over himself. How mankind hates itself!" Jim said, "We don't hate ourselves, we hate the invested capital that keeps us down." "The other side is made up of men, Jim, men like you. Man hates himself. . . ."[28]

Nevertheless, Doc's loneliness invalidates this certainty, and he ends by asking Jim for the secret of happiness.

A similar ambiguity governs Lisa's view of the good life.

25. *IDB*, p. 161.   26. *IDB*, p. 348.
27. *IDB*, p. 348.   28. *IDB*, p. 259.

Her recall of a simpler, agrarian world is concrete in its detail; its weakness is its utter nostalgia, its lack of reference. Lisa's pragmatism forces her to accept violence only if it is a means to a good end: "I wisht we lived in a house with a floor, an' a toilet close by. I don't like this fightin'."[29] Her point of view becomes fully relevant when it implies the chance of love. It is no accident that Lisa is paired nearly always with Jim. Her indifference to the strike and her concentration on her baby are counterparts to Jim's inhuman avowal of violence. Her admission that she "likes" Jim, near the end of the novel, balances Jim's accusation of Mac: "Sometimes I get the feeling that you're not protecting me for the Party but for yourself."[30]

This dialectic between Mac, Doc, and Lisa involves then a rather complete range of human affection, from male friendship or its lack to female love, and it suggests that Jim's avowal of violence denies his humanity. Within this very human context, it is significant that Mac's response to Jim's murder is sorrow for the death of a man, not regret for the loss of a superior Party man. Mac has, to be sure, a duty to the Party. Hence, he tries to stir the strikers by showing them Jim's faceless body, and in speaking to them he repeats essentially a speech he made earlier, over Joy's body. All of this devotion to the Party would seem to lend credence to the opinion of several critics that *In Dubious Battle* is too impersonal to convey much ultimate meaning.[31] Such critics fail to observe that Mac's addition of a single word, "Comrades," to his basic speech is an expression of personal loss, stated in the only way possible for a field organizer, and all the more affecting because of its context of official duty:

> Mac shivered. He moved his jaws to speak, and seemed to break the frozen jaws loose. His voice was high and monotonous. "This guy didn't want nothing for himself——" he began. "Comrades! He didn't want nothing for himself——"[32]

29. *IDB*, p. 271.   30. *IDB*, p. 343.
31. This general view is considered and rejected by Lisca, pp. 126–27. There is a good summary by Moore, pp. 41–42.
32. *IDB*, p. 349.

The initial adjectives and verbs indicate great emotional turmoil in themselves; they are a context for the use of "Comrades!" The term cannot be taken wholly as an invitation to join the Party, for London has become a member in a calmer atmosphere; nor can it be understood simply as a stab at creating group-man, since "blood," Jim's faceless, propped-up body, is mainly what is required. Instead, the term is universal: brothers. It expresses the best of Jim. His most human aspect has been his wish to help "the poor bastards." So Mac delivers a dirge for Jim that is in excess of the strict needs of the occasion. Nor is irony missing. Mac balances the inhumanity of capitalism, not Jim's inhumanity, against the idealized portrait of the dead man. Sentimentality is avoided through irony, not by coldness. Jim's desire to "use" himself fully had tended to separate him from humanity; Mac's "use" of Jim's corpse tends to return Jim to humanity. Therefore, a seeming impersonality is in fact an aspect of Steinbeck's control of structure and materials.

Mac's dirge ends the novel at a high point, but the ending is not an inconclusive suggestion that what we have witnessed will go on. Personalities do not repeat exactly. Nor does Steinbeck squeeze a stupidly optimistic wedge into the ending; there is no implication that the future is rosy or that a return to the happy preindustrial past is in view. The one encouraged hope is that human feelings may survive— at a price. Jim must die before he can return to humanity. The paradox is Christian rather than Marxian, and toughminded rather than optimistic. It brings to mind Steinbeck's own vision of "a terrible kind of order" in the novel, before it was published, and his postpublication comment that "he was trying to write this story without looking through 'the narrow glass of political or economic preconception.' "[33] Such objectivity precludes mere optimism as well as a merely brutal or cynical interpretation that would strip the novel of any moral content, reduce Mac to a rawly opportunistic revolutionary, and so forth. André Gide is correct, I think, in his estimation of the novel's dialogue: "The variegated

33. Moore, p. 41; Lisca, p. 127.

aspects of the problem are set forth without the discussion's ever cluttering and interrupting the action."[34] For the dialogue has a sustained dramatic quality which is in keeping with the functional unity of the novel.

A dramatic quality is characteristic of this novel in other respects. It governs the arrangement of huge forces into opposing pairs: city and country, orchard and bank, Party and capitalism, even life and death. The flaw in this arrangement is that representatives of the propertied class are handled rather abstractly and are dimly characterized vis-à-vis more fully realized and complex figures like Jim, Mac, or Doc. Nevertheless, Steinbeck maintains a number of points of view regarding the strike and the power situation in general. The resulting sense of complexity and specification contributes greatly to preventing the novel from any collapse into an unsuitable simplicity. The pairing of characters is equally a contribution to the novel's dramatic quality. Mac and Jim are leaders in the field, but they are sharply distinguished in spite of their common function. London and Dakin are "natural" leaders, but they are quite different from each other. Dakin is like Anderson, who lets the men camp on his small holding, and both men break up when their loved possessions are destroyed in the course of the strike. London is like Al, Anderson's son, and both men join the Party as a result of their experience in the strike. Even the men of violence are distinguished from each other. They include such different types as Jim's father, Sam, Joy, and Burke. Group-man is an especially complex entity. It is "good" so far as it is the strikers' main weapon, but "evil" so far as its basis in violent emotion leads to a repulsive and dangerous lack of moral direction as the strike develops. Consequently, group-man becomes the main symbol of the "dubious battle."

All phases of the use of language are governed by the novel's dramatic quality. The fruit pickers speak an uncensored, idiomatic language that is their own in expression

34. André Gide, *The Journals of André Gide*, trans. Justin O'Brien (New York: Alfred A. Knopf, Inc., 1951), 27 September 1940. Reprinted by permission of Alfred A. Knopf, Inc.

and in rhythm. Mac is an unconsciously expert mimic. Jim begins with lyrical outbursts of speech that do not disappear altogether, although in time he tends to use more frequently a flat but forceful diction that represents the progress of his education. Doc speaks the somewhat abstract language of ideas. The languages of "the other side," of the owners and of business, are represented by the orchard superintendent and by the new president of the Fruit Growers' Association. Their brusque or unctuous diction is tonally patriotic, hearty, and threatening by turns. Whatever the range of the spoken language, Steinbeck takes care to use the exact word, tone, and rhythm. The people are *made* to talk, to reveal themselves through their speech.[35] The defect of this objectivity is evident in the remote quality of the language whenever there is observation from the author's point of view, as in descriptive passages. Steinbeck was aware that a dramatic structure could not include an explicit control: "In one of his first letters about the work in progress, he wrote, 'I guess it is a brutal book, more brutal because there is no author's moral point of view.' "[36]

The question is whether the novel suffers seriously from this lack of warmth in description and from the concentration on suspense in the events. An answer involves two points. First, motivation and characterization are sufficiently complex, and there is adequate specification in the detailed narratives of the strike and of Jim's education as well as in the language the various characters use. Second, the brutal objective tone is an organic part of the whole tissue of the "dubious battle." But the concentration on suspense is a genuine limitation of the objective dramatic quality. It prevents the novel from attaining a thoroughly philosophical

35. Consult Lisca, pp. 110–12, for a letter in which Steinbeck discusses "the speech of working men" in the novel. Steinbeck seems to be as aware of dialects and speech rhythms here as Mark Twain was in *The Adventures of Huckleberry Finn*. This awareness is evident, or self-conscious, as far as I can discover, for the first time in connection with *In Dubious Battle*. Except for *Tortilla Flat*, the earlier novels suffer more or less for lack of an adequate language, and in practice language accounts for much of the "adequacy of specification" both in *In Dubious Battle* and *The Grapes of Wrath*.

36. Lisca, p. 114.

level of absolute insight, and it provides some justification for Freeman Champney's suggestion that Steinbeck's materials are peculiar to California—are local rather than universal.[37] But, as we have seen, the novel's permanence is a measure of its artistic value.

Thus, by aiming for and largely achieving a harmony between structure and materials, by selecting and arranging events in terms of a design, and by subordinating characterization, thematic motifs, symbols, and style to those considerations, Steinbeck was able to create particular kinds of people in the context of a certain historical situation. This situation, in the paradox of art, lies outside history although the environment that permits the artistic construct to assume its necessary shape is history.

37. Freeman Champney, "John Steinbeck, Californian," *The Antioch Review*, 7:3 (Fall 1947), 345–62.

4

The Fully Matured Art

The Grapes of Wrath

The enormous contemporary social impact of *The Grapes of Wrath*[1] can encourage the slippery reasoning that condemns a period novel to die with its period.[2] But continuing sales and critical discussions suggest that *The Grapes of Wrath* has outlived its directly reportorial ties to the historical past; that it can be considered as an aesthetic object, a good or a bad novel *per se*. In that light, the important consideration is the relative harmony of its structure and materials.

The Grapes of Wrath is an attempted prose epic, a summation of national experience at a given time. Evaluation proceeds from that identification of genre. A negative critical trend asserts that *The Grapes of Wrath* is too flawed to command serious attention: The materials are local and temporary, not universal and permanent; the conception of life is overly simple; the characters are superficial types (except, perhaps, Ma Joad); the language is folksy or strained by turns; and, in particular, the incoherent structure is the weakest point—the story breaks in half, the nonorganic, editorializing interchapters force unearned general conclusions, and the ending is inconclusive as well as overwrought and sentimental.[3] The positive trend asserts that *The Grapes*

---

1. John Steinbeck, *The Grapes of Wrath* (New York: The Viking Press, Inc., 1939). Hereafter cited as *GW*.

2. Louis Kronenberger, *The Nation*, 148 (April 15, 1939), 440. "It is, I think, one of those books—there are not very many—which really do some good."

3. I list a typical range of such criticism by date of publication.
   a. James T. Farrell, "The End of a Literary Decade," *The American Mercury*, 48 (December 1939), 408–14.
   b. Edmund Wilson, "The Californians: Storm and Steinbeck," *The New Republic*, 103 (December 9, 1940), 784–87.
   c. Stanley Edgar Hyman, "Some Notes on John Steinbeck,"

of Wrath is a great novel. Its materials are properly universalized in specific detail; the conception is philosophical; the characters are warmly felt and deeply created; the language is functional, varied, and superb on the whole; and the structure is an almost perfect combination of the dramatic and the panoramic in sufficient harmony with the materials. This criticism admits that overwrought idealistic passages as well as propagandistic simplifications turn up on occasion, but these are minor flaws in an achievement on an extraordinary scale.[4] Relatively detached studies of Steinbeck's ideas comprise a third trend. These studies are not directly useful in analytical criticism; they do establish that Steinbeck's social ideas are ordered and legitimate ex-

---

Antioch Review, 2 (Summer 1942), 185–200.

    d. Maxwell Geismar, *Writers in Crisis* (Boston: Houghton Mifflin Company, 1942), pp. 237–70.

    e. Alfred Kazin, *On Native Grounds* (New York: Harcourt, Brace & Co., 1942), pp. 393–94.

    f. W. M. Frohock, "John Steinbeck's Men of Wrath," *Southwest Review*, 31 (Spring 1946), 144–52.

    g. John S. Kennedy, "John Steinbeck: Life Affirmed and Dissolved," in *Fifty Years of the American Novel*, ed. H. C. Gardiner, S.J. (New York: Charles Scribner's Sons, 1951), pp. 217–36.

    h. Frederick J. Hoffman, *The Modern Novel in America: 1900–1950* (Chicago: Henry Regnery Company, 1951), pp. 146–53.

    i. Edmund Fuller, "The New Compassion in the American Novel," *The American Scholar*, 26 (Spring 1957), 155–63.

    j. Walter Fuller Taylor, "*The Grapes of Wrath* Reconsidered," *Mississippi Quarterly*, 12 (Summer 1959), 136–44.

    4. I list a typical range of such criticism by date of publication.

    a. Harry Thornton Moore, *The Novels of John Steinbeck* (Chicago: Normandie House, 1939), pp. 53–72.

    b. Frederic I. Carpenter, "The Philosophical Joads," *College English*, 2 (January 1941), 315–25.

    c. Joseph Warren Beach, *American Fiction: 1920–1940* (New York: The Macmillan Company, 1941), pp. 327–47.

    d. Chester E. Eisinger, "Jeffersonian Agrarianism in *The Grapes of Wrath*," *University of Kansas City Review*, 14 (Winter 1947), 149–54.

    e. Peter Lisca, "*The Grapes of Wrath* as Fiction," *PMLA*, 72 (March 1957), 296–309.

    f. Eric C. Carlson, "Symbolism in *The Grapes of Wrath*," *College English*, 19 (January 1958), 172–75.

    g. Theodore Pollock, "On the Ending of *The Grapes of Wrath*," *Modern Fiction Studies*, 4 (Summer 1958), 177–78.

tensions of biological fact, hence scientific and true rather than mistaken or sentimental.[5]

The two evaluative positions are remarkable in their opposition. They are perhaps overly simple in asserting that *The Grapes of Wrath* is either a classic of our literature or a formless pandering to sentimental popular taste. Certainly these extremes are mistaken in implying (when they do) that, somehow, *The Grapes of Wrath* is *sui generis* in relation to Steinbeck's work.

Trends so awkwardly triple need to be brought into a sharper focus. By way of a recapitulation in focus, consider a few words of outright praise:

> For all of its sprawling asides and extravagances, *The Grapes of Wrath* is a big book, a great book, and one of maybe two or three American novels in a class with *Huckleberry Finn*.[6]

Freeman Champney's praise is conventional enough to pass unquestioned if one admires *The Grapes of Wrath*, or, if one does not, it can seem an invidious borrowing of prestige, shrilly emotive at that. Afterthought emphasizes the serious qualification of the very high praise. Just how much damage is wrought by those "sprawling asides and extravagances," and does *The Grapes of Wrath* survive its structural faults as *Huckleberry Finn* does, by virtue of its mythology, its characterization, its language? If the answers remain obscure, illumination may increase (permitting, as well, a clearer definition of the aesthetic efficacy of Steinbeck's ideas) when the context of critical discussion is the relationship of the novel's structure to its materials.

5. I list a typical range of such criticism by date of publication.

a. Woodburn Ross, "John Steinbeck: Earth and Stars," in *University of Missouri Studies in Honor of A. H. R. Fairchild* (XXI), ed. Charles T. Prouty (Columbia: University of Missouri Press, 1946), pp. 177–91.

b. Frederick Bracher, "Steinbeck and the Biological View of Man," *The Pacific Spectator*, 2 (Winter 1948), 14–29.

c. Woodburn Ross, "John Steinbeck: Naturalism's Priest," *College English*, 10 (May 1949), 432–37.

6. Freeman Champney, "John Steinbeck, Californian," *The Antioch Review*, 7:3 (Fall 1947), 355. Reprinted by permission of *The Antioch Review*.

Steinbeck's serious intentions and his artistic honesty are not in question. He had studied and experienced the materials intensely over a period of time. After a false start that he rejected (*L'Affaire Lettuceburg*), his conscious intention was to create an important literary work rather than a propagandistic shocker or a journalistic statement of the topical problem of how certain people faced one aspect of the Great Depression.[7] Therefore, it is an insult to Steinbeck's aims to suggest that somehow *The Grapes of Wrath* is imperfect art but a "big" or "great" novel nevertheless. In all critical justice, *The Grapes of Wrath* must stand or fall as a serious and important work of art.

The consciously functional aspect of Steinbeck's intentions—his working of the materials—is clarified by a comparison of *The Grapes of Wrath* with *In Dubious Battle*. Both novels deal with labor problems peculiar to California, but that similarity cannot be pushed too far. The Joads are fruit pickers in California, but not of apples, the fruit mentioned in *In Dubious Battle*. The Joads pick cotton, and in the strike novel the people expect to move on to cotton. The Joads become involved in a strike but as strikebreakers rather than as strikers. Attitudes are less easy to camouflage. The strikers in *In Dubious Battle* and the Okies in *The Grapes of Wrath* are presented with sympathy whereas the owning class and much of the middle class have no saving virtue. The sharpest similarity is that both the strikers and the Okies derive a consciousness of the need for

7. The main sources are:

a. John Steinbeck, "Dubious Battle in California," *The Nation*, 143 (September 12, 1936), 302–4.

b. John Steinbeck, "The Harvest Gypsies," *San Francisco News*, October 5–12, 1936. Reprinted with a 1938 epilogue and retitled *Their Blood Is Strong*, under the auspices of the Simon J. Lubin Society of California, Inc., April 1938. Reprinted in *A Companion to "The Grapes of Wrath*," ed. Warren French (New York: The Viking Press, Inc., 1963), pp. 53–92.

c. Lewis Gannett, "Introduction: John Steinbeck's Way of Writing," *The Viking Portable Steinbeck* (New York: The Viking Press, Inc., 1946), pp. xx–xxiv.

d. Moore, pp. 53–54, 85, 88, 90.

e. Peter Lisca, *The Wide World of John Steinbeck* (New Brunswick: Rutgers University Press, 1958), pp. 144–48.

group action from their experiences; but even here there is a difference in emphasis. The conflict of interest is more pointed and the lessons of experience are less ambiguous in *The Grapes of Wrath* than in *In Dubious Battle*. The fact is that the two novels are not similar beyond a common basis in California labor problems, and Steinbeck differentiates that basis carefully in most specific details. The really significant factor is that different structures are appropriate to each novel. The restricted scope of *In Dubious Battle* demands a dramatic structure with some panoramic elements as they are needed. The broad scope of *The Grapes of Wrath* demands a panoramic structure; the dramatic elements appear as they are needed. Therefore, in each case, the primary critical concern must be the adequacy of the use of the materials, not the materials in themselves.

Steinbeck's profound respect for the materials of *The Grapes of Wrath* is recorded in a remarkable letter in which he explained to his literary agents and to his publisher the main reason for his withdrawing *L'Affaire Lettuceburg,* the hurried, propagandistic, thirty-thousand-word manuscript novel that preceded *The Grapes of Wrath*:

> I know I promised this book to you, and that I am breaking a promise in withholding it. But I had got smart and cagey you see. I had forgotten that I hadn't learned to write books, that I will never learn to write them. A book must be a life that lives all of itself and this one doesn't do that. You can't write a book. It isn't that simple. The process is more painful than that. And this book is fairly clever, has skillful passages, but tricks and jokes. Sometimes I, the writer, seem a hell of a smart guy—just twisting this people out of shape. But the hell with it. I beat poverty for a good many years and I'll be damned if I'll go down at the first little whiff of success. I hope you, Pat, don't think I've double-crossed you. In the long run to let this book out would be to double-cross you. But to let the bars down is like a first theft. It's hard to do, but the second time it isn't so hard and pretty soon it is easy. If I should write three books like this and let them out, I would forget there were any other kinds.[8]

This is Steinbeck's declaration of artistic purpose—and his effort to exorcise a dangerous (and permanent) aspect of

8. Gannett, pp. xxii-xxiii.

his craft. Much of the motivation for Steinbeck's career is stated in this letter. After all, he did write *L'Affaire Lettuceburg*; and "tricks and jokes," detached episodes, and detached ironic hits, as well as a twisting of characters, are evident enough in much of Steinbeck's earlier work. But the Depression materials were too serious to treat lightly or abstractly, or to subject to an imposed structure (mistaken idealism, nature worship, a metaphysical curse, a literary parallel). Such materials need to be in harmony with an appropriate structure.

From that intentional perspective, the central artistic problem is to present the universal and epical in terms of the individual and particular. Steinbeck chooses to deal with this by creating an individual, particular image of the epical experience of the dispossessed Okies by focusing a sustained attention on the experience of the Joads. The result is an organic combination of structures. Dramatic structure suits the family's particular history; panoramic structure proves out the representative nature of their history. To avoid a forced and artificial "typing," to assure that extensions of particular detail are genuinely organic, Steinbeck postulates a conceptual theme that orders structure and materials: the transformation of the Joad family from a self-contained, self-sustaining unit to a conscious part of a group, a whole larger than its parts. This thematic ordering is not merely implicit or ironic, as it is in *The Pastures of Heaven*, or withheld to create mystery as in *Cup of Gold* or *To a God Unknown*. Steinbeck chances the strength of the materials and the organic quality of their structure. And he defines differences: The group is not group-man. The earlier concept is a "beast," created by raw emotion ("blood"), short-lived, unwieldy, unpredictable, mindless; a monster that produces indiscriminate good or evil. The group is quite different— rational, stable, relatively calm—because it is an assemblage of like-minded people who retain their individual and traditional sense of right and wrong as a natural fact. Group-man lacks a moral dimension; the group is a morally pure instrument of power. The difference is acute at the level of leadership. The leaders have ambiguous aims in *In Dubious Battle,* but they are Christ-like (Jim Casy) or attain moral insight (Tom Joad) in *The Grapes of Wrath.*

The Grapes of Wrath is optimistic; *In Dubious Battle* is not. That the living part of the Joad family survives, though on the edge of survival, is less than glowingly optimistic, but that survival produces a mood that differs considerably from the unrelenting misery of *In Dubious Battle.* Optimism stems from the theme, most openly in the alternation of narrative chapter and editorial interchapter. While the Joads move slowly and painfully toward acceptance of the group, many of the interchapters define the broad necessity of that acceptance. Arbitrary plotting does not produce this change. Its development is localized in Ma Joad's intense focus on the family's desire to remain a unit; her recognition of the group is the dramatic resolution.[9] Optimism is demonstrated also in experience that toughens, educates, and enlarges the stronger Joads in a natural process. On the simplest, crudest level, the family's journey and ordeal is a circumstantial narrative of an effort to reach for the good material life. Yet that is not the sole motive, and those members who have only that motive leave the family. On a deeper level, the family is attempting to rediscover the identity it lost when it was dispossessed; so the Joads travel from order (their old, traditional life) through disorder (the road, California) to some hope of a better, rediscovered order, which they reach in Ma's recognition and Tom's dedication. Their journey toward order is the ultimate optimistic, ennobling process, the earned, thematic resolution of the novel.

I do not intend to imply that Steinbeck pretties his materials. He does not stint the details of the family's various privations, its continual losses of dignity, and the death or disappearance of many of its members. On the larger scale, there is considerable objective documentation of the general economic causes of such misery—a circumstantial process that lifts *The Grapes of Wrath* out of the merely historic

9. *GW,* p. 606. "'Use' ta be the fambly was fust. It ain't so now. It's anybody. Worse off we get, the more we got to do."

genre of the proletarian novel. Optimism survives as the ultimate value because of the will of the people to understand
and to control the conditions of their lives despite constant
discouragement.

This value is essentially abstract, political. Steinbeck
deepens and universalizes it by developing the relationship
between the family unit and "the people." The family is
made up of unique individuals. "The people" embraces a
timeless entity, a continuing past, present, and future of
collective memory—but free of any social or political function.[10] Time-lag confounds the usefulness of "the people"
as a guide for the present. The Joads and others like them
know they may keep the land or get new land if they can
kill or control "the Bank," as the old people killed Indians
to take the land and controlled nature to keep it.[11] But "the
Bank" is more complicated an enemy than Indians or nature because it is an abstraction.[12] So the Okies submit to
dispossession in Oklahoma (forced by mechanized cheaper
production of cotton) and to the huge migration into California (encouraged by landowners to get cheap field labor),
motivated by the time-lag that confuses them, for none of
them comprehends the monstrous logic of modern economics. Despite their ignorance, in a process that is unifying in
itself and is second only to survival, the families work at
some way of prevailing against "the Bank." The older,
agrarian concept of "the people" is succeeded in time by the
new concept of the group, an instrument of technology
and political power—an analogue that works. Steinbeck
makes this succession appear necessary and legitimate by
a representation that excludes alternate solutions.[13] The

10. *GW*, pp. 37, 45–46, 73, 312, 535–36, 597–98.

11. *GW*, pp. 45–46, 406–7, 432.

12. *GW*, pp. 45–46, 50–53, 63–65. That buccaneering capitalism
is an abstract or allegorical monster of evil is left to implication in
In Dubious Battle. Steinbeck is far more directly allegorical in characterizing "the Bank" as an evil, nonhuman monster. Consequently
there is, I think, a gain in horror but a relative loss of credibility.

13. It would be too severe to blame Steinbeck for failing to fore-
see a quite different solution, a war that produced jobs for the Okies.
But a cropper does plead to keep his land because with so many wars
in sight cotton will go up (p. 44). That logic is rejected, possibly to

permitted solution seems a natural evolution, from people to group, because it is a tactic, not a fundamental change in folkways. Its process is long and painful because the emotive entity, "the people," needs to feel its way toward redefinition as the group—the abstract, political entity which emerges as an organic, particularized whole. This is brilliant literary strategy, in its grasp of operative metaphor and its avoidance of an overly obvious, loaded opposition. Steinbeck is scrupulously careful to keep to precise and exact circumstantial detail in this developed metaphor. Concretely, the panicky violence of "the Bank" is the reverse of the fact that (seemingly by habit) the Joads are kind to those who need their help and neighborly to people who are like them. The metaphor is persuasive.

Steinbeck is quite as scrupulous in the use of allegory as a way of universalizing an abstract particular. In his earlier work this method can produce a tangibly artificial, forced result, but allegory is a credible and functional device in *The Grapes of Wrath*. The turtle episode in Chapter III is justly famous. Objectively, we have a fully realized description of a land turtle's patient, difficult journey over dust fields, across a road and walled embankment, and on through the dust. The facts are the starting point; nature is not distorted or manipulated to yield allegorical meaning. The turtle seems awkward but it is able to survive, like the Joads, and like them it is moving southwest, out of the dry area.[14] It can protect itself against a natural danger like the red ant it kills, as the Joads protect themselves by their unity. The turtle's eyes are "fierce, humorous," suggesting force that takes itself easily; the stronger Joads are a fierce, humorous people.[15] When mismanaged human power attacks, as when a truck swerves to hit the turtle, luck is on the animal's side —it survives by luck. The Joads survive the mismanagement

---

motivate the emergence of the group—an insight that has turned out to be too shallow or too simple. *The Grapes of Wrath* has lost readers most often in our time because of its serious loss of historic relevance.

14. I am indebted to Harry Thornton Moore for the directional suggestion. See Moore, p. 55.

15. *GW*, p. 20.

that produced the Dust Bowl and the brutalizing man-made conditions in California as much by luck as by design. The relation to the Joads of the life-bearing function of the turtle is more obscure, or perhaps overly ambitious. The factual starting point is that, unknowingly, the turtle carries an oat seed in its shell and unknowingly drops and plants the seed in the dust, where it will rest until water returns. The most obvious link in the Joad family is the pregnant Rose of Sharon, but her baby is born dead. Perhaps compassion is "born," as in Uncle John's thoughts as he floats the dead baby down the flooding river in its apple box coffin:

> Go down an' tell 'em. Go down in the street an' rot an' tell 'em that way. That's the way you can talk. . . . Maybe they'll know then.[16]

But this appeal is strained, too greatly distanced from the factual starting point. The link works in the restricted sense that Ruthie and Winfield are "planted," and will perhaps take root, in the new environment of California. At this point the careful allegory collapses under its own weight, yet care is taken to join the device to the central narrative. In Chapter IV, Tom Joad picks up a turtle, and later Casy remarks on the tenacity of the breed:

> "Nobody can't keep a turtle though. They work at it and work at it, and at last one day they get out and away they go—off somewheres."[17]

This recognition of the turtle's purposeful tenacity interprets and places the preceding interchapter in the central narrative. Tom calls the turtle "an old bulldozer," a figure that works in opposition to the threatening insect life the tractors suggest as self-defeating, destructive tools of "the Bank."[18] Again, a purposeful turtle is opposed to homeless domestic animals, like the "thick-furred yellow shepherd dog" that passes Tom and Casy, to suggest precisely the ruined land and the destruction of the old ways of life on

---

16. *GW*, p. 609. The reversal of values is evident in the reversed symbolism; the river bears death—not life, the coffin—not water to seeds in the earth.

17. *GW*, p. 28.   18. *GW*, p. 28.

the most basic, animal level, where the wild (or free) animal survives best.[19] These and other supporting details extend the exemplum into the narrative; they continue and deepen Steinbeck's foreshadowing, moralizing insight naturally, within the range of biological imagery. It is true, allowing for the one collapse of the allegory, that none of Steinbeck's earlier work exhibits as profound a comprehension of what can be done to "place" an allegorical narrative device.

The turtle interchapter is masterful enough. Steinbeck does even more with an extended instance of allegorizing —the introduction of the lapsed preacher, Jim Casy, into the Joad family. Casy has a role that is difficult to present within the limits of credibility. Casy may look too much like his function, the Christ-like force that impels the family toward its transformation into the group. If the novel is to have more significance than a reportorial narrative of travel and hardship, Casy's spiritual insights are a necessary means of stating a convincing philosophical optimism. The technical difficulty is that Casy does not have a forthright narrative function. He drops out of the narrative for almost one hundred and fifty pages, although his presence continues through the Joads' wondering at times what has happened to him. When he reenters the novel, he is killed off within fifteen pages—sacrificed for the group in accord with his Christ-like function, with a phrase that recalls Christ's last words.[20] In spite of the obvious technical difficulty in handling such materials, Steinbeck realizes Casy as fully as any of the major Joads. Casy's struggle with himself to define "sin" to include the necessary facts of the natural world lends him a completely human aspect. He earns the right to make moral statements because he bases all judgments on his own experience. This earned right to "witness" serves to keep Casy human, yet it permits him to function as if he were an allegorical figure. This is a brilliant solution, and Casy is Steinbeck's most successful use of a functional allegorical figure in a major role. His narrative sharpness contrasts amazingly with the dim realization of Sir Henry Morgan or Joseph Wayne.

19. *GW*, p. 29.   20. *GW*, pp. 364, 520, 527.

Even Casy's necessary distance is functional rather than arbitrary. He exists outside the narrative in the sense that he travels with the Joads but he is not a member of the family, and there is no danger of confusing his adventures with theirs. Further, by right of his nature and experience, he has the function of being the living moral conscience of "the people." He travels with the Joads to witness the ordeal of the Okies, to understand its causes, and to do what he can to help. Steinbeck's convincing final touch is that, at the end, Tom Joad aspires to Casy's role. In this shift, Steinbeck manipulates allegory, he does not submit to its rigid quality, for Tom is not like Casy. Tom is far more violent, more capable of anger; having been shown the way, however, he may be more successful as a practical missionary than Casy. One might say that if Casy is to be identified with Christ, the almost human god, Tom is to be identified with Saint Paul, the realistic, tough organizer. The allegorical link by which Tom is "converted" and assumes Casy's role is deeply realized and rich with significance, not simply because it is a technical necessity, but because it is a confirmation of Casy's reality as a man and a teacher. The parallels to Christ and Saint Paul would be only arid technical facts if they were not realized so profoundly. The trivial fact that Casy has Christ's initials dims beside this more profound and sustained realization.

Function, not mere design, is as evident in the use of characterization to support and develop a conflict of opposed ideas—mainly a struggle between law and anarchy. The one idea postulates justice in a moral world of love and work, identified in the past with "the people" and in the present with the government camp and finally with the union movement, since these are the modern, institutional forms the group may take. The opposed idea postulates injustice in an immoral world of hatred and starvation. It is associated with buccaneering capitalism, which, in violent form, includes strikebreaking and related practices that cheapen human labor.

The Joads present special difficulties in characterization. They must be individualized to be credible and universalized to carry out their representative functions. Steinbeck meets these problems by making each of the Joads a specific individual and by specifying that what happens to the Joads is typical of the times. The means he uses to maintain these identities can be shown in some detail. The least important Joads are given highly specific tags—Grandma's religion, Grandpa's vigor, Uncle John's melancholy, and Al's love of cars and girls. The tags are involved in events; they are not inert labels. Grandma's burial violates her religion; Grandpa's vigor ends when he leaves the land; Uncle John's melancholy balances the family's experience; Al helps to drive the family to California and, by marrying, continues the family. Ma, Pa, Rose of Sharon, and Tom carry the narrative, so their individuality is defined by events rather than through events. Ma is the psychological and moral center of the family; Pa carries its burdens; Rose of Sharon means to ensure its physical continuity; and Tom becomes its moral conscience. On the larger scale, there is much evidence that what happens to the family is typical of the times. The interchapters pile up suggestions that "the whole country is moving" or about to move.[21] The Joads meet many of their counterparts or outsiders who are in sympathy with their ordeal; these meetings reenforce the common bond of "the people."[22] Both in the interchapters and the narrative, the universal, immediate issue is survival—a concrete universal.

On the other hand, the individualized credibility of the Joads is itself the source of two difficulties: the Joads are too different, as sharecroppers, to suggest a universal or even a national woe, and they speak an argot that might limit their universal quality.[23] Steinbeck handles these limitations with artistic license. The narrative background contains the Joads' past; their experience as a landless prole-

21. *GW*, pp. 6–7, 43–47, 65, 104, 196–97, 206, 236, 259, 264–70, 273, 279, 317–18, 324–25.

22. *GW*, pp. 165, 171, 174–75, 215–20, 245–46.

23. It is a curious fact that Steinbeck attempts to create a so-called "universal language" in *Burning Bright*, a far more theory-ridden novel than *The Grapes of Wrath*. In any event, the attempt produces a fantastic, wholly incredible language.

tariat is highlighted in the narrative foreground. The argot is made to seem a typical language within the novel in three ways: It is the major language; people who are not Okies speak variations of their argot; and that argot is not specialized in its relevance, but is used to communicate the new experiences "the people" have in common as a landless proletariat. However, because these solutions depend on artistic license, any tonal falseness undermines severely the massive artistic truthfulness the language is intended to present. So the overly editorial tone in several of the interchapters has a profoundly false linguistic ring, although the tonal lapse is limited and fairly trivial in itself.

The Joads are characterized further in comparison with four Okie types who refuse to know or are unable to gain the knowledge the family derives from its collective experience. They are the stubborn, the dead, the weak, and the backtrackers; they appear in the novel in that order.

Muley Graves is the stubborn man, as his punning name suggests. He reveals himself to Tom and Casy near the beginning of the novel. His refusal to leave Oklahoma is mere stubbornness; his isolation drives him somewhat mad. He is aware of a loss of reality, of "jus' wanderin' aroun' like a damn ol' graveyard ghos'," and his blind violence is rejected from the beginning by the strongest, who oppose his pessimism with an essential optimism.[24]

Deaths of the aged and the unborn frame the novel. Grandpa and Grandma are torn up by the roots and die, incapable of absorbing a new, terrible experience. Rose of Sharon's baby, born dead at the end of the novel, is an index of the family's ordeal and a somewhat contrived symbol of the necessity to form the group.

The weak include two extremes within the Joad family. Noah Joad gives up the struggle to survive; he finds a private peace. His character is shadowy, and his choice is directed more clearly by Steinbeck than by any substance within him.[25] Connie has plenty of substance. He is married

24. *GW*, pp. 67–71, 151.
25. Noah does not suggest earlier "idiot" characters—the two Burgundians in *Cup of Gold*, Willie in *To a God Unknown*, and

to Rose of Sharon and deserts her because he has no faith in the family's struggle to reach California. His faith is absorbed in the values of "the Bank," in getting on, in money, in any abstract goal. He wishes to learn about technology in order to rise in the world. He does not admire technique for itself, as Al does. He is a sexual performer, but he loves no one. Finally, he wishes that he had stayed behind in Oklahoma and taken a job driving a tractor. In short, with Connie, Steinbeck chooses brilliantly to place a "Bank" viewpoint within the family. By doing so, he precludes a simplification of character and situation, and he endorses the complexity of real people in the real world. (*In Dubious Battle* is similarly free of schematic characterization.) In addition, the family's tough, humanistic values gain in credibility by their contrast with Connie's shallow, destructive modernity. The confused gas station owner and the pathetic one-eyed junkyard helper are embodied variations on Connie's kind of weakness.[26] Al provides an important counterpoint. He wants to leave the family at last, like Connie, but duty and love force him to stay. His hard choice points the moral survival of the family and measures its human expense.

The Joads meet several backtrackers. The Wilsons go back because Mrs. Wilson is dying; the Joads do not stop, in spite of death. The ragged man's experience foreshadows what the Joads find in California; but they keep on. Some members of the Joad family think of leaving but do not, or they leave for specific reasons—a subtle variation on backtracking. Al and Uncle John wish deeply at times to leave, but they stay; Tom leaves (as Casy does) but to serve the larger, universal family of the group. Backtracking is a metaphor, then, a denial of life, but always a fact as well. The factual metaphor is deepened into complexity because the Joads sympathize with the backtrackers' failure to endure the hardships of the road and of California, in balance with where they started from—the wasteland—while know-

---

Tularecito in *The Pastures of Heaven.* Instead, Noah's shadowy, directed character recalls one aspect of Lennie in *Of Mice and Men.*

26. *GW*, pp. 170–74, 242, 343–44, 372.

ing they cannot accept that life-denying solution. All of these choices are the fruit of the family's experience.

A fifth group of owners and middle-class people are accorded no sympathetic comprehension, as contrasted with the Joads, and, as in *In Dubious Battle*, their simply and purely monstrous characterization is too abstract to be fully credible. The few exceptions occur in highly individualized scenes or episodes (Chapter XV is an example) in which middle-class "shitheels" are caricatures of the bad guys, limited to a broad contrast with the good guys (the truck drivers, the cook), who are in sympathy with a family of Okies.[27] This limitation has the narrative advantage of highlighting the importance and vitality of the Okies to the extent that they seem by right to belong in the context of epic materials, but the disadvantage of shallow characterization is severe. Steinbeck can provide a convincing detailed background of the conditions of the time; he cannot similarly give a rounded, convincing characterization to an owner or a disagreeable middle-class person.

On the whole, then, fictive strength and conviction are inherent in the materials of *The Grapes of Wrath*. The noticeable flaws are probably irreducible aspects of the time-context and of narrative shorthand, counterpointed by a complex recognition of human variety in language and behavior.

The ordering of the structure supports this conclusion. *The Grapes of Wrath* has three parts: Tom's return and his witnessing of events; the family's departure and experiences on the road; its arrival and experiences in California. The interchapters "locate" and generalize the narrative chapters, somewhat like stage directions. They supply, in a suitably dramatic or rhetorical style, information the Joads cannot possess, and they are involved more often than not

27. Fifteen years later, Steinbeck detailed this technique in a witty article, "How to Tell Good Guys from Bad Guys," *The Reporter*, 12 (March 10, 1955), 42–44. In that quite different, political context, Steinbeck demonstrates that he knows the technique is too bluntly black and white to permit any but the broadest cartoon characterization. There is every reason to think he knew as much in 1935 or 1939.

in the narrative.[28] This device provides for both precise detail and epic scope. The imagery fulfills the structural purpose of pitting life against death.

The first part contains ten chapters. The opening is a "location" interchapter. The dead land of the Dust Bowl in Oklahoma provides the imagery of a universal death, but at the close the women watch their men to see if they will break in the stress of that natural disaster. The men do not break; the scene is repeated in California at the close of the novel in a rising rhetoric.[29] The objective imagistic frame sets life against death, and life endures in the will of the people to endure. The following nine chapters center on Tom's return from a kind of death—prison. With Casy, Tom is an external observer, witnessing with fresh eyes the dead land and the universal dispossession. Death seems to prevail. The turtle interchapter is recapitulated ironically in the narrative. Pa carries handbills that promise jobs in California, an analogue to the turtle carrying a head of oats; but the handbills falsely promise renewal; their intention is to cheapen the labor market. Later events prove the group concept is the genuine renewal, the true goal. Immediately, death is associated with "the Bank," an abstraction presented concretely in symbolic form as the tractor—the perfect tool of the abstract "Bank," which dehumanizes its driver and kills the fertility of the land.

When he sees the abandoned Joad home, Tom says, "Maybe they're all dead," but Muley Graves tells Tom the family is alive, with Uncle John, and about to leave without him for California.[30] Tom is reborn or returned to life within the family, but its vital center has shifted (as represented in charged, frankly mystical terms) to a life-giving machine:

28. Because of that involvement, it is incorrect to think of the interchapters as choral. We see the difference in comparing the four deatched interchapters in *Cup of Gold* with any interchapters in *The Grapes of Wrath*, and we see as well Steinbeck's artistic growth in the organic integration of chapter and interchapter in the later novel. For an excellent analysis of style in the interchapters, see Lisca, pp. 160–65. The stylistic variety always suited to its content is further evidence of a conscious, intentional artistry.

29. *GW*, pp. 6, 592–94.   30. *GW*, p. 55.

> The family met at the most important place, near the truck. The house was dead, and the fields were dead; but this truck was the active thing, the living principle.[31]

The family's certainties develop from an ironically hopeful innocence, a failure to realize that a new basis for life has overtaken them, replacing family with group. The trek is an instinctive flight from death, but the economic system is more deadly than the drouth. The Joads accept the promise of the handbills, they are cheated when they sell their farm equipment, but they do not doubt that they will transplant themselves in California. The real certainty is the death of the past, as in the burning of relics by an unnamed woman in an interchapter, and by Ma herself, just before the trek begins.

All that is not dead is altered. Pa's loss of authority to Ma and Al's new authority (he knows automobiles) represent the shifts in value within the family. They retain a living coherence as farmers. They work as a unit when they kill and salt down the hogs in preparation for the trek. They are innocent of the disgusting techniques of close dealing in business, but Tom explains to Casy how the Joads can deal closely enough in their accustomed agrarian context. Their innocence, therefore, is touching, not comic, and their literal preparations support a symbolic preparation, a blindly hopeful striving to find life. Their journey is an expression, despite all shocks and changes, of the will to survive; hence, it has an epic dignity, echoing their retained, personal dignity.

In all the imagery of life and death, Steinbeck is consistent in that his symbols grow out of objective, literal facts. He thus achieves imagery in a more fully realized texture in this novel than in earlier work. This organically realized symbolism is maintained and developed in the seven chapters of the second section.

With the dead land behind them, the family carries the death of the past on its journey. Grandpa dies on the first night. Probably his stroke is caused, at least in part, by the "medicine" that Ma and Tom dope him with to take him

31. *GW*, p. 135.

away from the land—for the good of the family as a whole. An incipient group concept emerges in this overriding concern for the whole. Grandpa's death is offset by the meeting of the Joads and the Wilsons. At the beginning, Grandpa's illness and death join the two families in bonds of sympathy. There are other unifying forces; the language bar becomes senseless, and the two families help each other. Casy sees the emergence of the group, the whole absorbing the individual, in his sermon for Grandpa:

> Casy said solemnly, "This here ol' man jus' lived a life an' jus' died out of it. I don't know whether he was good or bad, but that don't matter much. He was alive, an' that's what matters. An' now he's dead, an' that don't matter. Heard a fella tell a poem one time, an' he says, 'All that lives is holy. . . .' "[32]

A modest dignity embodies the vitalistic dogma. As a further push from individual to group, the family decides to break the law by burying Grandpa secretly beside the road; a conventional funeral would eat up the money they need to reach California. Grandma's grisly, circumstantial death is delayed until the end of the section; it outweighs the achievement of reaching their destination and foreshadows the reality of California. True, the family can absorb death, even new kinds of death, into its experience. Ruthie and Winfield react most violently to the dog's death at the first stop on the road; they are less affected by Grandpa's death, still less by Grandma's. Late on the night of Grandpa's death, after the Joads and Wilsons have agreed to join forces, Ma remarks: "Grandpa—it's like he's dead a year."[33] Experience breeds a calm in the face of loss that fills in the past. Tom points this harshly realistic network of difference after Grandma's death:

> "They was too old," he said. "They wouldn't of saw nothin' that's here. Grampa would a been a-seein' the Injuns an' the prairie country when he was a young fella. An' Granma would a remembered an' seen the first home she lived in. They was too ol'. Who's really seein' it is Ruthie and Winfiel'."[34]

32. *GW*, p. 196.
33. *GW*, p. 203.   34. *GW*, p. 313.

Life matters. The narrative context supports this fruit of the family's private experience. Between the deaths of Grandpa and Grandma, the Joads meet several symbolically dead people on the road. The gas station owner is incapable of learning the meaning of his own experience even when it is explained to him. The one-eyed junkyard helper lives in a prison of self, inside his ugly face and unclean body. Tom (who was in an actual prison) tries unsuccessfully to force him from his death into life. The several returning sharecroppers have come to accept a living death as the only reality. They have cut themselves off from the inchoate struggle to form a group, admittedly against severe odds, so they have no choice but to return to the dead, empty land.

But to outsiders, seeing only the surface, the Joads are not heroic life-bearers but stupidly ignorant, as in a dialogue between two service station boys when the family leaves on the final lap of the trek, the night trip across the Mojave Desert:

> "Jesus, I'd hate to start out in a jalopy like that." "Well, you and me got sense. Them goddamn Okies got no sense and no feeling. They ain't human. A human being wouldn't live like they do. A human being couldn't stand to be so dirty and miserable. They ain't a hell of a lot better than gorillas." "Just the same, I'm glad I ain't crossing the desert in no Hudson Super-Six. . . ." "You know, they don't have much trouble. They're so goddamn dumb they don't know it's dangerous. And, Christ Almighty, they don't know any better than what they got. Why worry?"[35]

The dialogue is exactly true, but the truth is ironic. The Joads do have the appearance of death, and ignorant, dirty, dispossessed yokels seem to be unlikely carriers of an affirmation of life. The ironic truth defines the heroism of the Joads. The family is aware of the dangers of the desert crossing, and Grandma dies during it, "for the fambly," as Ma says.[36] In general the family is more aware than the boys at the service station are allowed to know. After meeting a second returning sharecropper, the Joads are even aware of the actual conditions in California; Uncle John, the fam-

35. *GW*, pp. 301–2.   36. *GW*, pp. 311–12.

ily's weakest moral agent, voices the family's rejection of despair when he says, "We're a-goin' there, ain't we? None of this here talk gonna keep us from goin' there."[37] The service-station boys express, so we can dismiss, a superficially sentimental view of the Joads. The ironic truth is that the family goes ahead, knowing the dangers and aware that California may not be Eden. Their genuine heroism and nobility are all the more valid for being tested by irony.

Yet there is no suggestion that the Joads are merely deterministic formulae. They are pawns of circumstance up to a point. They react to events they do not understand fully, and no doubt partial ignorance and pure necessity keep them on the road and get them to California. But Ma and Tom undergo certain developments of character that exclude determinism. Ma's constantly increasing moral authority is her response to the forces that are tearing the family apart, but she acts out of a love that is restricted to the family, that is not universalized until very near the end of the novel. Tom's role is more extensive and more complex. He begins by regarding himself as a creature of necessity—"I ruther jus'——lay one foot down in front a the other"—but his quietism relates to a prison experience he does not want to live "over an' over."[38] His natural understanding of why and how people behave forces him into a moral concern that is larger but as intense as Ma's. His knowledge of people is established at the beginning of the novel, in his shrewd, unflattering understanding of the truck driver who gives him a lift, and it widens subsequently with experience on the road. His disdain for the gas station owner precedes his tough moral lecture to the one-eyed junkyard helper and an equally tough lecture to Al. That is to say, Tom is involved. His moral development follows Casy's, with the significant difference that his is the more difficult to achieve. Casy is a relatively simple character; he can express moral concern easily. Tom's emotional numbness following his time in prison does not permit meditation or cancel personality, so the awakening of his moral consciousness on the road is a more rigorous, more painful experience than

37. *GW*, p. 283.   38. *GW*, p. 241.

Casy's time in the desert. Consequently, because of its special quality, Tom's growing awareness of good and evil is a highly credible mirror of the general experience that drives the family toward the group. The logic is paradoxical, but the artistic insight is realized deeply in Tom's circumstantial journey from moral quietism to moral concern for the group.

Enduring all the harsh experiences of their journey, the family gains moral stature and finds that it can function as a unit in the new environment of the road. Its survival in California is a result in part of its redefinition gained on the road.

The interchapters underscore and generalize these particulars. Chapter XIV states the growth of the group concept as a shift in the thinking of the migrants from *I* to *we*. The narrative context is Grandpa's death and the unity of the Joads and Wilsons. Chapter XV suggests that the Joads' ordeal is a moral experience that affects society at large. Chapter XVII continues the theme that the road furthers the growth of the group concept:

> Every night relationships that make a world, established; every morning the world torn down like a circus. At first the families were timid in the building and tumbling worlds, but gradually the technique of building worlds became their technique. Then leaders emerged, then laws were made, then codes came into being. And as the worlds moved westward they were more complete and better furnished, for their builders were more experienced in building them.[39]

The formation of a group is a "technique" with its basis in the older agrarian order. As with the Joads, the experience of building produces a new moral stature and a redefinition of the family.

In the relation of these events and changes, the narrative chapters and interchapters cohere in an organic unity. Their common theme is movement from and through death to a new life inherent in the group concept. The symbolic level extends the narrative level of movement on the road through time and space. The texture is fully realized. No generaliza-

39. *GW*, p. 265.

tion violates narrative particulars or exists apart from them. Steinbeck's work is careful, convincing, flawless.

The third part—the family's arrival and experience in California—marks an artistic decline. The materials alter and at times the structure is defective.

The chief difference in the materials is an absolute focus on man-made misery. In Oklahoma and on the road, survival can seem to be mainly a struggle against natural conditions. Drouth is the cause of the migration. "The Bank" dispossesses the Okies, but it is not the effective cause of the drouth. In California the struggle is almost entirely against men, and there is no possibility of an escape by further migration. The chief difference in structure stems from Steinbeck's need to begin to think of how to conclude the novel, which presents structural choices and manipulations not present in the first two parts of the novel. For a time the narrative thrust remains coherent, an organic unity, disguising these changes.

Grandma's undignified burial establishes the pattern of the family's experience in California. Her pauper's funeral by the state contrasts with the full dignity and free will the family expressed in burying Grandpa. Landless poverty is a moral insult to family pride, and it affects their will to survive. For the moment, as their moral spokesman, Ma expresses a will to recover as quickly as possible for the sake of the future:

> "We got to git," she said. "We got to find a place to stay. We got to get to work an' settle down. No use a-lettin' the little fellas go hungry. That wasn't never Granma's way. She always et a good meal at a funeral."[40]

The conserving lesson of the past is negated by the present economic reality. Ma's brave gesture fails as the family learns that California is a false goal. The imagery associated with California indicates these negations. Peter Lisca and Joseph Fontenrose have pointed to the major biblical parallels in *The Grapes of Wrath*, including those associating California and the Promised Land.[41] The parallels are in-

40. *GW*, p. 328.
41. Lisca, pp. 169–70; Joseph Fontenrose, *John Steinbeck: An In-*

tensive, even more so than Lisca and Fontenrose suggest, and their function is ironic rather than associative. To begin with, California evokes images of plenty to eat and drink. The ironic fact is that California is the literal reverse of Canaan; there is little to eat and drink, at least for Okies; but California *is* the Promised Land so far as the family's experience there forces the full emergence of the group concept. Appropriately, the family enters California with a foreboding that runs counter to their expectations:

> Pa called, "We're here—we're in California!" They looked dully at the broken rock glaring under the sun, and across the river the terrible ramparts of Arizona.[42]

They have crossed over, but the physical imagery foreshadows their actual human environment. The land is green across the river, but the biblical lists of landscape features are framed by the fact that they have been carrying Grandma's corpse. The human reality of Californian life is a living death, as the first camp, the Hooverville, suggests: "About the camp there hung a slovenly despair," everything is "grey" and "'dirty," there is no work, no food, and no evident means of overcoming "despair."[43] The deadly economic reality is explained by a young man in the Hooverville, when Tom asks why the police "shove along" the migrants:

> "Some says they don' want us to vote; keep us movin' so we can't vote. An' some says so we can't get on relief. An' some says if we set in one place we'd get organized."[44]

That reply announces the political solution, the humanly possible way of countervailing power through organization. But the words are programmatic, not a revelation of character.

The difference in materials and in structure begins to appear at this point. The root of the matter is that Steinbeck is so compelled by the documentary facts that he permits

---

troduction and Interpretation (New York: Barnes & Noble, Inc., 1963), pp. 74–83.

42. *GW*, p. 275.   43. *GW*, pp. 327–29.
44. *GW*, pp. 332–33.

their narration to take precedence over the central theme of the family's transformation into the group. And in moving the novel toward an affirmation of life in response to the facts, Steinbeck allows the Joads' experience in California to become a series of allegorical details within a panoramic structure. The narrowed scope of the materials and the schematic handling of the structure are visible in nearly every event in this part of the novel.

Casy's alternative to "despair," sacrificing himself for "the people," is almost wholly an allegorical solution. It is so abstractly schematic that at first none of the family understands its meaningful allegorical force—that loss of self leads to the group concept and thus to power to enforce the will of the group. Instead, the narrative is largely an account of the family's efforts to avoid starvation. The phrase "We got to eat" echoes through these concluding chapters.[45] Ma's changing attitude toward hungry unknown children is ambiguous: "I dunno what to do. I can't rob the fambly. I got to feed the fambly."[46] Ma grows more positive, later, when she is nagged by a storekeeper in the struck orchard:

> "Any reason you got to make fun? That help you any?"
> ... "A fella got to eat," he began; and then, belligerently, "A fella got a right to eat." "What fella?" Ma asked.[47]

Ma asserts finally that only "the poor" constitute a group that practices charity:

> "I'm learnin' one thing good," she said. "Learnin' it all a time, ever' day. If you're in trouble or hurt or need—go to poor people. They're the only ones that'll help—the only ones."[48]

"The poor" are identified with "the people," who, in turn, are the emerging group. Their purity is allegorical, and, in its limitation, incredible. Steinbeck's handling of "the poor" in *In Dubious Battle* is much less schematic, and therefore far more credible. In general, romanticizing "the poor" is more successful in an outright fantasy like *Tortilla Flat*,

---

45. *GW*, pp. 479, 483, 487, 497, 512–13.
46. *GW*, p. 351.   47. *GW*, p. 512.
48. *GW*, pp. 513–14.

but Steinbeck commits himself to a measure of realism in *The Grapes of Wrath* that does not sort well with the allegorical division of "good" from "evil."

Romanticizing "the poor" extends beyond Ma's insight to an idealization of the "folk law" that Tom envisions as the fruit of his own experience in California—at a great distance from the "building" experience on the road:

> "I been thinkin' how it was in that gov'ment camp, how our folks took care a theirselves, an' if they was a fight they fixed it theirself; an' they wasn't no cops wagglin' their guns, but they was better order than them cops ever give. I been a-wonderin' why we can't do that all over. Throw out the cops that ain't our people. All work together for our own thing—all farm our own lan'."[49]

Presenting the reverse of Tom's beatific vision in an interchapter, Steinbeck draws on the imagery of the novel's title:

> This vineyard will belong to the bank. Only the great owners can survive. . . . Men who can graft the trees and make the seed fertile and big can find no way to let the hungry people eat their produce. . . . In the souls of the people the grapes of wrath are filling and growing heavy, growing heavy for the vintage.[50]

It is not vitally important that Steinbeck's prediction of some kind of agrarian revolt has turned out to be wrong. The important artistic fact is that "good," divided sharply, abstractly, from "evil," argues that Steinbeck is not interested in rendering the materials in any great depth. Consider the contrast between the people in the government camp and in the struck orchard. Point by point, the camp people are described as clean, friendly, joyful, and organized, while in the struck orchard they are dirty, suspicious, anxious, and disorganized by the police.[51] Credibility gives way to neat opposites, which are less than convincing because Steinbeck's government camp is presented openly as a benevolent tyranny that averages out the will of "the people" to live in dignity and excludes people unable or unwilling to accept that average.

49. *GW*, p. 571.
50. *GW*, p. 476.   51. *GW*, pp. 389–491, 558.

Neat opposites can gather fictive conviction if they are realized through individuals and in specific detail. There is something of that conviction in specific action against specific men, as when the camp leaders exclude troublemakers hired by business interests to break up the camp organization. There is more awkwardness in the exclusion of a small group of religious fanatics obsessed with sin. An important factor is that these people are genuinely Okies, not tools of the interests; another is that the exclusion is necessary, not realistic, if the secular values of the group concept are to prevail. Allowing for his selection and schematic treatment of these materials, Steinbeck does engineer his manipulated point with artistic skill. Fanaticism is considered a bad thing throughout the novel, both as a religious stance and as a social phenomenon. Tom's first meeting with Casy identifies "spirit" with emotional release, not a consciousness of sin, and Casy announces his own discovery, made during his time in the desert, of a social rather than an ethical connection between "spirit" and sexual excitement.[52] Further, fanaticism is identified repeatedly with a coercive denial of life. Rose of Sharon is frightened, in the government camp, by a fanatic woman's argument that dancing is sinful, that it means Rose will lose her baby. The woman's ignorance is placed against the secular knowledge of the camp manager:

> "I think the manager, he took [another girl who danced] away to drop her baby. He don' believe in sin. . . . Says the sin is bein' hungry. Says the sin is bein' cold."[53]

She compounds ignorance by telling Ma that true religion demands fixed economic classes:

> "[A preacher] says 'They's wicketness in that camp.' He says, 'The poor is tryin' to be rich.' He says, 'They's dancin' an' huggin' when they should be wailin' an' moanin' in sin.'"[54]

These social and economic denials of life are rooted in ignorance, not in spiritual enlightenment, and they are countered by the materialistic humanism of the camp manager.

52. *GW*, pp. 27, 29, 30, 31–32.
53. *GW*, p. 423.   54. *GW*, p. 437.

So fanaticism is stripped of value and associated with business in its denial of life. The case is loaded further by the benevolent tyranny of the group. Fanatics are not punished for their opinions, or even for wrongdoing. They are merely excluded, or they exclude themselves.

A similar process is apparent in the group's control of social behavior, as when Ruthie behaves as a rugged individual in the course of a children's game:

> The children laid their mallets on the ground and trooped silently off the court. . . . Defiantly she hit the ball again. . . . She pretended to have a good time. And the children stood and watched. . . . For a moment she stared at them, and then she flung down the mallet and ran crying for home. The children walked back on the court. Pig-tails said to Winfield, "You can git in the nex' game." The watching lady warned them, "When she comes back an' wants to be decent, you let her. You was mean yourself, Amy."[55]

The punishment is directive. The children are being trained to accept the group and to become willing parts of the group. The process is an expression of "folk law" on a primary level. There is no doubt that Ruthie learned her correct place in the social body by invoking a suitably social punishment.

Perhaps the ugliness implicit in the tyranny of the group has become more visible lately. Certainly recent students of the phenomenon of modern conformity could supply Steinbeck with very little essential insight. The real trouble is precisely there. The tyranny of the group is visible in all of Steinbeck's instances (its ambiguity is most evident in Ruthie's case), which argues for Steinbeck's artistic honesty in rendering the materials. But he fails to see deeply enough, to see ugliness and ambiguity, because he has predetermined the absolute "good" of group behavior—an abstraction that precludes subtle technique and profound insight, on the order of Doc Burton's reservations concerning group-man. The result is a felt manipulation of values and a thinning of credibility.

Given this tendency, Steinbeck does not surprise us by dealing abstractly with the problem of leadership in the gov-

55. *GW*, pp. 433–34.

ernment camp. Since there is minimal narrative time in which to establish the moral purity of Jim Rawley, the camp manager, or of Ezra Huston, the chairman of the Central Committee, Steinbeck presents both men as allegorical figures. Particularly Jim Rawley. His introduction suggests his allegorical role. He is named only once, and thereafter he is called simply "the camp manager." His name is absorbed in his role as God. He is dressed "all in white," but he is not a remote God. "The frayed seams on his white coat" suggest his human availability, and his "warm" voice matches his social qualities.[56] Nevertheless, there is no doubt that he is God visiting his charges:

> He put the cup on the box with the others, waved his hand, and walked down the line of tents. And Ma heard him speaking to the people as he went.[57]

His identification with God is bulwarked when the fanatic woman calls him the devil:

> "She says you was the devil," [says Rose of Sharon]. "I know she does. That's because I won't let her make people miserable. . . . Don't you worry. She doesn't know."[58]

What "she doesn't know" is everything the camp manager does know; and if he is not the devil, he must be God. But his very human, secular divinity—he can wish for an easier lot, and he is always tired from overwork—suggests the self-sacrifice that is Casy's function. The two men are outwardly similar. Both are clean and "lean as a picket," and the camp manager has "merry eyes" like Casy's when Tom meets Casy again.[59] These resemblances would be trivial, except for a phrase that pulls them together and lends them considerable weight. Ezra Huston has no character to speak of, beyond his narrative function, except that when he has finished asking the men who try to begin a riot in the camp why they betrayed "their own people," he adds: "They don't know what they're doin'."[60] This phrase foreshadows Casy's words to his murderer just before he is

56. *GW*, pp. 415–16.
57. *GW*, p. 416.   58. *GW*, p. 424.
59. *GW*, pp. 25–26, 415, 521.   60. *GW*, p. 470.

killed in an effort to break the strike: "You don't know what you're a-doin'."[61] Just as these words associate Casy with Christ, so they associate the leaders in the government camp with Casy. Steinbeck's foreshortening indicates that, because Casy is established firmly as a "good" character, the leaders in the government camp must resemble Casy in that "good" identity.

The overall process is allegorical, permitting Steinbeck to assert that the camp manager and Ezra Huston are good men by definition and precluding the notion that leadership may be a corrupting role, as in *In Dubious Battle*. It follows that violence in the name of the group is "good," whereas it is "evil" in the name of business interests. The contrast is too neat, too sharp, to permit much final credibility in narrative or in characterization.

A still more extreme instance of Steinbeck's use of allegory is the process by which Tom Joad assumes the role of a leader. Tom's pastoral concept of the group is fully developed, and as the novel ends, Tom identifies himself through mystic insight with the group. Appropriately, Tom explains his insight to Ma because Tom's function is to act while Ma's function is to endure—in the name of the group. More closely, Ma's earlier phrase, "We're the people—we go on," is echoed directly in Tom's assurance when Ma fears for his life:

> "Well, maybe like Casy says, a fella ain't got a soul of his own, but on'y a piece of a big one—an' then——" "Then what, Tom?" "Then it don' matter. Then I'll be all aroun' in the dark. I'll be ever'where—wherever you look. . . . See? God, I'm talkin' like Casy. Comes of thinkin' about him so much. Seems like I can see him sometimes."[62]

This anthropomorphic insight, borrowed from *To a God Unknown* and remotely from Emerson, is a serious idea, put seriously within the allegorical framework of the novel's close. Two structural difficulties result. First, Tom has learned more than Casy could have taught him—that identification *with* the group, rather than self-sacrifice *for* the group, is the truly effective way to kill the dehumanized

61. *GW*, p. 527.   62. *GW*, p. 572.

"Bank." Here, it seems, the Christ/Casy, Saint Paul/Tom identifications were too interesting in themselves, for they limit Steinbeck's development of Tom's insight to a mechanical parallel, such as the suggestion that Tom's visions of Casy equate with Saint Paul's visions of Christ. Second, the connection between the good material life and Tom's mystical insight is missing. There is Steinbeck's close attention to Tom's political education and to his revival of belief in a moral world. But, in the specific instance, the only bridge is Tom's sudden feeling that mystical insight connects somehow with the good material life. More precisely, the bridge is Steinbeck's own assertion, since Tom's mystical vision of pastoral bliss enters the narrative only as an abstract announcement on Steinbeck's part.

Characterization is, as might be assumed, affected by this abstracting tendency. Earlier, major characters such as Tom and Ma are "given" through actions in which they are involved, not through detached, abstract essays; increasingly, at the close, the method of presentation is the detached essay or the extended, abstract speech. Steinbeck's earlier, more realized presentation of Tom as a natural man measures the difference. Even a late event, Tom's instinctive killing of Casy's murderer, connects organically with Tom's previous "social" crimes—the murder in self-defense, for which Tom has finished serving a prison term when the novel begins, and the parole that Tom jumps to go with the family to California. In all of these crimes, Tom's lack of guilt or shame links with the idea that "the people" have a "natural" right to unused land—not to add life, liberty, and the pursuit of happiness—and that "the Bank" has nothing but an abstract, merely legal right to such land. Tom's mystical vision is something else; it is a narrative shock, not due to Tom's "natural" responses, but to the oversimplified type of the "good" man that Tom is made to represent in order to close the novel on a high and optimistic note. Tom is a rather complex man earlier on, and the thinning out of his character, in its absolute identification with the "good," is an inevitable result of allegorizing.

Style suffers also from these pressures. Tom's speech has

been condemned, as Emerson's writing never is, for mawk-ishness, for maudlin lushness, for the soft, rotten blur of intellectual evasion.[63] Style is a concomitant of structure; its decline is an effect, not a cause. Tom's thinking is em-barrassing, not as thought, but as the stylistic measure of a process of manipulation that is necessary to close the novel on Steinbeck's terms.

The final scene, in which Rose of Sharon breastfeeds a sick man, has been regarded universally as the nadir of bad Steinbeck, yet the scene is no more and no less allegorical than earlier scenes in this final part. Purely in a formal sense, it parallels Tom's mystical union or identification with the group: It affirms that "life" has become more important than "family" in a specific action, and, as such, it denotes the emergence of the group concept. In that light, the scene is a technical accomplishment. Yet it is a disaster from the outset, not simply because it is sentimental; its execution, through the leading assumption, is incredible. Rose of Sharon is supposed to become Ma's alter ego by taking on her burden of moral insight, which, in turn, is similar to the insight that Tom reaches. There is no preparation for Rose of Sharon's transformation and no literary justification ex-cept a merely formal symmetry that makes it desirable, in spite of credibility, to devise a repetition. Tom, like Ma, undergoes a long process of education; Rose of Sharon is characterized in detail throughout the novel as a protected, rather thoughtless, whining girl.[64] Possibly her miscarriage produces an unmentioned, certainly mystical change in character. More likely the reader will notice the hand of the author, forcing Rose of Sharon into an unprepared and purely formalistic role.

Once given this degree of manipulation, direct senti-mentality is no surprise. Worse, the imagistic shift from anger to sweetness, from the grapes of wrath to the milk of human kindness, allows the metaphor to be uplifted,

---

63. See references in footnote 3.

64. *GW*, p p. 129–30, 134–35, 175–77, 285–86, 343–44, 366, 371–72, 378–79, 413–14, 420–225, 440, 460–61, 482–85, 504, 508, 537, 539, 548, 580–81, 586–88.

but at the cost of its structural integrity. The novel is made to close with a forced image of optimism and brotherhood, with an audacious upbeat that cries out in the wilderness. I have no wish to deny the value or the real power of good men, optimism, or brotherhood. The point is that Steinbeck imposes an unsupported conclusion upon materials which themselves are thinned out and manipulated. The increasingly grotesque episodes (and their leading metaphors) prove that even thin and manipulated materials resist the conclusion that is drawn from them, for art visits that revenge on its mistaken practitioners.

To argue that no better conclusion was available at the time, granting the country's social and political immaturity and its economic innocence, simply switches the issue from art to politics. No artist is obliged to provide solutions to the problems of the socio-politico-economic order, however "engaged" his work may be. Flaubert did not present a socioeducational program to help other young women to avoid Emma Bovary's fate. The business of the artist is to present a situation. If he manipulates the materials or forces them to conclusions that violate credibility—especially if he has a visible design upon us—his work will thin, the full range of human possibility will not be available to him, and to that extent he will have failed as an artist.

We must not exclude the likelihood, not that Steinbeck had no other conclusion at hand, but that his predisposition was to see a resolution in the various allegorical and panoramic arrangements that close out *The Grapes of Wrath*. Steinbeck's earlier work argues for that likelihood.

Yet that is not all there is to John Steinbeck. If he becomes the willing victim of abstract, horrendously schematic manipulations as *The Grapes of Wrath* nears its close, still he is capable of better things. He demonstrates these potentialities particularly in minor scenes dealing with minor characters, so the negative force of the imposed conclusion is lessened.

Consider the scene in which Ruthie and Winfield make their way (along with the family) from the flooded boxcar to the barn where Rose of Sharon will feed the sick man.

The intention of the scene is programmatic: the children's identification with the group concept. The overt content is the essentially undamaged survival of their sense of fun and of beauty. Significantly, the action makes no directly allegorical claim on the reader, unlike the rest of the concluding scenes.

Ruthie finds a flower along the road, "a scraggly geranium gone wild, and there was one rain-beaten blossom on it."[65] The common flower, visualized, does not insist on the identity of the beaten but surviving beauty in pure nature with the uprooted, starved children of all the migrants. The scene is developed implicitly, in dramatic, imagistic terms. Ruthie and Winfield struggle to possess the petals for playthings, and Ma forces Ruthie to be kind:

> Winfield held his nose near to her. She wet a petal with her tongue and jabbed it cruelly on his nose. "You little son-of-a-bitch," she said softly. Winfield felt for the petal with his fingers, and pressed it down on his nose. They walked quickly after the others. Ruthie felt how the fun was gone. "Here," she said. "Here's some more. Stick some on your forehead."[66]

The scene recapitulates the earlier scene on the playground of the government camp. Here, as there, Winfield is the innocent, and Ruthie's cruelty is changed by external pressure (the other children, Ma's threat) to an official kindness that transcends itself to become a genuine kindness when "the fun was gone." The observed basis of the present scene is the strained relationship that usually exists between an older sister and a younger brother. There is no visible effort to make the scene "fit" a predetermined allegorical scheme. Ruthie's kind gesture leads into Rose of Sharon's, as child to adult, and both scenes project the affirmative values—the survival of optimism, brotherhood, kindliness, goodness—that are the substance of the group concept at the conclusion. The children's quarrel and reconciliation is a relatively unloaded action, an event in itself. Tom's affirmation is nondramatic, a long, deeply mystical speech to Ma. Rose of Sharon's affirmation is out of character and frankly

65. *GW*, p. 615.   66. *GW*, pp. 615–16.

incredible. Uncle John's symbolic action derives from his own guilt but expresses a universal anger.

As the scene between the children is exceptional, Steinbeck's development of the flood scene is typical. Allegorical intentions override narrative power: The family's struggle against the flood is intended to equate with its surviving will to struggle against hopelessness; Pa, Uncle John, and Al are exhausted but not beaten. Tom's insight precedes the flood; Rose of Sharon's agreement to breastfeed the sick man follows it. In the larger frame, neither extreme of drouth or flood can exhaust the will and the vitality of the people. The dense texture of these panoramic materials is impressive. They lie side by side, at different levels of the "willing suspension of disbelief," depending on whether they are convincing narrative actions or palpable links in an arranged allegory. Hence, there is no great sense of a concluding "knot," an organic fusion of parts; there is no more than a formulated ending, a pseudoclose that does not convince because its design is an a priori assertion of structure, not the supportive and necessary skeleton of a realized context. Here structure and materials fail to achieve a harmonious relationship.

These final scenes are not hackwork. We cannot apply to Steinbeck, even here, the slurring remark that F. Scott Fitzgerald aimed at Thomas Wolfe: "The stuff about the GREAT VITAL HEART OF AMERICA is just simply corny."[67] Steinbeck's carefully interwoven strands of character, metaphor, and narrative argue a conscious, skillful intention, not a sudden lapse of material or of novelistic ability. Even in failure, Steinbeck is a formidable technician. His corn, here, if it exists, is not a signal of failed ability.

Steinbeck's feeling that *The Grapes of Wrath* must close on an intense level of sweetness, of optimism and affirmation, is not seriously in doubt. His ability to use the tech-

---

67. F. Scott Fitzgerald, *The Letters of F. Scott Fitzgerald*, edited, with an introduction by Andrew Turnbull (New York: Charles Scribner's Sons, 1963), p. 97. Reprinted by permission of Charles Scribner's Sons. Copyright © 1963 Frances Scott Fitzgerald Lanahan.

niques of structure to this end is evident. The earlier novels demonstrate his able willingness to skillfully apply an external structure, to mold, or at least to mystify, somewhat recalcitrant materials. The letter withdrawing *L'Affaire Lettuceburg* suggests that Steinbeck is aware of having that willing skill—"just twisting this people out of shape"—and of having to resist its lures in this most serious work. So for the critic there is a certain horrid fascination in Steinbeck's consistent, enormously talented demonstration of aesthetic failure in the last quarter of *The Grapes of Wrath*.

The failure is not a matter of "sprawling asides and extravagances," or the more extreme motivational simplicities of naturalism, or a lapse in the remarkably sustained folk idiom and the representative epic scope. The failure lies in the means Steinbeck utilizes to achieve the end.

The first three quarters of the novel are masterful. Characters are presented through action; symbolism intensifies character and action; the central theme of transformation from self to group develops persuasively in a solid, realized documentary context. The final quarter of the novel presents a difference in every respect. Characters are fitted or forced into allegorical roles, heightened beyond the limits of credibility, to the point that they thin out or become frankly unbelievable. Scenes are developed almost solely as links in an allegorical pattern. Texture is reduced to documentation, and allegorical signs replace symbolism. The result is a hollowed rhetoric, a manipulated affirmation, a soft twist of insistent sentiment. These qualities deny the conceptual theme by simplifying it, by reducing the facts of human and social complexity to simple opposites.

The reduction is not inherent in the materials, which are rendered magnificently in earlier parts of the novel. The reduction is the consequence of a structural choice—to apply allegory to character, metaphor, and theme. In short, *The Grapes of Wrath* could conceivably have a sweetly positive conclusion without an absolute, unrestrained dependence on allegory. Yet the least subtle variety of that highly visible structural technique, with its objectionably simplified, manipulative ordering of materials, is precisely the element that prevails in the final part of *The Grapes of Wrath*.

Why? Steinbeck is aware of various technical options, and he is able to make use of them earlier in the novel. As we have seen in the previous novels, with the exception of *In Dubious Battle*, Steinbeck draws on allegory to stiffen or to heighten fictions that are too loose—too panoramic— to achieve the semblance of a dramatic structure purely by means of technique. Apparently Steinbeck was not offended aesthetically by the overwhelming artificiality that results from an extreme dependence on allegory. That the contemporary naturalistic or symbolic novel requires a less simple or rigid structure clearly escapes Steinbeck's attention.

On the contrary, Steinbeck is greatly attracted to some extreme kind of external control in much of the immediately preceding work and in much of the succeeding work. During the rest of his career, Steinbeck does not attempt seriously, on the massive scale of *The Grapes of Wrath*, to achieve a harmonious relationship between structure and materials. He prefers some version of the control that flaws the last quarter of *The Grapes of Wrath*.

This judgment offers a certain reasonableness in the otherwise wild shift from *The Grapes of Wrath* to the play-novelettes.

5

Three Play-Novelettes

John Steinbeck's only published excursion into literary theory is an effort to justify the form of the play-novelette —a term he invented. Also, in the span of thirteen of the middle years of his career, Steinbeck published three play-novelettes. These facts suggest that for Steinbeck the play-novelette is an important novelistic form. It is therefore appropriate to consider the theory and the practice of the form as well as its implications in the larger frame of Steinbeck's development of a simplified novelistic structure in longer fiction after about 1940.

Steinbeck presented the theory in an oddly titled article, ". . . the novel might benefit by the discipline, the terseness . . .," in the January 1938 issue of *Stage*.[1] Steinbeck's view is that a play-novelette is a pure dramatic structure— in the theatrical, not in the Jamesian, sense. He argues that if a novelist can simplify narrative and characterization by ordering a novel as if it were a play, the result must be an immediately powerful communication of theme and an enormous intensification of all the other novelistic values. He adds that *Of Mice and Men*, one of his efforts in the genre, is a failure as a play-novelette.

One can praise Steinbeck's intention to vitalize the novel through a new form, but without doubt his theory is absurd.[2] (It should be added that Steinbeck's practice does little to redeem the theory.) Foremost, a novel is not a play, and terms do not make it so. Consider a key passage in Steinbeck's argument:

1. John Steinbeck, ". . . the novel might benefit by the discipline, the terseness . . . ," *Stage*, 15 (January 1938), pp. 50–51. Excerpts from this work are quoted by permission of McIntosh and Otis, Inc.

2. Antonia Seixas was Steinbeck's secretary for a time, and the wife of Steinbeck's close friend, Edward Ricketts; she speaks with authority from within the circle. Consequently, her opinion—published in March 1947—that *Of Mice and Men* is a great novel primarily on philosophic grounds is a fascinating echo of Steinbeck's low view of the actual novel and his high view of the abstract theory of the form presented in the *Stage* article.

> For some years the novel has increasingly taken on the attributes of the drama. . . . To read an objective novel is to see a little play in your mind. All right, why not make it so you can see it on a stage? This experiment, then, is really only a conclusion toward which the novel has been unconsciously heading for some time.[3]

The argument is serious, as the tone suggests. But the logic is unconvincing because the analogy is false. To know that Henry James and his literary heirs succeed in making the novel a direct rendering of experience does not mean that a novelist can remove every vestige of form and, in that sense, "make it so you can see it on a stage." Steinbeck takes the issue beyond the limits of analogy in an effort to sharpen a point; he confuses what a novel and a play are and can do; in short, he loads the argument in his favor.

The logical trick is not worth consideration, as Steinbeck seems to know, since he uses a second argument that is based on a quite different theory: The best way to reach an audience is by a direct effect. He asserts that the trouble with the novel as a form is that it is made for the individual "alone under a reading lamp," whereas a play depends on a group response:

> Now if it is true, and I believe it is, that the preoccupation of the modern novelist lies in these themes which are most poignantly understood by a group, that novelist limits the possibility of being understood by making it impossible for groups to be exposed to this work.[4]

Again the logic is unconvincing because the analogy is false. The argument rests only on Steinbeck's feeling that the group responds to a literary effect with more emotional validity than any individual can generate. Even if a measure of emotion could be devised, and if the private reading of drama were outlawed, the fact remains that a play is not a novel. Finally, the analogy is qualified by the direction of much modern writing, including the novel, into private or subjective content and form.

The *Stage* article is an aberration of logic and of literary

3. *Stage*, p. 51.   4. *Stage*, p. 51.

history, but it is more illuminating to consider how deeply the aberration is rooted in Steinbeck's practice.[5]

Much of the longer fiction is organized around some abstraction, a technical device or an intellectual point of view that operates as a "universal," giving a spurious dramatic structure to panoramic materials. Steinbeck can overcome this tendency by accident (as in *Tortilla Flat*) or by exorcising a part of his skill that is dangerous to cultivate (as in *The Grapes of Wrath*—but only in part). The excellent work and the aberrant work are both characteristic. Dates of publication alone prevent critical simplicity: *Of Mice and Men* and the *Stage* article were published between *In Dubious Battle* and *The Grapes of Wrath*. It is quite probable, as Moore and Lisca suggest, that the beginnings of the play-novelette form can be seen in the more objectively rendered chapters of *In Dubious Battle*.[6] The factual and probable evidence indicates that the play-novelette form, aberration as it may be, nevertheless is rooted deeply in some of the best of Steinbeck's previous work. Further, the evidence suggests why Steinbeck engages in so patently absurd a confusion of form over a period of thirteen years. He tries to achieve a harmony between structure and materials in every novel, but the effort is a constant struggle, open in part to accident. Now, the play-novelette form is eminently a way to *formulate* a harmony—to remove accident and struggle by a formula. To a novelist like Steinbeck, afflicted with artistic ambitions but limited in structural insight, the attraction of the play-novelette form is obvious. Its theory may rest on false analogy, may be only a gimmick, may indicate Steinbeck's lack of judgment with a terrifying clarity. But we must keep in mind that the theory and the

5. The aberration is embarrassing. Tedlock and Wicker omit the *Stage* article from an otherwise important collection of Steinbeck's observations on his craft. E. W. Tedlock, Jr., and C. V. Wicker, eds., *Steinbeck and His Critics: A Record of Twenty-Five Years* (Albuquerque: University of New Mexico Press, 1957).

6. Harry Thornton Moore, *The Novels of John Steinbeck* (Chicago: Normandie House, 1939), pp. 48–49; Peter Lisca, *The Wide World of John Steinbeck* (New Brunswick: Rutgers University Press, 1958), pp. 132–33.

practice of the play-novelette, in Steinbeck's hands, is a continuation of his constant effort to achieve a harmony between structure and materials. To do less is to limit criticism to a club.

These various matters can be understood more deeply and perhaps more clearly through analysis of the three play-novelettes.

Of Mice and Men

Despite Steinbeck's disclaimer in *Stage*, *Of Mice and Men*[7] is certainly a play-novelette according to Steinbeck's own theory. Biographical information supports this view. Steinbeck reported to his agents, at the beginning of his work in February 1935, "I'm doing a play now," and Harry Thornton Moore records several illuminating contemporary facts:

> After *Of Mice and Men* was published and the suggestion was made that it be prepared for the stage, Steinbeck said it could be produced directly from the book, as the earliest moving pictures had been produced. It was staged in almost exactly this way in the spring of 1937 by a labor-theater group in San Francisco, and although the venture was not a failure it plainly demonstrated to Steinbeck that the story needed to be adapted to dramatic form. . . . But when Steinbeck transferred the story into final dramatic form for the New York stage he took 85% of his lines bodily from the novel. A few incidents needed juggling, one or two minor new ones were introduced, and some (such as Lennie's imaginary speech with his Aunt Clara at the end of the novel) were omitted.[8]

It would seem that the novel was intended to function as a play, and Steinbeck did not alter the novel in any essential during the tinkering in preparation for the New York stage production. Aesthetic considerations support the biographical information, as in Moore's observation:

> Structurally, the novel was from the first a play: it is divided into six parts, each part a scene—the reader may observe that

7. John Steinbeck, *Of Mice and Men* (New York: Covici, Friede, Inc., 1937). Hereafter cited as *OMM*.

8. Moore, p. 49; Lisca, p. 130.

the action never moves away from a central point in each of these units.[9]

And clearly the novel does "play": Characters make entrances and exits; plainly indicated parallels and oppositions that are characteristic of the drama exist in quantity and function as they should; suspense is maintained; characters are kept uncomplicated and "active" in the manner of stage characterization; since there is little internal or implicit development, events depend on what is said or done in full view; the locale is restricted mainly to one place; the span of time is brief; the central theme is stated and restated— the good life is impossible because humanity is flawed— and in itself is deeply poignant, as Steinbeck had defined a play-novelette theme. In short, I do not see how *Of Mice and Men* could meet more completely the specifications of a play-novelette as Steinbeck listed them. If critics have been displeased with *Of Mice and Men*, as Steinbeck was, the trouble cannot lie in the application of the theory but in the assumption that inspired the theory. I shall explore this point in detail.

As a dramatic structure, *Of Mice and Men* is focused on Lennie and occurs within the context of the bunkhouse and the ranch. Within these confines, Steinbeck develops theme and countertheme by exploring the chances for the good life against the flawed human material that Lennie symbolizes most completely and the code of rough justice that most people accept. Even this initial, limited statement points to the central difficulty in the novel. The "well-made" dramatic form that Steinbeck defined in *Stage* and did construct in *Of Mice and Men* is conducive to abstraction because it is limited to visible action. Lennie is limited in much the same way. As a huge, powerful, semi-idiot who kills when he is frightened or simply when he is thoughtless, Lennie is a reduction of humanity to the lowest common denominator. It may be possible to construct a parable out of so limited a structure and materials, but it is impos-

9. Moore, p. 48.

sible to handle complex human motives and relationships within those limits. *Of Mice and Men* is successful to the extent that it remains a parable, but the enveloping action is more complex than the parable form can encompass.

Lennie is the most fully realized character, yet he is presented necessarily as a personification, an exaggerated, allegorized instance of the division between mind and body; the sketch that is Lennie is incapable of conveying personality. The other characters are personified types rather than realized persons. Though less pathetic than Lennie, they do not have his moral impact. In short, every structural device except personification is sacrificed to highlight Lennie's moral helplessness. The sacrifice is much too great. It thins out the parable. The stripped language furthers this effect of extreme thinness. For example, Lennie's one friend, George, is not a realized man but a quality that complements Lennie's childlike innocence. George fills out Lennie's pattern to complete a whole man. He is a good man, motivated to protect Lennie because he realizes that Lennie is the reverse image of his own human nature. George is a representation of humanity that (unlike Lennie) is aware of evil. An extended abstract passage (pages 70–76), makes this clear.

Everything in the development of the novel is designed to contribute to a simplification of character and event.

The opening scene of the green pool in the Salinas River promises serenity, but in the final scene the pool is the background for Lennie's violent death. George's initial hope that Lennie can hide his flawed humanity by seeming to be conventional is shattered in the end. Lennie's flaw grows into a potential for evil, and every evil is ascribed to him after his unwitting murder of Curley's wife. The objective image of the good life in the future," a little house and a couple of acres an' a cow and some pigs," is opposed sharply to the present sordid reality of the bunkhouse and the ranch.[10] Minor characters remain little more than opposed types, identifiable by allegorical tags. Curley is the unsure hus-

10. OMM, pp. 28–30, p. 60.

band, opposed to and fearful of his sluttish, unnamed wife. Slim is a minor god in his perfect mastery of his work. His serenity is contrasted sharply with Curley's hysterical inability to please or to control his wife, and it contrasts as easily with the wife's constant, obvious discontent. Candy and Crooks are similar types, men without love. Both are abused by Curley, his wife, and the working crew. (Lennie might fall into this category of defenselessness, if he were aware enough to realize the situation; but he is not.) These sharp oppositions and typed personae restrict the development of the novel. The merely subordinate characters, such as Carlson and Whit, who only begin or fill out a few scenes, are strictly nonhuman, since they remain abstract instruments within a design.

The climax of that design is simplified in its turn, since it serves only to manipulate Lennie into a moral situation beyond his understanding. The climax is doubled, a pairing of opposites. In its first half, when Curley's wife attempts to seduce Lennie as a way to demonstrate her hatred of Curley, Lennie is content (in his nice innocence) to stroke her soft hair; but he is too violent, and he snaps her neck in a panic miscalculation as he tries to force her to be quiet. In the second half, George shoots Lennie to prevent a worse death at the hands of others. The melodramatic quality of these events will be considered at a later point. Here, it is more important to observe, in the design, that the climax pairs an exploration of the ambiguity of love in the rigid contrast between the different motives that activate Curley's wife and George. Curley's wife wants to use Lennie to show her hatred for Curley; George shoots Lennie out of a real affection for him. The attempted seduction balances the knowing murder; both are disastrous expressions of love. Lennie is the unknowing center of the design in both halves of this climax. Steinbeck's control is all too evident. There is not much sense of dramatic illumination because the quality of the paired climax is that of a mechanical problem of joining two parallels. Lennie's necessary passivity enforces the quality of a mechanical design. He is only the man to whom things happen. Being so limited, he is incapable of providing that sudden widening insight which alone justifies an artist's extreme dependence on a rigid design. Therefore, in general, *Of Mice and Men* remains a simple anecdote.

It would be a mistake to conclude that the limited scope of the materials is the only or the effective cause of the simplification. Writers frequently begin their work with anecdotal materials. Most often, however, they expand the reference of such materials through a knowing exercise of their medium.[11] It is Steinbeck's inability to exercise his medium or, perhaps more fundamentally, to select a proper medium, which ensures the limited reference, the lack of a widening insight.

In his discussion of the play-novelette form in *Stage*, Steinbeck dismisses the objection that allegory is an overly limited form,[12] but the objection is serious. *Of Mice and Men* is not merely a brief novel. It is limited in what its structure can make of its materials. Moreover, Steinbeck hoped to achieve precisely that limitation—the *Stage* essay leaves no doubt of this—although, it is true, he felt the form would ensure a concentration, a focus, of the materials. Instead, there is a deliberate thinning of materials that are thin (or theatrical) to begin with.

In fact, Steinbeck uses every possible device to thin out the effect of the materials. Foreshadowing is overworked. Lennie's murder of Curley's wife is the catastrophe that George has been dreading from the start. It is precisely the fate that a fluffy animal like Curley's wife should meet at the hands of Lennie, who has already killed mice and a puppy with his overpowering tenderness.[13] When Curley's wife makes clear her intention to seduce the first available man and the course of events abandons Lennie to her, the result is inevitable. But that inevitability does not have tragic qualities. The result is merely arranged, the characters

---

11. Mark Schorer, "Technique as Discovery," *Hudson Review*, 1 (Spring 1948), 67–87. I am much indebted to Schorer's argument.
12. *Stage*, p. 51.   13. *OMM*, pp. 15, 151.

merely inarticulate, and the action develops without illumination. Lennie can hardly distinguish between a dead pup and the dead woman:

> Lennie went back and looked at the dead girl. The puppy lay close to her. Lennie picked it up. "I'll throw him away," he said. "It's bad enough like it is."[14]

The relative meaninglessness of his victims substitutes pathos for tragedy. Curley's rather shadowy wife underlines the substitution: She is characterless, nameless, and constantly discontent, so her death inspires none of the sympathy one might feel for a kind or a serene woman. Others respond to her death wholly in light of Lennie's predicament—from George's loving concern to Curley's blustering need for revenge—not his character. Everything that is excellent in the novel tends to relate, intensely if narrowly, to that emphasis. Within these limits, much that Steinbeck does is done excellently. The essential question is whether the treatment of the materials is intense enough to justify their evident manipulation, their narrowed pathos.

The novel communicates most intensely a theme of unconventional morality. Lennie does commit murder, but he remains guiltless because he is not responsible for what he does.[15] Yet the morality is only a statement of the pathos of Lennie's situation, not an exploration of guilt and innocence. A development through parallels and juxtapositions does little to expand the stated theme. Carlson parallels Lennie's violence on a conventional level when he insists on killing Candy's ancient, smelly dog. Carlson's reasoning is that the group has a right to wrong the individual. Lennie is incapable of any logic, even of this twisted sort, and he is never cruel by choice; that potential moral complexity is neglected in the design to permit the brutal simplicity of the

14. *OMM*, p. 159.
15. This paradox is the "moral" of the poem by Robert Burns which supplies the title of the novel; the title indicates Steinbeck's own concentration on a thematic development, not on characters or events as important in themselves. Further: A "moral" does tend to be simple.

group's response to Carlson's argument and to Lennie's crime. Carlson's crime is approved by the group: He abuses power to invade another man's desire for affection, reduced to a worthless dog. Lennie's crime is an accident in an attempt to express affection; murder is too serious for the group to ignore, so Lennie is hunted down. We are intended to notice the irony that Carlson's crime inverts Lennie's. That simple, paralleled irony substitutes for a possible, intense, necessarily complex, and ambiguous development of the materials. The rendered development, not the materials themselves, produces this simply mechanical irony.

Certainly the theme of unconventional morality offers tragic possibilities in a dimension beyond the anecdotal or the sketch of a character or event. From that viewpoint, the oppositions can expand into tragic awareness, at least potentially. They can even be listed, as follows. Lennie is good in his intentions, but evil in fact. The group is good in wanting to punish a murderer, but evil in misunderstanding that Lennie is guiltless. Counterwise, George, Candy, and Slim are endowed with understanding by their roles as the friend, the man without hope, and the god, but they are powerless against the group. Curley's wife is knowingly evil in exploiting Lennie's powerful body and weak mind. Curley is evil in exploiting all opportunities to prove his manhood. These two are pathetic in their human limitations, not tragic. George enacts an unconventional morality less by accident than any of the others. He feels strongly that, in being compelled to look after Lennie, he has given up the good times he might have had, but he knows the sacrifice is better, that he and Lennie represent an idealized variety of group-man. Slim's early, sympathetic insight makes this explicit:

> "You guys travel around together?" [Slim's] tone was friendly. It invited confidence without demanding it. "Sure," said George. "We kinda look after each other." He indicated Lennie with his thumb. "He ain't bright. Hell of a good worker, though. Hell of a nice fella, but he ain't bright. I've knew him for a long time." Slim looked through George and beyond him. "Ain't many guys travel around together," he mused. "I

don't know why. Maybe ever'body in the whole damn world
is scared of each other." "It's a lot nicer to go around with a
guy you know," said George.[16]

This important passage centers the theme of unconventional
morality. It celebrates a relationship "the whole damn
world" is incapable of imagining, given the ugly context of
ranch life and sordid good times, and it locates the good life
in friendship, not in the material image of the little farm.
This passage is the heart of the novel.

But a novel cannot be structured solely on the basis of a
theme, even a fundamental theme. Too much else must be
simplified. Worse, the unconventional morality located in
friendship produces Lennie's death, not only because Steinbeck can see no other way to conclude. Lennie dies necessarily because friendship can go no further than it does go,
and nothing can be made of the dreamlike ideal of the
little farm. The extreme simplification is that Steinbeck can
do nothing with Lennie after he has been exhibited. These
limitations derive from the simplification required by the
play-novelette form. Steinbeck appears to be aware that
formal limitations need some widening, since he imbeds
Lennie's happiest and most intense consciousness of the good
life of friends in an ironic context:

> George said, "Guys like us got no fambly. They make a little
> stake an' then they blow it in. They ain't got nobody in the
> worl' that gives a hoot in hell about 'em——" "*But not us,*"
> Lennie cried happily. "Tell about us now." George was quiet
> for a moment. "But not us," he said. "Because——" "Because
> I got you an'——" "An' I got you. We got each other, that's
> what, that gives a hoot in hell about us," Lennie cried in
> triumph.[17]

16. *OMM*, pp. 63–64. After Lennie's death, Slim invites George to
go into town, to enjoy the good times now in reach (drinking, gam-
bling, whoring). From the weary tone of aftermath, these good times
are clearly an entirely inadequate substitute for friendship. Yet the
special world of Mack and the boys (in *Cannery Row*) has its creative
basis in this passage. Steinbeck protects and ensures the survival of
that later world precisely by making it special—and somewhat incredible, or overly simple, even on its own terms. Steinbeck can destroy or sentimentalize; his treatment of such materials occurs within
those limits.

17. *OMM*, pp. 180–81. This is a repetition of an earlier passage in

The passage extends friendship beyond its boundary; it celebrates a species of marriage, minus the sexual element, between Lennie and George. But the content of the passage is qualified heavily by its position; George shoots Lennie after retelling the story about the little farm that always quiets Lennie. As further irony, precisely the responsibilities of a perfect friendship require George to shoot Lennie. The mob that would hang Lennie for murder is in the background throughout the scene. The situation is moving, but the effect is local. The ironies relate only to Lennie's pathetic situation; they do not aid an understanding of Lennie or account (beyond plot) for his death. Too, the scene is melodramatic; it puts aside the large problems of justifying the event in order to jerk our tears over the event itself.

To say that Steinbeck avoids the problems of structure by milking individual scenes is not to say that *Of Mice and Men* is a total failure. As mature work, it is not a depot for the basic flaws in Steinbeck's earliest work. Many of the scenes are excellently constructed and convincing in themselves. Considerable attention is given to establishing minor details. For example, George shoots Lennie with the Luger that Carlson used to kill Candy's old dog. The defenseless man is linked by the weapon with the defenseless dog in the group's web of created power. George does his killing as a kind of ritual. If the police or the mob had taken Lennie, the death would have been a meaningless expression of group force, the exaction of an eye for an eye rather than an expression of love. The background of language is the workingman dialect that Steinbeck perfected in *In Dubious Battle,* realized here to express a brutally realistic world that negates idealism and exaggerates the sadistic and the ugly. Its perfection is enhanced by a factual context—the dependence of the men on their shifting jobs, the explicit misery of their homelessness, and the exposure of their social and economic weaknesses. The more sensitive men dream of escape into some kind of gentleness. The thread of possible realization of that dream tends to hold the novel in a focus.

---

a less sinister context (pp. 28–29). Compare the close of *In Dubious Battle.*

The opposite pole of man's imperfect moral nature motivates Curley's wife and Carlson. Steinbeck's fine web of circumstance reaches from the ideal possibility to the brutal fact.

Of Mice and Men is strongest in precisely this plot sense, in a sequence and linkage of events controlled by ironic contrast and juxtaposition. The result is limited to the rendering of a surface, yet the necessarily external devices of plot are used with artistic care and skillful tact.

Just after George, Lennie, and Candy agree to realize the dream of the little farm by pooling their savings and earnings, Curley appears, searching for his wife. Frustrated, Curley punches Lennie without mercy until (on George's order) Lennie grabs and crushes Curley's hand. This violent event suggests that Curley's sadistic vision of the world will not be shut out by the idealized vision of cooperative friends. More closely, the ugly inversion of "the good, clean fight" serves to contrast Lennie's innocence with his surprise and helplessness before evil. The other men in the bunkhouse are unconcerned; violence is an ordinary element in their lives. The incident enacts and announces the implicitly universal moral imperfection of humanity—an insight that broadens and becomes more overt in the following scenes. When Curley has to go to town to have a doctor care for his crushed hand, the men take the chance to go into town for a spree. Crooks, Candy, and Lennie—the Negro, the old man, and the idiot—are left on the ranch with Curley's wife. The circumstances provide her with an opportunity to seduce Lennie; she hates Curley, and the Hollywood ideal of the seductive movie queen is her only standard of love. Crooks cannot protect Lennie because his black skin leaves him open to sexual blackmail; Candy's feeble efforts are useless; and Lennie does not understand what is happening. The ultimate irony in this tangle of violence is that none of the characters is evil or intends to do evil. The irony is more explicit and more powerful than the crux of the Munroe family in *The Pastures of Heaven*, in that all of them are trying to express some need of love. In her need as in her amoral unawareness of good and evil, Curley's wife is not unlike Lennie, just as the various moral defects of other people conspire by chance to leave Lennie alone and defenseless with Curley's wife. Yet "love" has different meanings for Lennie and for Curley's wife; the clash of meanings ensures their deaths.

The death of Curley's wife switches the narrative focus to George and to the device of the split hero. Steinbeck is fond of this device of a divided (not a duplicated) hero, usually two men of opposite nature, one distinctly secondary to the other, but both sharing the center of the novel. For a few suggestive, not inclusive, examples: Henry Morgan, Jim Nolan, and Aaron Trask are coldly thoughtful, knowing men, either selfish or idealistic in what they do; Coeur de Gris, Mac, and Caleb Trask are relatively warmer men, possibly as knowing as their opposites, but usually more subject to their emotions. Jim Casy and Tom Joad extend and complicate the pattern as they become suggestive types of Christ and Saint Paul, the human god and the coldly realistic organizer, but they do not break the pattern. There are obvious narrative virtues of clarity in a device that is recognizable as well as flexible. The secondary hero is subordinate in Steinbeck's fiction—except in *Of Mice and Men*. There, Lennie's murder propels George into a sudden prominence that has no structural basis. Is the novel concerned with Lennie's innocence or George's guilt? The formal requirements of a play-novelette mandate a structural refocus. Steinbeck needs a high point to ring down the curtain. With Lennie dead, Steinbeck must use and emphasize George's guilt. The close is formulated—the result of a hasty switch—not structured from preceding events, so it produces an inconclusive ending in view of what has happened previously. And the ideal of the farm vanishes with Lennie's death, when George tells Candy the plan is off.

Here the difficulty is with a structure that requires a climax which cannot be achieved once Lennie, the center of the novel, is removed; but Lennie must be killed off when his existence raises problems of characterization more complex than the play-novelette form can express. Materials and structure pull against each other and finally collapse into an oversimplified conclusion that removes rather than faces the central theme.

The abrupt "solution" rests on melodrama, on sudden, purely plot devices of focus and refocus. Such overt manipulation indicates that in its practice the play-novelette is not a new form. Steinbeck's experience, his mature technical skill do not finally disguise his wish to return to his earliest fictional efforts to realize complex human behavior by way of an extreme simplification of structure and materials. His deliberate avoidance of an organic structure and his consequent dependence on a formula, on the exercise of technique within an artistic vacuum, exhausts the significance of the play-novelette theory. His practice, as in *Of Mice and Men*, does not lead to serious efforts and to a real achievement in the art of the novel. Rather, it leads to manipulations designed to effect a simplification of structure and materials. So much skill, directed toward so little, is disturbing. But the skill is absolutely there.

The Moon Is Down

Steinbeck's conception of the aftermath of a military conquest emphasizes the aesthetic inadequacy of the play-novelette's innocent simplifications. Possibly *The Moon Is Down*[18] is a purer play-novelette than *Of Mice and Men*, for Steinbeck does avoid reverberations and complexities in the propagandistic war novel more successfully than in the earlier sentimental novel. Lennie is given a depth of pathos beyond the strict needs of the plot; Colonel Lanser is not. Yet in both novels the formula remains unchanged in all essentials. James Thurber, scathingly reviewing *The Moon Is Down*, refers to its sentimentality and theatrical atmosphere as though Steinbeck were attempting some new crime.[19] The crime, if there is one, is hardly new in substance; everything Thurber objects to in *The Moon Is Down*

18. John Steinbeck, *The Moon Is Down* (New York: The Viking Press, Inc., 1942). Hereafter cited as *MID*.

19. James Thurber, "What Price Conquest," *The New Republic*, 106 (March 16, 1942), 370.

is present in *Of Mice and Men*, but less nakedly. And surely the perfected skill is impressive.

The basic situation and the plot grew out of Steinbeck's "serious discussion with Colonel William J. Donovan of the Office of Strategic Services on techniques for aiding resistance movements in the occupied countries."[20] Steinbeck had suggested earlier that dropping counterfeit marks on Germany could disrupt her financial system and thus collapse her war effort.[21] This becomes Mayor Orden's idea to have the British drop dynamite sticks with attached instructions to the people in the unnamed occupied country—which seems to be Norway. Here, then, an original idea bears fruit as they do not in many of the earlier novels. Often, too, in working out the earliest novels, Steinbeck had announced an intention that was not accomplished in the actual development of the materials by the structural techniques on which he relied. So far as origins and intention are realized in form, Steinbeck is a more capable technician here than in any of the earliest novels.

Perhaps the war-inspired origins of *The Moon Is Down* draw too much attention to direct force, to dynamite in the hands of an occupied people. Steinbeck is interested as much —perhaps more—in the occupied people themselves as the important elements of power. The idea that a people is strong, and the corresponding biological metaphor, that an individual's power is the unity of the group, have their origins at the beginning of Steinbeck's career. In the earlier work, an ironic or simply an alien context measures the sometimes ambiguous, sometimes inchoate power of the group, which then can assume a dramatic role; the individual can be perceived in the round within the actions of the group.[22] *The Moon Is Down* draws on these backgrounds—

20. Lewis Gannett, "Introduction: John Steinbeck's Way of Writing," *The Viking Portable Steinbeck* (New York: The Viking Press, Inc., 1946), p. xxvi.

21. John Steinbeck, "The Secret Weapon We Were Afraid to Use," *Collier's*, 131 (January 10, 1953), 9–13.

22. A group produces evil in *The Pastures of Heaven, In Dubious Battle*, and *Of Mice and Men*. A group is outlined against a hostile context in *To a God Unknown* and *Tortilla Flat*. A group loses its

with a radical difference. The group concept becomes an unambiguous abstraction. The characters are not individuals but aspects of group function and teamwork. The theory of the play-novelette encourages such characterization, and the simplicities of war seem to provoke its full development in Steinbeck's novelistic thinking. Or: The group is good at the close of *The Grapes of Wrath*, but it is still composed of individuals. Significantly, an extreme of abstract characterization is not present for the first time in *The Moon Is Down*, but it is an element in Steinbeck's report on the Air Corps Training Program, *Bombs Away*, which appeared in the same year.[23] The members of the "typical bomber training crew" do not exist as individuals. They are presented almost wholly in their functions as crew members. The narrative fits easily into a dramatic structure—in the stage sense—of the selection, training, and final testing of the crew. Finally, they are presented flatly, precisely because they are significant as the group, not as the individual. This transformation fits into the theory of simplified characterization that Steinbeck advanced in *Stage*.

Other theatrical shorthand devices and conventions are evident in *The Moon Is Down*. The central theme—that a free people cannot be conquered by force—is pure theatre, absurd only in historical fact; the main characters are abstractions while the minor characters are whimsical; the scenes are limited to a few sets, so there is a good deal of reporting "off stage"; the elapsed time is brief and the language mostly clipped dialogue, so there is not much novelistic depth of time or tone; the play-novelette form requires brief panoramic scenes; a concentration of effect is apparent only as universal design, never as a dramatic structure of minute, unique particulars. Notably, the novel has a theatrical structure of three parts or sequences: the conquest, the slow awakening of resistance, and the intimation

---

identity in *The Grapes of Wrath*, and a puzzled, determined search for redefinition by individuals and families is much of the content of the novel.

23. John Steinbeck, *Bombs Away* (New York: The Viking Press, Inc., 1942).

that the resistance will conquer. These sequences are paced by a constant equation of individual and group action. The invaders are seen as the air fleets, the detachment that attacks the twelve local troops, and the occupying forces. The awakening of the resistance is signaled by Molly Morden's murder of Lieutenant Tonder and the first parachute drop of dynamite. The intimation of triumph for the resistance is spelled out by Colonel Lanser's decision to shoot Mayor Orden and by Orden's recognition of his universal role as a free man. The complication is the two groups, "invaders" and "natives," instead of the one group in *Bombs Away*. Necessarily arbitrary distinctions must be made, so nearly everyone is a type in his language and his actions. The one complex man is the quisling, George Corell, but only because his situation is complex. He lives in a moral no man's land, since he cannot belong (after the conquest) to either the invading group or the native group. His potentially ambiguous role is not developed beyond the irony that he is unable to recognize, after the conquest, that he is useless to the invaders and hateful to the natives. There is no mistaking the typed, abstracted quality of the other personae. The invaders themselves are soldiers designated by rank, and only the officers are outlined to any extent (last name only) beyond their rank. Colonel Lanser, the oldest and the commander, exhibits a certain amount of insight, which reflects experience rather than a personality. The other officers are known by their engineering or police functions or by their attitudes toward war:

> Major Hunter thought of war as an arithmetical job to be done so he could get back to his fireplace; Captain Loft as the proper career of a properly brought-up young man; and Lieutenants Prackle and Tonder as a dreamlike thing in which nothing was very real . . . only Colonel Lanser knew what war really is in the long run.[24]

Similarly, the natives are typed in their roles of resistance to the conquest.

All of the characters are presented by the essay method as in the earliest novels. Steinbeck does present and develop

24. *MID*, pp. 46–47.

characters organically through actions, notably in *In Dubious Battle* and *The Grapes of Wrath*. Here the essay method is purposeful, an aspect of characterization, not a mark of the author's awkwardness or lack of skill, for the inability to humanize is the strength of the natives and the weakness of the invaders. Anyone somewhat outside the group is in danger. Captain Bentick, with ideals and pleasures beyond his function as a soldier, is murdered almost at once and by mistake. Captain Loft is a professional soldier, the intended victim of an attack by the native, Alex Morden. Loft's report is chilly, abstract, and brisk, suggesting that function is a necessary virtue, not an absolute strength, in the circumstances of war:

> Loft . . . said, "I had some trouble about a recalcitrant miner who wanted to quit work. He shouted something about being a free man. When I ordered him to work, he rushed at me with his pick. Captain Bentick tried to interfere." He gestured slightly toward the body.[25]

Function is dehumanizing. The invaders come to operate a coal mine; they do not find glory in war. So if Captain Bentick's humanism is deadly, Captain Loft's professionalism is absurd in its inhuman pomp, its stiff denial of emotion. Alex Morden's fury brings to the surface the group identity of the natives as a difference in function. The essay method, hovering above specific individuals, permits this generalized reduction of character to function.

Obviously, the fusion of typed man and mechanical function has a definite propagandistic impact. The invaders are hateful because they are not human; the natives are admirable because they hate the invaders. This contrived logic does not make for a convincing development of the plot, so far as character is made a typed, functional abstraction.

This bad logic is restricted, perhaps to personalize the typical event, to the episode of Lieutenant Tonder and Molly Morden. Tonder falls in love with Molly, the widow of the miner who was executed for killing Captain Bentick. The coincidence is a necessity. As a native and widow, Molly's only function is to exact revenge; she uses Tonder's lapse

25. *MID*, pp. 70–71.

into humanity—his feelings of love—to murder him. Her loss of function as a wife equates with the natives' growing hatred and balances Tonder's emotive lapse of strength within a context of the invaders' decreasing moral strength. The murder is echoed rather than enlarged by surrounding events. At first the other natives have only domestic functions. One is a butler, another a doctor, and so on. But they discover quickly that, like Molly, they must resist the invaders. Resistance becomes their function; it justifies everything they do. Molly's revenge is personal, not private. Other natives lack Molly's immediate goad; a recollection of freedom is their moral strength, as the dynamite is their literal strength. The abstract quality of that motivation equates fully with their reduction to function. On the other hand, the invaders are not given moral strength, and every lapse into humanity (Captain Bentick, Lieutenant Tonder) is restricted to their side.

The abstraction of function does not permit the creation of credible individuals but furthers (as its central purpose) an allegorical division of function, and so of individuals, into opposing categories. Such division is typified in the person of Mayor Orden; it is the extent of Colonel Lanser's personality. Hence, the process of becoming absorbed in the abstract idea of one's function is "good" and suggests "strength" in the case of Mayor Orden, but is "bad" and suggests "weakness" in the case of Colonel Lanser. The process of distinguishing values is outlined frankly toward the end of the novel:

> "But they can't arrest the Mayor," she explained to him. Orden smiled at her. "No," he said, "they can't arrest the Mayor. The Mayor is an idea conceived by free men. It will escape arrest."[26]

Steinbeck asserts that such practical details as arrests do not affect a strength that has a moral basis. Colonel Lanser's conviction that wars cannot be won stems from his cause's lack of a moral basis. The invaders cannot police the natives, in spite of their military power, because the invaders lack an insight into the moral basis of a people's strength. This

26. *MID*, p. 186.

process of determining value is not credible because it depends on a merely arranged logic. We must admire Mayor
Orden's optimism or deny the principles of freedom, and
we must hate Colonel Lanser's despairing obedience or accept the principles of a police state. The aesthetic result of
such arranged logic is a flattening of character, of choice.
Steinbeck's artistic integrity is at issue. The fact is that in
war each side destroys the other side as it can. Steinbeck's
real point is that war is morally good on Our Side, but
morally bad on Their Side; consequently, by a logical jump,
Our Side is strong, but Their Side is weak. The point and
the jump are strictly propagandistic. The practical result is
that the meaning of war is falsified, since any ironic or tragic
insights into the horror that really is war are blanked out by
the contrived logic.

These observations apply to Steinbeck's handling of the
two groups, invaders and natives, throughout the novel.
Just here a number of critics have been sidetracked into
discussing the literal honesty of Steinbeck's representation
of life in Norway under the German occupation, on the assumption that no occupied town has been so strong, no
conquering army so weak as Steinbeck would have us believe.[27] That issue is a widely indirect approach to the central
point, the question of a fruitful relationship between structure and materials, given Steinbeck's loaded contrast between the two groups.

The invaders are efficient at conquest, but their inability
to govern the conquered is prefigured in their amoral military planning, which depends on a quisling, and in their
motives for conquest—the theft of the coal mine operation.
The rhythm of the first two chapters is determined by the
invaders' dubious methods of conquest and rule. Colonel
Lanser's insistence that "this is more like a business venture
than anything else" is contradicted by repeated instances of
the invaders' moral inferiority.[28] Simply, they are bad men:
"Their war so far had been play—fine weapons and fine

27. For a summary of contemporary quarreling over Steinbeck's
reportorial accuracy, see Lisca, p. 187.
28. *MID*, p. 33.

planning against unarmed, planless enemies."[29] So, in the strange logic that Steinbeck advances, the invaders rule badly or uncertainly because they are bad men. Especially as the people become acquainted with the moral inferiority of the invaders and begin to resist the conquest through personal coldness or outright sabotage, the invaders tend to lose much of their initial efficiency. Steinbeck develops this idea by linking together various repeated motifs. For example, the invaders arrive with helmets and automatic weapons among a defenseless people, but, within a few chapters, they are being killed off by the natives at a great rate:

> Now it was that the conqueror was surrounded, the men of the battalion alone among silent enemies, and no man might relax his guard for even a moment. If he did, he disappeared, and some snowdrift received his body. If he went alone to a woman, he disappeared and some snowdrift received his body. If he drank, he disappeared.[30]

These lines typify the rhetorical method that Steinbeck depends on: A single idea is repeated in a number of balanced, linking phrases that generalize rather than specify the idea in actions. The incremental, rather hypnotic rhythms soothe the mind into something of a blur, so that embarrassing questions—such as why policing is not in force, or why entertainment is lacking—do not rise to the surface of the mind. The rhetorical method is akin to a propaganda method. The unacceptable implication is that an invader can be driven out of his collective mind by a defenseless population. Steinbeck never quite states that notion, but it is always implicit in his descriptions of the invaders. They become increasingly pathetic (although Colonel Lanser has this quality from the start) as they recognize with alarming clarity after the opening chapters the irony that divides their seeming power from their actual weakness. Numerous details establish this point. A few typical examples will serve to indicate the texture of the whole. Lieutenant Tonder at first thinks of settling there, with the innocence of a robber. "If four or five [of the local farms] were thrown together, it would be a nice place to

29. *MID*, pp. 46–47.   30. *MID*, pp. 101–2.

settle, I think."[31] The violence implied by the first verb contradicts the pacific, overt sense of Tonder's idea. When the subject recurs, fifty-two pages later, in the context of the growing resistance, its purpose is to mark a pathetic breakdown of morale:

> "Well," Tonder went on, "I would like to get out of this god-forsaken hole!" Prackle broke in, "I thought you were going to live here after the war?" And he imitated Tonder's voice. "Put four or five farms together. . . . Isn't that the way it was, Tonder?" As Prackle spoke, Tonder's hand dropped. Then he clasped his temples with his hands and he spoke with emotion. "Be still! Don't talk like that! These people! These horrible people! These cold people! They never look at you." He shivered.[32]

Or, in a much simpler contrast that covers about the same space, Major Hunter is seen designing a bridge for his model railroad line "in my back yard at home," just after the conquest, for lack of anything else to do; as the resistance gathers and the war goes on, Major Hunter has more work:

> His drawingboard was permanently ready now, for the bombs tore out his work nearly as fast as he put it in. And he had little sorrow, for to Major Hunter building was life and here he had more building than he could project or accomplish.[33]

The irony is plain. Major Hunter's "little sorrow" is an index to the growing weakness of the invaders, their growing failure to survive. The contrast extends to the setting itself. Just after the conquest, Prackle had suggested pinning up a photograph of a "something" girl, but in the later scene "from the upstairs room of the Mayor's palace the comfort seemed to have gone."[34] The officers have two gasoline lanterns for light because the dynamo has been wrecked; Lieutenant Prackle's arm is in a sling as a result of an attempt on his life; and, in general, the officers express the same loneliness, fear, and hysteria as the common soldiers. They have grown pathetic at the same rate as their inability

31. *MID*, p. 58.
33. *MID*, pp. 52, 106.
32. *MID*, p. 110.
34. *MID*, pp. 53, 105.

to survive in so hostile an environment. That, in turn, is the measure of their moral inferiority. The invaders are simply not able to endure any degree of defeat. Colonel Lanser's contempt for the "children" he has as officers loads the case even more heavily toward a simplified view of character as malfunction.[35] That simplification is the key to Steinbeck's rhetorical method, for it permits the novel to develop along the lines of a one-dimensional, cartoonlike series of contrasts.

Steinbeck's loaded case against the invaders dimly reflects the moral ambiguity that Doc Burton saw in group-man. How dim the reflection is, after being simplified to suit a propagandistic aim, is suggested by the firmly opposed categories that Mayor Orden finds when he knows he is to be killed:

> "The people don't like to be conquered, sir, and so they will not be. Free men cannot start a war, but once it is started, they can fight on in defeat. Herd men, followers of a leader, cannot do that, and so it is always the herd men who win battles and the free men who win wars."[36]

The loaded terms, *free men* and *herd men*, preclude argument, and Mayor Orden's opinion is delivered as the truth, not as a partial opinion among others in a context, as in *In Dubious Battle*, that is subject to an interplay of contradictory facts.

Oddly, then, the play-novelette form does not encourage the best sense of theatre, the revelatory give-and-take of the lines, of building through partial truths to a rounded close. There is not much theatre in Steinbeck's novelistic version of a play.

One scene succeeds in breaking through the simplicities of the form: Lieutenant Tonder's expression of the invaders' ambiguous position, given as an insect metaphor in the nature of a parable:

> "I dreamed the Leader was crazy. . . . Conquest after conquest, deeper and deeper into molasses." His laughter choked

35. *MID*, p. 58.   36. *MID*, pp. 185–86.

him and he coughed into his handkerchief. "Maybe the Leader is crazy. Flies conquer the flypaper. Flies capture two hundred miles of new flypaper!" His laughter was growing more hysterical now. . . . And gradually Loft recognized that the laughter was hysterical and he stepped close to Tonder and slapped him in the face. . . . Suddenly Tonder's laughter stopped and the room was quiet except for the hissing of the lanterns. Tonder looked in amazement at his hand and he felt his bruised face. . . . "I want to go home," he said.[37]

Ostensibly this scene is the climax of a series of details which record a breakup of the invaders' morale, but the scene is more profound than its immediate purpose would suggest. Tonder's hysteria is caused by his recognition that group-man is a monster that produces death, murdering itself simultaneously, when its controls are the amoral drives of the Leader. That recognition generates a real terror, in excess of the stage direction that cues a breakup of morale. The dream is Tonder's rejection of group-man and a recognition of his ties, not to the nonhuman image of paradox, "flies conquer flypaper," but to the deepest sense of humanity. On this level of insight, Tonder's dream defines two possible ways of leaving group-man. One is "to go home," where one was an individual; the other is to find that love is a relationship between individuals. Tonder does not realize either possibility. He cannot "go home" because he has grown to manhood by helping the Leader organize the homeland in the image of group-man. The point is sharpened in a later conversation between two common, nameless soldiers. One states that to conserve food in the interest of group-man, "they took my dog when they took the others."[38] "They" is the authentic form of reference to group-man, and significantly the all-too-humanitarian type, Captain Bentick, is "a lover of dogs."[39] As for love, there is none in the occupied town. Steinbeck uses a profound irony, not a simple parallel, to give this enactment a dramatic structure. Appropriately, Tonder is murdered in a violation of love, the most individualistic of human emotions, by a unit of group-man on the native side, where he expects to

37. *MID*, pp. 118–19.   38. *MID*, p. 148.
39. *MID*, p. 43.

find a woman—Molly Morden. The scene is chillingly successful.

Lieutenant Tonder comes nearest, among the invaders, to being a realized character, as he is furthest from being an allegorical type. His search for humanity and his denial of group-man provide a felt, dramatic means of understanding why the invaders are hateful. Tonder's personal failure allows Steinbeck to create more than a type in the process of demonstrating the power and the weakness of group-man.

There is no Tonder in the opposing group, because the townspeople think and feel as one, as do all the natives in the country. Hence, the townspeople do not have to undergo an extensive transformation from the individual to group-man. They simply become aware in time of their practical and moral strength and the corresponding weakness of the invaders. Steinbeck is unable or unwilling to create a dramatic focus for these assertions, so they remain assertions, delivered generally by Mayor Orden. Their static quality is noteworthy. Yet there is plenty of action. George Corell is attacked several times, Captain Bentick is killed, Lieutenant Prackle is shot in the arm, and Lieutenant Tonder is stabbed to death. If anything, violence is too much in view. What is missing is any great effort on Steinbeck's part, beyond asserting that free men will not be conquered, to put the violent actions in a context that rationalizes the process by which individuals become group-man or to explain how group-man resists conquest when the people are unarmed and starved. He repeats, to be sure, the assertion that moral integrity is more conducive to unity and strength than submachine guns in the hands of robbers. For example, in Chapter One Colonel Lanser's explanation of *macht politik*, addressed to Mayor Orden, is interrupted by the butler's reports from the kitchen, that the cook does not like having soldiers on her back porch; these reports undercut the Colonel's various orders to Mayor Orden to maintain order; Annie's personal resistance, expressed by throwing boiling water on the soldiers, corresponds to Mayor Orden's refusal to accept a willing show of obedience.[40] The intention of

40. *MID*, pp. 30–40. We *hear* about Annie's resistance in accord

the passage is clear in the interplay which suggests that every native dislikes and resists conquest, and that boiling water, if thrown by a free woman, is effective against guns. One may admire the structural precision of this scene as a development of the premise that guns cannot frighten a free people whose shared moral integrity is the basis of a rising, unified resistance. Admirable as the structure is in its clarity, the basic situation is comic in its misunderstandings as the Colonel pleads for order so he can fulfill his assignment and the Mayor points out that free men do not control their servants, who are also free. In short, the scene requires a simplification of structure and materials into neat parallels to avoid the fact that invaders enforce discipline—a restriction of freedom. If this relatively complex scene is fatuously comic, many of the briefer proofs that moral integrity subverts guns are plainly incredible. For example, later in the novel, Major Hunter points out that he has arrested all of the five men who might have wrecked the dynamo and he has increased the guard. Shortly, the dynamo is wrecked again. Here is the same neat clarity in the structure and the same moral basis for a selection of the materials. There is no doubt of the excellent development of these materials, but they are selected beyond credibility to support the assertion that somehow the natives are superior to arrest and to guards.[41]

The development of the central action, the dropping of dynamite and the results of its possession by the natives, exemplifies both the fatuous and the incredible development of a simplified, arranged logic. Having the dynamite, the natives become more efficient at terror and killing than the invaders. A recollection of freedom is their moral justification for the creation of terror, but the recollection has no organic connection with the terror or the mechanics of group-man. Another way of putting this is that the natives kill the invaders because they are there, not because they

with stage convention, and we tend to be told what is happening even when the action is visible. Thus, both stage and fictional conventions further the process of simplification.

41. *MID*, pp. 108, 112.

restrict freedom. This distinction produces a gap between the facts of war and the moral quality Steinbeck attempts to give to the resistance. Doubtless a resistance may have a moral quality. The fact is that the natives become so efficient at terror and killing that moral justification tends to disappear on the level of action, much as it does in a Hollywood gangster film. In consequence, Mayor Orden's noble final speeches are melodramatic, since there is no intellectual or moral reason to attribute their quality to the resistance (violence is but violence), and Steinbeck does not provide a metaphor or a point of view to fuse the two. So far as Mayor Orden's final speeches merely assert the nobility of the resistance, then, they are not a figuring forth, and their intended function is spurious as well as melodramatic.

Viewed as a work of art, *The Moon Is Down* presents a paradox. Unquestionably, its structure and materials are thoroughly controlled. Steinbeck says exactly what he means to say and performs exactly what he sets out to perform. There is none of the vague, confusing imprecision of *Cup of Gold*, the inoperative framework of *The Pastures of Heaven*, or the detached, mythological overlay of *To a God Unknown*. Nevertheless, the rigid categorizing of characters and causes promotes an allegorical stiffness, increased by the restriction of action to rather simple parallels and contrasts. The result is not quite truth or art, but a skillful manipulation of selected materials. As one example: the inherent ambiguity in the group-man concept is untouched in this war novel, although it is as relevant here as in the more objective strike novel, *In Dubious Battle*. An abstraction of opposites is Steinbeck's only artistic purpose. The purchase of that kind of propagandistic clarity is essentially fraudulent. Still, *The Moon Is Down* is everything a play-novelette can be. A direct communication of ideas, the purpose of the play-novelette, combines nicely with a wartime imperative that limits artistic perception to simple assertion. Correspondingly, the contrivances of propaganda limit the potential complexities of the various scenes. The formal perfection is mechanical, not organic; manipulated, not created. The devices of form are imposed on the materials of history. A fuller, more honest craft would not require restrictive devices—simple parallels, loaded contrasts, typed characters, arranged logic, false rhetoric, or a sentimental grasping at abstractions like freedom. The balanced result is this paradox: *The Moon Is Down* is one of Steinbeck's thinnest, yet most formally perfect novels.

Burning Bright

Burning Bright[42] is an absolutely pure play-novelette, an excursion into artifice, freed of any novelistic considerations. The plot is simple. Joe Saul is a highwire performer in a circus. He is sterile, but he has a compulsion to father children. Mordeen, his wife, becomes pregnant by a younger man, Victor, in a casual relationship, out of her great love for Joe Saul. When Joe sees a medical report that proves his sterility, he must choose to accept or deny the child and Mordeen's infidelity. (This major theme of affirming life or death is present in much of Steinbeck's work, in novels as seemingly different as *To a God Unknown* and *The Grapes of Wrath*.) Joe affirms life, after considerable nudging by Friend Ed, who is a manifestation of God. Victor develops possessive feelings toward Mordeen and the child, and Friend Ed murders him.

This strange plot contains many of Steinbeck's customary materials. Mordeen is a goddess of life, much like Ma Joad. Friend Ed has the godlike role of the camp manager in *The Grapes of Wrath* or of Slim in *Of Mice and Men*. Joe Saul begins as a deluded seeker of truth, like Henry Morgan, but he arrives at last at complete awareness, like Tom Joad. The three characters are a unit, a benevolent variety of groupman, like the *paisanos* in *Tortilla Flat* or the natives in *The Moon Is Down*. Victor is the merely selfish and appetitive enemy, like the owning or the middle class. Or he is the snake in Eden, forcing man into a knowledge of life and death and a celebration of life through an awareness of death. Adam, Eve, and God play opposite to Victor's snake.

42. John Steinbeck, *Burning Bright* (New York: The Viking Press, Inc., 1950).

Steinbeck's purpose is lucid enough in the novel and in his several comments.[43] He wishes to construct a universal story, an allegorical parable of man's life. The purpose is admirably ambitious and serious; the execution is something less. Allegory is seldom a good friend to Steinbeck, who seems unable to resist its promise of clarity at the price of simplified and manipulated materials.

The peculiar "universal" language that Steinbeck invents as the proper linguistic vehicle for this play-novelette exemplifies the inner confusion of the overtly lucid purpose. Peter Lisca has summed up the "universal" language in fitting terms as "a kind of incredible hash of realism, coined archaisms, and poetic rhetoric."[44] Such as it is, this language suits the allegorical aim, intended to reach universal truths not available to Steinbeck's superb colloquial diction. In keeping with other aspects of this novel, it is an abstraction of language. Steinbeck is more than consistent; he glories in the loss of a functional language and restates that view in "Critics, Critics Burning Bright":

> Third on the list of hazards [others are the theme of sterility and the universalizing of the materials] was the use of a kind of universal language. . . . While I had eminent authority for this method from Aeschylus down through O'Neill, it was still problematical whether audiences used to the modern realistic theatre would accept such expression. The language did not intend to sound like ordinary speech, but rather by rhythm, sound, and image to give the clearest and best expression to what I wanted to say.[45]

He makes a straw man of the protest "of a middle-aged woman" that "circus people don't talk that way" by pointing out that "a New Haven housewife" is no authority, and, in any case, diction is a convention we can accept if we "try to leap a gulf of unreality and . . . join the company in creating a greater reality."[46] To cite authority and blame

43. See the "Foreword" to *Burning Bright*, and John Steinbeck, "Critics, Critics Burning Bright," *The Saturday Review of Literature*, 33 (November 11, 1950), 20.
44. Lisca, p. 256.
45. "Critics, Critics Burning Bright," p. 20.
46. Ibid., pp. 20–21.

audiences does not excuse language as silly as this typical example:

> He held her tight. "Oh, my God! My God, Mordeen! You're a burning flower in my heart. See—I am harsh breathing like a boy. I'm full of you."[47]

The completely abstract purpose drowns out even a momentary glimpse of a functioning style.

To be sure, the play-novelette form permits only a conflict of ideas, life against death—so there is no dramatic conflict. Plot and character are contrivances without a context, as Steinbeck points out in the Foreword:

> There can be no waste, no long discussion, no departure from a main theme, and little exposition.[48]

He believes his structure is so informing that the usual tasks of the novelist, the "waste" of a credible rendering, can be foregone. But he confuses abstraction with universal insight or parabolic truth, so he sacrifices content to form. Even then, form is a mere abstraction. *Burning Bright* is subtitled "a play in story form." There are three "acts," and each "act" is located in one place and limited to one major event which rises to a climax—Mordeen's seduction; her struggle to convince Victor that to her he is only a stud; Victor's murder, paralleled by Joe Saul's acceptance of the newly born child. In these episodes there is no great sense of the unfolding of character and event that is characteristic of the novel. That limitation would be serious enough in itself, but place is similarly limited. The acts occur in locales that are named—a circus tent, a farmhouse, and the cabin of a freighter. Named as they are, the places do not exist because they are not realized descriptively. As in characterization, Steinbeck leaps across the need for realized particulars and strikes at once for universalization. His explanation of this process leaves no doubt of his intentions:

> In an attempt to indicate a universality of experience I placed the story in the hands of three professions which have long

---

47. *Burning Bright*, p. 35.   48. Ibid., "Foreword," p. 12.

and continuing traditions, namely the Circus, the Farm, and the Sea.[49]

So much universalizing makes any particular impossible to discover. The novel is uniquely a fictional void.

One puzzle is whether to be more impressed by the thoroughness of the failure of this theory-ridden novel or by Steinbeck's evident care to ensure that failure and to insist that it is success. What must be understood is that *Burning Bright* is a spectacular but logical result of an important aspect of Steinbeck's view of the art of the novel, of his rooted interest in the simplification of structure and of materials in order to achieve a controlled harmony. His sustained interest in the play-novelette form is not, then, merely an aberration but evidence of his continued interest in a formal solution to his enduring difficulty in structuring materials coherently and significantly.

Steinbeck wrote no play-novelettes after *Burning Bright*, but he did not abandon that direction, and he did not understand fully what had failed inside a novel that should have attained perfection. His high expectations are expressed in the Foreword to *Burning Bright*, and his wildly bitter response to the critical and popular failure of that effort is expressed in "Critics, Critics Burning Bright." These strange documents affirm the importance to Steinbeck of the play-novelette form by reflecting his bitterly unconverted disappointment at the failure of the purest example of the form. The seriousness of the entire episode is the measure of the artist, for Steinbeck is no hack.

Rather, he strives to produce significant, experimental fiction, expressive of the core of humanly significant values. The play-novelette form is an intensification of this effort, concentrated on a dramatic structure and complete with a self-developed theory of the novel that rationalizes the author's shortcomings. The central significance of *Burning Bright* is that it recapitulates and releases tensions that are present in much of Steinbeck's earlier work; it is not a new departure in the theory or even the practice of his longer fiction.

49. "Critics, Critics Burning Bright," p. 20.

In the end, knowing the question cannot be answered finally, we may ask why Steinbeck embarked on so odd an excursion as the play-novelettes and (even more pressingly) why he persisted beyond the point of excess. Clearly, the sequence of the play-novelettes marks Steinbeck's determined and self-assured choice, around 1940, to create fiction in terms of a theory that assumes the validity of an extreme panoramic structure or an extreme dramatic structure (once the theory is accepted, which extreme is selected makes little difference in the result), and this thrust continues into the later novels. But why? I think the theory of the play-novelette flatters Steinbeck's weakness in organic construction by asserting that a schematic, imposed structure is a strength. At the extremes, either episodic or allegorical structures appear, intended to engage Steinbeck's continuing thematic concerns without the problem of devising organic forms that harmonize structure and materials. This tendency exists plainly in much of Steinbeck's work before 1940. Steinbeck's view of the structure of *Tortilla Flat* and his letter withdrawing *L'Affaire Lettuceburg* mark crucial stages of development in a theory of the novel. The play-novelettes are not important works, but they focus the power of Steinbeck's continued tendency to substitute mechanics and manipulation for organic form.

Steinbeck's extensive and angry public defense of the play-novelette as a form survives the partial or entire failure of any specific play-novelette. His defense argues a serious loss of a basic honesty. If the artist is incapable of applying an accurate, illusionless self-criticism to his work, he cannot organize a significant engagement with particular materials.

I suggest that Steinbeck's rapid artistic decline in the postwar years is related closely to the experiment, trivial in itself, with the play-novelette: formally, and as a critical aftermath. It has been said, often enough, that Steinbeck ran out of materials after the Depression years. I suggest, on the contrary, that a structural bias in shaping and giving finality to materials is the crucial element in Steinbeck's varied career. The postwar materials continue to be current and universal; the structural quality of the execution too often declines. That decline is focused in the play-novelette so far as it is either a pure form or a pure type of a tendency that is discernible in much of Steinbeck's earlier work. *Burning Bright* is the exemplification of a structural crisis, a concentration of external form imposed on materials for its own sake, which distorts them in the process of manipulation or the denial of all other novelistic considerations. As a form, the play-novelette has no other significant function, and that function is absolute in *Burning Bright*. Its tensions place a stumbling-block in the path of Steinbeck's effort to achieve form.

Steinbeck does not disown the extremes of tight or loose structure in his later work; he asserts the virtue of those extreme controls; he believes they guarantee a vital, harmonious art.

6

"Is" Thinking

Cannery Row

In the wake of the experiment with the play-novelette form, Steinbeck manipulates and simplifies structure and materials more freely or less self-consciously than in his earlier work. He does not solve the old problems; he ignores them with an authority that derives from their apparent resolution through insights he had gathered by developing the theory and attempting the practice of the play-novelette —a form that exalts manipulation and simplification for any purpose.

That sense of authority is evident in *Cannery Row*,[1] and distinguishes that work from such forerunners as *The Pastures of Heaven* and *Tortilla Flat*. *Cannery Row* is the first side effect, as it were, of Steinbeck's long experiment with the play-novelette form. Structure and materials are not fused into a harmonious unity; but in its loose relaxation, *Cannery Row* enjoys a more coherent thematic development than either of these forerunners.

Cannery Row puzzled contemporary reviewers who judged the new work from the perspective of the Depression novels, rather than in the light of the still-developing influence of the play-novelette form. Steinbeck's aims frankly puzzled F. O. Matthiessen; Malcolm Cowley dismissed the novel as "a poisoned cream puff"; Edmund Wilson found it the Steinbeck novel he "most enjoyed reading," although he scored its sentimentality.[2] These and other similarly am-

1. John Steinbeck, *Cannery Row* (New York: The Viking Press, Inc., 1945). Hereafter cited as *CR*.

2. F. O. Matthiessen, "Some Philosophers in the Sun," *The New York Times Book Review*, December 31, 1944, p. 1; Malcolm Cowley, "Steinbeck Delivers a Mixture of Farce and Freud," *PM*, Magazine Section, January 14, 1945, p. 15; Edmund Wilson, "John Steinbeck's Newest Novel and James Joyce's First," *The New Yorker*, 20 (January 6, 1945), 62. Only *The Moon Is Down* intervened between *The Grapes*

biguous evaluations indicate a failure of criticism rather than a proper judgment of *Cannery Row*, in that they tease rather than grip the novel.

Cannery Row is a strange novel to follow *The Grapes of Wrath* if one makes no allowance for Steinbeck's developing interest in the play-novelette form. The fact is that *Cannery Row* does not follow *The Grapes of Wrath* in time or spirit; it is quite another kind of novel. Its totally panoramic structure is an extreme development, complementary to the play-novelette form.

The theory of nonteleological or "is" thinking relates significantly to *Cannery Row*. "Is" thinking is presented in *Sea of Cortez*, Steinbeck's discursive diary of a marine biology collecting trip with Edward Ricketts down the Gulf of California in early 1940.[3] "Is" thinking demands a willing acceptance of whatever is observed in the natural world; it forbids imposing on experience any prior values or systems. So far as this theory permits the recording of purely objective events in an untouched sequence of apprehension, it enthrones an extreme variety of panoramic structure, for the theory is a means of arriving at literary form.

An entirely objective narration is not a new element in Steinbeck's work. Rather, "is" thinking exaggerates a number of Steinbeck's deeply rooted tendencies. *The Pastures of Heaven* and *Tortilla Flat* may be read as objective studies of small groups, *In Dubious Battle* and *The Grapes of Wrath* as objective reports of events that affect masses of people, and the play-novelettes can be read as efforts to achieve a total objectivity in the presentation of a leading idea. Likewise with certain characterizations and with certain actions by characters. Doc Burton's study of group-man may be considered similar in its objective method to Jim Casy's pragmatic study of the migrant people in flight from "death" to "life." Many other examples might be cited, but these are

of *Wrath* and *Cannery Row*, and it was considered a minor wartime novel. No doubt *The Grapes of Wrath* got Steinbeck reviewers of such caliber for *Cannery Row*, and perhaps they expected a novel of social concern.

3. John Steinbeck and Edward F. Ricketts, *Sea of Cortez* (New York: The Viking Press, Inc., 1941).

typical enough. If the literary application of "is" thinking is not new in Steinbeck's work, certainly its exaggeration in *Cannery Row* is unique. The play-novelettes and *Cannery Row* are mutations in their exaggerated purity of structure, and as with biological mutation, the link between the present and the preceding creation can be seen or deduced.

Cannery Row enjoys an enormous freedom in narration, a release from the necessity to hedge the novel with a plot. Consequently, it is a delightful novel, and a successful one within its limitations. Steinbeck is concerned in *Cannery Row*, as in many earlier novels, with a definition of the good life. At the same time, he aims more frankly at entertainment than he does in many of the earlier novels:

> I saw a piece of war as a correspondent, and following that wrote *Cannery Row*. This was a kind of nostalgic thing, written for a group of soldiers who had said to me, "Write something funny that isn't about the war. Write something for us to read—we're sick of war."[4]

This warming purpose distinguishes *Cannery Row* immediately and obviously from *The Moon Is Down*; that bleakness is gone. The purpose of creating an overtly escapist entertainment relieves Steinbeck of the often embarrassing necessity, felt in the earlier comic novels, to associate a comic invention with a literary model or with some outright philosophic position that might lend a certain value that, presumably, the specific novel did not have in its own right. Consequently, there is a supporting reason to improvise, to depend thoroughly on a panoramic structure.

Cannery Row begins as a story about the pure in heart, as a fairy tale in never-never land, made credible and realized as a fiction by sharp narrative detail. Unlike *Tortilla Flat*, "the story of Danny and of Danny's friends and of Danny's house," presented in that rather discursive fashion, *Cannery Row* is stated in very sharp images that pinpoint a profusion of places and objects, a typical sorting of the Monterey slum named Cannery Row:

4. John Steinbeck, "My Short Novels," *Wings* (October 1953), p. 8. Reprinted by permission of McIntosh and Otis, Inc.

Tin and iron and rust and splintered wood, chipped pave-
ment and weedy lots and junk heaps, sardine canneries of
corrugated iron, honky tonks, restaurants and whore houses,
and little crowded groceries, and laboratories and flophouses.[5]

The rendering is governed by "is" thinking. Its unity lies
only in the fact that it really exists. The effect is analogous
to a panning camera, registering everything in its range
after the initial close-up.

All of the inhabitants of the Row are the pure in heart,
but Mack and the boys are especially pure. This reasoning
follows the initial panoramic view:

> [The] inhabitants are, as the man once said, "whores, pimps,
> gamblers, and sons of bitches," by which he meant Every-
> body. Had the man looked through another peephole he
> might have said, "Saints and angels and martyrs and holy
> men," and he would have meant the same thing.[6]

This paradox refers directly to "is" thinking, to a point of
view that permits but does not judge. As a narrative control,
the paradox suggests that a point of view means only that
we are complex enough to need various, even opposed,
meanings if we are to deal with the truth. So the viewer
is also viewed. The cliché, "as the man said," and "peephole" with its implication of spying, suggest that the man
is not thinking very clearly, like most people, and that his
own character, not the objective facts or the facts available
to someone else, creates his point of view and his specific
judgment. Therefore, purity equates with the complexities
of human nature. Mack and the boys are especially pure,
in the sense that they are children of nature like Tularecito,
Junius Maltby, Tom Joad, Jim Casy, Lennie, and all *paisanos*; their unique existence is unquestioned and unargued.
Precisely that certainty, that lack of debate, or any need
on Steinbeck's part to excuse or defend the materials, sets
Cannery Row apart from his earlier efforts to establish what
may be considered credible nature gods.[7] Steinbeck simply

5. *CR*, p. 1.   6. *CR*, p. 1.
  7. This would include such different novels as *To a God Unknown*
and *Tortilla Flat*.

asserts that God is "our Father who art in nature."[8] Nature is Steinbeck's key to "is" thinking, and his use of nature determines the development of the panoramic structure of the novel.

This perspective gives drive and buoyancy to the frame by involving its detail in image and paradox, and it cancels the inert essay method. Many contemporary reviewers were misled, however, by an analogy placed at the close of this initial frame. They concluded that *Cannery Row* must be altogether casual in its structure. This is the analogy:

> When you collect marine animals there are certain flat worms so delicate that they are almost impossible to capture whole, for they break and tatter under the touch. You must let them ooze and crawl of their own will onto a knife blade and then lift them gently into your bottle of sea water. And perhaps that might be the way to write this book—to open the page and to let the stories crawl in by themselves.[9]

The issue is Steinbeck's own artistic preoccupations, not the opposition in literary history between naturalistic and symbolistic method. The analogy does not imply that Steinbeck abandons the responsibility of selection and arrangement to wallow in mere reporting, but that he abandons for the time his contemporary effort in the play-novelettes to execute an absolutely predetermined story—an effort that hopes by the force of a formula to create, not just to capture, the delicate, self-revealing order of the fully realized work of art. Here, Steinbeck knows that a story eludes all effort except a willing suspension of disbelief, for author as for reader. Here, then, Steinbeck exorcises a self-recognized, controlling tendency that is embalmed in the play-novelettes, just as he had exorcised earlier (another self-recognition) a merely clever, propagandistic tendency in withdrawing *L'Affaire Lettuceburg*.[10] Hence, the flat worm analogy rises from allegory to metaphor.

8. *CR*, p. 15.   9. *CR*, p. 15.

10. To realize that Steinbeck was exploring the extremes of dramatic structure and of panoramic structure at the same moment is to realize that his development is more reasoned and self-conscious than hasty observers believe.

In fact, there is an explicit narrative method in *Cannery Row* in the controlling metaphor of the tide pool, the collection of natural life which parallels Cannery Row. The tide pool is savage; but, viewed through "is" thinking, it is not judged nor is its outward beauty contrasted with its savage reality. Simplified oppositions are not characteristic of *Cannery Row*. Instead, adjectives associate nature and the human town; starfish "squat" over prey, nudibranchs have "skirts waving like the dresses of Spanish dancers," black eels "poke their heads out of crevices and wait for prey," and "hermit crabs like frantic children scamper on the bottom sand," but Steinbeck does not sentimentalize either children or crabs ("is" thinking forbids), since "here a crab tears a leg from his brother."[11] As an analogue of human life, the tide pool is too complex to be condemned or sentimentalized; as a natural phenomenon, it does not recall the abstract codes of human morality. Yet distinctions are drawn in terms of function, as in Steinbeck's descriptions of killing. The anemones use narcotic stings on prey that then "grows weak and perhaps sleepy while the searing caustic digestive acids melt its body down," but the octopus is "a creeping murderer" that kills by stealth, "leaps savagely" and "runs . . . ferociously."[12] So morality exists in the tide pool as in human life, as a result (not a judgment) of function, but it is more complex than we imagine, more involved in relationships that human tender-mindedness likes to allow: "[In the tide pool] the smells of life and richness, of death and digestion, of decay and birth, burden the air."[13]

The tide pool operates as a symbol of the complexity that is nature. This central insight justifies—demands— the objective narrative extreme of "is" thinking. As an objective, realized metaphor, the tide pool passage exhausts its purpose. It is not a detached essay, nor does it require an allegorical parallel between the swarming natural life and the human town. In being relaxed and amoral, or suggestive

11. *CR*, pp. 31–32.
12. *CR*, pp. 31–32.   13. *CR*, p. 32.

rather than dogmatic, the passage differs from much of Steinbeck's earlier work—and for the better.[14]

Steinbeck is fully aware of his purpose. The tide pool is carefully "placed" as an organic part of the total world of Cannery Row. Everyone on the Row is an eccentric. Doc is a lovable intellectual, making a curious, individualistic living as a marine biologist; he regards people and the specimens he collects from the tide pool with the same cool, warm eye. Doc is a fuller, less tortured version of Doc Burton. Lee Chong regards the mathematics of business with a philosophic detachment; his grocery is a humanly mysterious institution. Dora operates a whorehouse, an illegal, necessary business, uniquely illogical in its social mathematics, for Dora must contribute heavily to worthy community projects and charities and must preserve an abnormally solid front of obedience to the law as the price of an uncertain social and police toleration. Less developed characters are privately eccentric. But these three people are the pillars of Cannery Row society; their oddity upholds and defines the social order, since they exemplify a social adjustment of logic to eccentric necessity, to the way things are. At the center of this society, at the hub of its universe, Steinbeck places the extreme eccentrics, Mack and the boys. Their communal life suggests an adjustment to ecology, a Thoreaulike fronting of the essentials, a heroic withdrawal from the world. Their anarchistic goodness measures the inadequacy of bourgeois values. The existence of this community—its adventures, its relationships—recapitulates in the human sphere the complexities of the tide pool community. Both

14. In this the tide pool metaphor differs from the more rigidly conceived turtle passage in *The Grapes of Wrath*, as that passage resembles the gopher episode in *Cannery Row*. Steinbeck does not use metaphor extensively or splendidly in much of his work. Potential metaphors become rigid abstractions too often, as in the scene in *To a God Unknown* in which Joseph and Elizabeth pass through a valley. But the symbolic function of the rose bush in the Pat Humbert episode in *The Pastures of Heaven* suggests Steinbeck's practice in *Cannery Row*. The early example is impressive in its singularity. There is a good deal of incidental metaphor in the novels, but Steinbeck is far more prone to utilize metaphor and symbolism for structural purposes in his short stories.

are strange and alive, but that insight is symbolic and implicit, never an allegorical, one-to-one simplification or a forced identity. Steinbeck's earlier rigidities vanish here, for "is" thinking insists that to see is better than to be told. Steinbeck has a purpose, which he enacts rather than defines.

What appear to be attempts at definition turn out to be enactments, dramatic encounters. Almost half way through the novel, after a number of events have occurred, Steinbeck permits something like a debate when Doc explains to Richard Frost that Mack and the boys are "your true philosophers."

> "I think they survive in this particular world better than other people. In a time when people tear themselves to pieces with ambition and nervousness and covetousness, they are relaxed. All our so-called successful men are sick men, with bad stomachs, and bad souls, but Mack and the boys are healthy and curiously clean. They can do what they want. They can satisfy their appetites without calling them something else."[15]

Frost, an intellectual friend whose chilly name suggests the quality of "the world," replies skeptically: "They're just like anyone else. They just haven't any money." Doc disagrees by distinguishing the natural man from the corrupt, corrupting world that Frost represents:

> "They could get it," Doc said. "They could ruin their lives and get money. Mack has qualities of genius. They're all very clever if they want something. They just know the nature of things too well to be caught in that wanting."[16]

The natural man comprehends the true nature of things. Through Doc's peephole, then, Mack and the boys are "saints and angels and martyrs and holy men" who have chosen to renounce "the world." Through Frost's peephole, they are, if not "whores, pimps, gamblers, and sons of bitches," at least unsuccessful wooers of the bitch goddess success. The intensity of Doc's defense and the chilly inadequacy of Frost's denial enact the intellectual removal of our doubt.

15. *CR*, pp. 148–49.   16. *CR*, p. 149.

A prior, significant action certifies Doc's side of the debate. Mack and the boys encounter a man whose wife is plainly a horror of perfect adjustment to "the world." Her house is the image of her soul, a revelation of her values:

> [Mack and the boys] were unconsciously glad she wasn't there. The kind of women who put papers on shelves and had little towels like that instinctively distrusted and disliked Mack and the boys. Such women knew that they were the worst threats to a home, for they offered ease and thought and companionship as opposed to neatness, order, and properness.[17]

The puritanic lady is unnatural. She replaces the tide pool metaphor ("dirt" that has to be cleaned up) with an inhuman abstraction of neatness and cleanliness, and she abandons her husband for the abstractions of a political career. Mack and the boys restore the henpecked husband to an almost forgotten delight in dogs, corn whiskey, and good companionship, but they leave a mess.[18]

The persistent thematic motif identifies the good life with any of the possibilities of love. Opposing views—Richard Frost's cash nexus, the puritanic wife's frigid order—are not so much debated as dismissed with contempt. This dismissal of manipulation, of argument, frees Steinbeck's improvisational comic style to prove on our pulses that Mack and the boys are truly the Beauties, the Virtues, the Graces:

> In the world ruled by tigers with ulcers, rutted by strictured bulls, scavenged by blind jackals, Mack and the boys dine delicately with the tigers, fondle the frantic heifers, and wrap up the crumbs to feed the sea gulls of Cannery Row. What can it profit a man to gain the whole world and to come to his property with a gastric ulcer, a blown prostate, and bifocals? Mack and the boys avoid the trap, walk around the poison, step over the noose while a generation of trapped, poisoned, and trussed-up men scream at them and call them no-goods.[19]

The enormous release of verbal energy in this intensely playful passage is rare in Steinbeck's work. Some earlier examples exist—the vacuum cleaner in *Tortilla Flat* and

17. *CR*, pp. 93–94.
18. *CR*, p. 98.   19. *CR*, pp. 14–15.

the "shitheels" passage in *The Grapes of Wrath* suggest the typical range—as incidental or decorative elements in a design. They are the center in *Cannery Row,* drawing their relevance and power from the central metaphor of the tide pool. That vitality embodies its own value. Similarly, we credit the value of Mack and the boys because we must believe the sharp, realized imagery they provoke. We can disbelieve argument; we cannot help but accept whatever exists in energized images, since they preclude argument. "Is" thinking releases metaphor; it fleshes concepts and characters in an imagistic development of theme, as it rejects any externalized, allegorical ordering.

Style and imagery can have structural qualities, but they are not structural in themselves. There is some minimal sense of plot, however, in the efforts of Mack and the boys to organize a party worthy of Doc, but only enough to delude the unwashed. The effective structure is the interaction of panoramic scene and thematic motif. The seemingly loose development is a suitably organic way to represent the complexity of the tide pool and its analogue, "the poem and the stink and the grating noise" that is Cannery Row, as viewed by the controlled vagaries of "is" thinking.[20]

In working out the segments of *Cannery Row,* Steinbeck shows marvelously what can be done with a panoramic structure that is organized consciously to develop a particular theme.

The first six chapters and interchapters scan the important inhabitants of the Row. Little episodes, not abstract statement, register the nature of love in each man. The unstated theme remains implicit in what the inhabitants are. Lee Chong supplies food and is paid, but his "kindness and understanding" establish the humane quality of life in Cannery Row.[21] Dora provides women or womanly affection, a decent sexuality for hire at the Bear Flag Restaurant. Doc supplies his exotic, bearded, completely natural self, casual medical care, occasional wages, and the glamour of the arts and sciences through his female visitors, his books and music, and his operation of Western Biological, a firm

20. *CR,* p. 15.   21. *CR,* p. 9.

that "deals in strange and beautiful wares . . . the lovely animals of the sea."[22] Among them, these three people cover most of the hungers and needs that love can involve. At the center of the community, Mack and the boys contain an absolutely unworldly, unselfish love that is odd at times even in Cannery Row. Three interchapters are attached to the three chapters in which these people are seen, and they establish in their turn the totality that love produces. Everything is image. Chapter Two draws on the figure of the spinning universe in orbit around "our Father who art in nature" to universalize Lee Chong in brilliant specifics:

> Lee Chong is more than a Chinese grocer. He must be. Perhaps he is evil balanced and held suspended by good—an Asiatic planet held to its orbit by the pull of Lao Tze and held away from Lao Tze by the centrifugality of abacus and cash register—Lee Chong suspended, spinning, whirling among groceries and ghosts.[23]

The brilliance is persuasive—linguistic magic—in its own right. Further, it is functional, not decorative or merely whimsical. Love is also defined by its reverse, and all of the events occur on two planes, the specific and the general, in "the hurried mangled craziness of Monterey and the cosmic Monterey."[24] Evil is particularized in the octopus in the tide pool and in the mysterious, ancient Chinaman, able to draw out the mind of a "brave and beautiful boy of ten named Andy" who insults him.[25] The precise interchange of specific and general allows a clear view of the lesser evil that is social maladjustment or too much acceptance of the standards of "the world." Horace Abbeville kills himself (Chapter One) because he thinks he is a failure after he sells his only property to Lee Chong to pay off a huge grocery debt; and Dora's watchman, William, kills himself (Chapter Three) because he accepts the disgrace of being a pimp. Twice mistaken, his gloomy nature sets him apart and forces him to drive an ice pick into his heart in a desperate effort to elicit the cook's interest.

Mack and the boys survive. Mack gets Horace's ware-

22. *CR*, p. 25.
24. *CR*, p. 15.
23. *CR*, p. 14.
25. *CR*, p. 23.

house as an unpaid rental from Lee Chong (*paisano* economics!) in Chapter One, and the communal life is explained in Chapter Six in a long conversation between Doc and Hazel. These plot strands are embedded in thematic material, the existence of love and hate in the literal and cosmic Monterey, as in chapter and interchapter. The seeming anarchy of the narrative method is an analogue of the seeming anarchy of life. In fact, there is a narrative pattern, consisting of individual attempts to adjust to a given environment. Some are able, some are not. Not that adjustment means a simple, animal easiness, Edmund Wilson's insight notwithstanding.[26] There is no love in the tide pool, only in the human place, Cannery Row. Also, values are ultimately human, as in the cap to a discussion between Doc and Hazel concerning black stink bugs. No study notes that black stink bugs "put their tails up in the air." Doc thinks they are praying, and adds: "We can only use ourselves as yardsticks. If we did something as inexplicable and strange we'd probably be praying—so maybe they're praying."[27] Notice that Steinbeck has moved from the specific facts (the bugs act in a certain way, and no authority has observed this activity) to the general, universalizing conclusion that knowledge is limited to self-knowledge. The passage embodies the general in the specific, it relates love and hate to deductions made from human values in obedience to "is" thinking (not pathetic fallacy), and it develops a thematic rather than a plot line. Doc's conceit draws on fantasy, but the insight is realistic, not fanciful. Just so, Mack and the boys are realists. Their self-created fairyland, on enchanted ground, is no whimsical conception, but a serious, reverse image of "the world." Similarly, Doc, Dora, and Lee Chong are realists, and Cannery Row is quite real to its inhabitants. Like love, it is a fantasy only in relation to "the world" that is too much with us. Like love, Cannery Row is a creation of its inhabitants. They choose to live there, and they make their lives the creation of love in any of its forms.

26. Edmund Wilson, "The Californians: Storm and Steinbeck," *The New Republic*, 103 (December 9, 1940), 784–87.

27. *CR*, p. 38.

"Is" thinking provides a realistic narrative method and a completely realized narrative surface—a context in which fantasy is most likely to flourish. The resulting narrative complexity can absorb ironic contrast within the narrative pattern, producing an organic unity, not the incidental ironic hits characteristic of *The Pastures of Heaven*. Thus, in Chapters Seven and Eight, the fantastic interior of the warehouse "home" assembled by Mack and the boys sets off a parody of the values of "the world" in terms of the close description of the boiler home of the Malloys. The contrast extends into action when Mrs. Malloy insists on lace curtains, a symbol of genteel living, after Mr. Malloy has become a landlord of sorts.

Several episodes risk an appeal to sentimentality, but "is" thinking promotes narrative objectivity this side of the sentimental. For example, Doc shelters Frankie, a semi-idiot boy. That is the fact. But as the day of the party for Doc approaches, Frankie wishes to give something; he steals a clock and is put away, after telling Doc that he took the clock because "I love you," a phrase he uses often.[28] Doc's tragic association with Frankie balances the impersonal benevolence of the authorities, who are right about Frankie —without comment. And when Dora and her girls, at Doc's suggestion, look after sick people during a flu epidemic, the result is not the "heart of gold" device so dear to sentimental writers but an ironic weighing of the complexities of the good life. The irony that Dora has more business than ever during the epidemic is only a fact along with the fact of the epidemic:

> The girls slipped out the back door, and sometimes staying with the sleeping children the girls dropped to sleep in their chairs. They didn't use makeup for work any more. They didn't have to. Dora herself said she could have used the total membership of the old ladies' home. It was the busiest time the girls at the Bear Flag could remember. Everyone was glad when it was over.[29]

The girls' good deeds and their relief at the eventual slack in business are separate items, one as true as the other, and

28. *CR*, pp. 58–62, 183–86.   29. *CR*, p. 103.

they mingle as they will. No sentimental or moralistic claims mar the human data. The factual language presents irony for inspection.

The varieties of love range from the two cheerfully drunken soldiers and their girls, unable to hear the "dark and surly" watchman ordering them off the dawn-lit beach of the Hopkins Marine Station, to the drowned girl Doc comes upon, wedged in the rocks on the La Jolla tidal flat.[30] Pleasure and violence, beauty and horror, comprise a range of human possibility, a further analogue to the tide pool's nonhuman fury, which extends beyond moral judgment. But people intrude judgment. The watchman judges the lovers; they judge him. Doc sees a fearful beauty in the drowned girl's face, a pull of death, and endures its reduction to cash nexus when a passing man tells him there is a bounty for finding a body, a human fact that Doc rejects with teleological disgust.

The tall tale about the undignified disposal of Josh Billings's "tripas" is a comic reduction of human values concerning death. Steinbeck reproduces the poker-faced delivery that Mark Twain recommended for the tall tale.[31] The human pomp of embalming the dead, celebrated author does not quite conceal the liver and intestines of the human animal, and the objective report attains its grotesque comic revelation by exposing the strain of pretending otherwise. Official piety betrays communal hypocrisy. The living author does not elicit the concern, the love, the pretense, the leaden box that fearsome death and commercial "honor" evoke. The Ur-version may be the seven Greek cities' regard for Homer alive and dead.[32] The Josh Billings episode is an interchapter; the frog hunt follows it, as an extended tall tale; Doc's "beer milk shake" is a minute tall tale. The strangeness, the fantasy of humankind can be expressed with particular flavor in the tall tale; Steinbeck may have had its

30. *CR*, pp. 88–91, 114–16.

31. Mark Twain, "How to Tell a Story," *Literary Essays* (New York: Harper and Brothers, 1899), pp. 11–12.

32. Epigrams by Thomas Heywood and Thomas Seward, in *Familiar Quotations*, ed. John Bartlett (Boston: Little, Brown and Company, 1955), p. 227a.

potential in mind. Each tall tale concerns or reacts to the existence of death, but plot linkage is not stressed. Thematic values, the duality of human experience and motive, knit up the plot of *Cannery Row* as they sustain the most extensive tall tale, namely, the fabula of the birthday party for Doc.

Mack is fond of Doc, as everyone is, but Mack's fondness is expressed by insisting that Doc must have a party. The effort permits several thematic developments that evolve slowly across the face of the novel, avoiding the frantic, un-motivated climax that mars *Tortilla Flat*. Doc is "a fine fel-low" to Mack, perhaps his other half, not his reverse self:

> His face is half Christ and half satyr and his face tells the truth. . . . His mind had no horizon—and his sympathy had no warp. . . . He lived in a world of wonders, of excitement. He was concupiscent as a rabbit and gentle as hell. Everyone who knew him was indebted to him.[33]

Despite a kindly understanding, Doc is a detached, essen-tially lonely observer of the good life. He is particularly detached—socially, economically, and intellectually—from Mack and the boys. He has unusual guests, he pays Mack and the boys for work, and for the ruined party as well as for the party that succeeds, but when he praises them he looks down on them from his laboratory windows.[34] They are interesting to him, as everyone is, but his interest in them is much like that he pays to the specimens he finds in the tide pools. He helps them as much as he can, but he does not love them.

The thematic development requires that Mack and the boys must desire strongly to pull Doc into the humane commune they have created for themselves. This desire is a metaphor, not a plot device. The two halves of the good life must be fused, like mind and body. Precisely the splintered nature of the plot, so far as it is the creation of a party for Doc, ensures the primacy of theme and avoids the tyranny of a schematic order. Plot seems to get lost, both in such self-contained episodes as the frog hunt (where Mack has to remind himself and the others that Doc's party is what

33. *CR*, pp. 28–29.
34. *CR*, pp. 43, 44, 45, 148, 181.

they are working at, despite all the fun they are having) and in the apparent interruptions of the interchapters and Doc's own work.

In fact, theme is never in doubt; it points directly to the enormous climax of the successful party, which is both a real event and a symbolic ceremony of uniting opposites, resolving contradictions, and fusing what plot elements there are. The prefix of the failed party is an objective means of demonstrating that unities are not simple or easy to achieve. The two parties are not so very different on the narrative surface of detail: the drinking, the music, the food, the violence. But they are distinguished in their artfulness. The first party is a purely spontaneous event, a failure of planlessness. The second party is an elaborate conspiracy, a preparation, a framework, that grows into spontaneity within the bounds of a due regard for the complexity of good and evil. The human duality that finds its most complete expression in the comic revelation of the tall tale, like the fantastic, jumbled "is" of the tide pool, is really what is invoked and celebrated at Doc's birthday party.

Transformations are the key to this mystery. Doc transforms his somewhat detached intellectualism by a preparty preparation of listening to sadly sentimental, Romantic music, appropriate to the emotional anarchism, the simplistic naturalness of his quasi-hosts. Mack and the boys are uncommonly formal—to begin with—careful to keep their irrationalism and disorder within polite bounds. Dora's prostitutes are carefully girlish, wistfully virginal. And so forth.

But the transformations are necessarily partial and temporary. They vanish as the party loses its stiffness, and reverse man emerges. The party celebrates the felicitous, unforced complexity of Cannery Row. For example, Doc seems to impose his tastes—good whiskey, classical music, Sanskrit poetry—on much of the affair and to return to his customary isolation on the morning after. But that is only as it may seem to a hurried eye. Social decency prevails. Doc's whiskey is good, his music is softly romantic, and the Sanskrit poetry is an idealistic praise of love-making.

None of that is Doc's usual mode. His thoughts are of the others, as in the kindly irony of his laying in food and drink for the "surprise" he is given. The morning-after mood is a continuation of this softness, counterpointed by the sharper and harsher realities in Doc's life—his playing Gregorian music that would not have suited the party and his awareness of the cases of white rats and rattlesnakes that he had locked in a room to prevent lethal accidents on the night of the party. That is to say, Doc accommodates his nature to the measure of his guests and hosts, as Mack and the boys, Dora's whores, and the others accommodate their natures to Doc's measure. Everyone is a little wrong, but right enough. The fistfights are communal affairs, not the private affairs of the failed party. They also wreck Doc's house; the difference is in the emotion. The explosion of Lee Chong's gift, a twenty-foot string of firecrackers, completes the event, for in that act the inscrutable businessman's mentality bursts out of itself. The traditional anarchy of the wise Chinese prank is the ultimate send-up or blow-up—the genuine climax of the party.

The humanly momentary resolution of opposites, of doubleness, and the attainment of the completion that is happiness are figured in the metaphor of the tide pool; and "our Father who art in nature" is the true object of the celebration, in all His complex creation of human nature.

The party's success is defined further and extended literally into nature by its negation in the interchapter that follows. This objective, self-contained animal fable avoids allegory but achieves illumination, much like the turtle episode in *The Grapes of Wrath*. The fable contemplates the usefulness of security without love. The gopher's construction of a perfect home is in vain, and his reproductive urge is frustrated; he is too far away from gopherdom. In sexual desperation "he had to move two blocks up the hill to a dahlia garden where they put out traps every night."[35] This comedy of mischance and misfortune is a suggestive analogue of the human condition. The gopher's need is limited to a sexual urge. Human affection is broader and more ex-

35. *CR*, p. 204.

tensive, ranging from the accommodations of friendship to the simplicities of lust. Given these differences in scale, animal need and human need are similarly imperative. Love is a fragile, transformational concept and dangerous to self-definition, to the security of a firm isolation; but we invoke and risk love, as the two parties do, because we have no better way to become fully human, complete, communal. The gopher's achievement of perfection fails, but Mack and the boys imperfectly succeed. Lee Chong and Doc agree on this in the aftermath of the party and in the happiness of implication; they had been the community's firmest isolates, but they (like the simplest folk) have been given a vision of momentary wholeness in the nature of things, through the medium of the second party.

Although this vision occurs, it has its limitations. The party is a high point, a fragile construct, not a pattern of conduct. The victory over isolation or lovelessness is a metaphor, not a legal or social handbook. The entire thematic development risks a sentimental pumping, a romantic haze that can distort fictional reality by its soft-hearted selection of the available data. Yet "is" thinking minimizes these possibilities in two ways: by the objective rendering it demands, and by the narrative restraint, the absence of special claims, of any imposed value system; for these factors are the essence of "is" thinking. By these means we see the love, the goodness, the strange, communal unity of Cannery Row without blinking the incidental negations of love, goodness, and community that are imbedded in the narrative. What is missing is a schematic opposition of these poles along a rigid plot line, which had been Steinbeck's earlier strategy. *Cannery Row* is a successful version, then, of *The Pastures of Heaven* and *Tortilla Flat*. The positive virtue of joyfulness, the enchantment of style, and the praise of whimsical or eccentric behavior do not deny the more sombre aspects of reality. "Is" thinking includes in its compass the puritanical woman, the drowned girl, the failed party, heartless intellectual curiosity, destructive hypocrisy, and the impermanence of any apparent victory over the human isolation and twistedness which are the overt symptoms of these negative realities. "Is" thinking records the partial human success. The unmitigated, absolute fusion of these opposites is possible only in the simpler, value-free animal context, but only because we cannot comprehend the tide pool. A humanized animal, as in the gopher fable, suffers the despair of thwarted desire, as humanized animals always have. "Is" thinking is only the method of the novel; teleological cruxes afflict the characters and shape the events which "is" thinking contemplates serenely.

A value-free narrative system, a loose commingling of thematic materials and panoramic structure, suits the authorial purpose: to "set down alive" the delightful, complex unity of Cannery Row.[36] The shaping, recording instrument of "is" thinking is a better friend to Steinbeck than the allegory which he relies on in many of the late novels. But at some expense. Most important, the revealed fragility of human felicity reduces the scope, the resonance, of what Cannery Row can signify. The evocation of pastoral serenity permits a lucid and convincing demonstration of a specific fantasy, a particularized association of the good life with the life of Cannery Row. But all of it is unique to the Row, to a special mood, or time, or place. The details of a fantasy must be realistic, as they are here, if they are to be convincing. Yet the realized novel does not pertain finally to human concerns beyond the range of a special creation or discovery. The tide pool is repeatedly called a fantastic world, and so is Cannery Row. Even the enormous, climactic party is a limited event, both in its necessarily imperfect, momentary, and somewhat ironic celebration of a god in nature and its inability to supply a universal, even a repeatable, pattern of conduct. Steinbeck is perfectly aware of these limitations. They are inherent in "is" thinking, in the modesty of setting down alive a unique, improvised pattern of how things can be. Steinbeck does not strain for a larger, less convincing claim, and that is the glory of *Cannery Row*.

The dismay of the contemporary reviewers can be appreciated as a measure of the reduction Steinbeck accepts in

36. *CR*, p. 15.

order to create the perfection of *Cannery Row*. After all, Tom Joad's discovery of a mystical wholeness, a pastoral felicity, lays claim to immediate social relevance. Doc's discovery of a similar wholeness and felicity is hedged by its privateness, its irony, its incompleteness. Probably that aspect of *Cannery Row* is more honest than its parallel in *The Grapes of Wrath*. Certainly it is more aesthetically rounded, more convincing as a fictive statement than the mystico-allegorical straining after conviction at the close of *The Grapes of Wrath*.

Cannery Row is a small, restrained fictive universe, but perfected within its limits. Steinbeck may relinquish too much to attain the elegance of perfection. A more extreme version of "is" thinking may cause the disintegration of the comfortable looseness of the merest thematic unity. The immediate fact is that *Cannery Row* delights and persuades more thoroughly, more profoundly than any of Steinbeck's work that utilizes external devices and techniques to formulate a simulacrum of aesthetic unity.

The dividing line is thin between the most extreme and the most relaxed of Steinbeck's narrative forms. If much of the delight and persuasion of *Cannery Row* depends on its restraint, its modesty, its reduced scale, still the materials of a potential allegory are at hand. The tide pool, "the Beauties, the Virtues, the Graces," Doc, Lee Chong as more than a Chinese grocer, the balance of love and hate, and the adjustment to environment—all these could become the instrumental units of a full-scale allegory. They do not because Steinbeck refrains from pressing their connections on the level of plot. "Is" thinking insists on an organic presentation of materials—without allegory, without authorial comment. That degree of trustful objectivity is a most unusual commitment in Steinbeck's fiction. The only complete parallel in the preceding novels is *In Dubious Battle*, at the other end of the thematic and structural scale. Uniqueness does not bear repetition, in either case.

A final point of distinction lies somewhat outside the novel but is highly relevant to the nature of its success: The materials of the Great Depression are put to various, even opposed uses in Steinbeck's fiction. The Joads in *The Grapes of Wrath* are harrowed by their immediate, brutalizing problem of physical survival. For less needy people, the Depression could bring the exhilaration of a relative freedom—in the virtual absence of any need to strive, to want to possess things, to be competitive. The emphasis could be, since it could not be otherwise, on the self-containment of happiness, of simply being, of doing one's thing. That mood is evoked and celebrated in *Cannery Row* with the honesty, the objectivity, the creative depth and force of Steinbeck's fictive powers at their best.

7

The Natural Parable

The Pearl

The Pearl[1] fulfills the best literary possibilities of "is" thinking: a parable realized in objective, imagistic detail, the abstract fleshed by the particular. The tight dramatic structure is the reverse of Cannery Row's panoramic technique, but there is improvement, not a falling off. Masterfully, The Pearl exhibits a compact precision, a completeness in the Aristotelian sense, and the force of convincing thematic materials.

Kino's discovery, defense, and final disposal of the pearl fits into one hundred and twenty-two pages—about five days of elapsed time. The key to the narrative method is balance. A spare, impersonal narration concentrates the richly implicational materials. Particularly the pearl suggests various meanings to different people at different times. The highly suggestive quality of the precise object, the pearl, keeps the narrative from collapsing into a narrowed allegory. As the simplicity of the structure balances the complexity of the materials, so the allegorical thrust of the parable balances the precise, enriching details that result from "is" thinking.

The evidence is that Steinbeck worked out most of his novels, but that he thought out The Pearl. Elsewhere, he can seem to give most attention to the superficial, surface aspects of structure, to "pattern" in the pettiest sense. His evaluative, technical comments tend to be vague or puzzled when he remarks on such novels as The Pastures of Heaven or Tortilla Flat. But with The Pearl he is fully aware of the artistic problem, and astutely in professional command.

The basic plot came to Steinbeck in the process of com-

1. John Steinbeck, The Pearl (New York: The Viking Press, Inc., 1947). Hereafter cited as TP.

posing *Sea of Cortez*.[2] He added several important critical observations to the plot summary, recorded there, indicating his awareness of a need to establish a literal credibility, not merely a formal order as in the concurrent play-novelettes:

> This seems to be a true story, but it is so much like a parable that it almost can't be. This Indian boy is too heroic, too wise. He knows too much and acts on his knowledge. In every way, he goes contrary to human direction. The story is probably true, but we don't believe it; it is far too reasonable to be true.[3]

So, for Steinbeck, the basic plot is a natural, made-to-order parable. Further, as he knows here, a parable can be either absurdly self-evident or richly suggestive as an insight into human nature, depending entirely on its treatment. The sophisticated accuracy of this critical judgment is most uncommon, especially as foresight, among Steinbeck's comments on his own work.

His emphasis on adequate characterization is reflected in the finished novel; the increased range of character in the shift from an Indian boy to an Indian family demands more complexity than allegory would permit. Character joins the reasonable with the true. The allegorical implications of particular events become mythical—or absolutely true—because they emerge from an objective, realized context through "is" thinking; the characters exist in that context but without severe dislocation as in *Tortilla Flat* or (more grimly) *Burning Bright*. Therefore, Steinbeck's artistic aims in *The Pearl* tend to fuse the two main kinds of storytelling, the tightly controlled dramatic structure and the wider range of panoramic structure. The allegory is located in details that are realized beyond any doubt, and the allegory benefits in credibility. The play-

---

2. John Steinbeck and Edward F. Ricketts, *Sea of Cortez* (New York: The Viking Press, Inc., 1941), pp. 102–3.

3. *Sea of Cortez*, p. 103. This passage is a rare example of Steinbeck's critical foresight. Yet it predates *Cannery Row*, to which it might seem relevant. This suggests once more that Steinbeck does not learn from one novel to another, that he perceives each novel as a separate problem.

novelettes, *The Wayward Bus*, and *East of Eden*—those other allegorical and semiallegorical novels of Steinbeck's—are less distinguished than *The Pearl* because the allegory is in itself uncertain, incredible in its detail, or both. So it is highly significant that Steinbeck conceived of *The Pearl* as a parable that is foremost an objective, credible narrative, a tight structure capable of expanded belief.[4]

The Pearl is superior to most of the author's contemporary works primarily because of Steinbeck's good fortune, his lucky discovery of a natural parable, a structure that could be worked up, rearranged, even cut or expanded at points to reveal itself most fully—but above all a structure, a preexisting order. As previously noted, Steinbeck does not have an easily stimulated feel for an organic form unless the circumstances are unusual in their urgency (as with the Depression novels). So his delight in discovering an essential structure in the embryo version of *The Pearl* is far more than the artist's simple joy in a gift that can be used; the delight is in the prior resolution of his weakest capability.

"Is" thinking is most likely to produce a panoramic structure, or at its worst, a miscellaneous, journalistic surface of details. Used in a tight structure, it can be a means of validating insight in combination with artful aids to order and artful devices that alone are merely artifices. In joining his natural parable to the technique of "is" thinking, heightened by various artifices, Steinbeck chances the best of everything.

There is no pretense of artlessness in his technique, no suggestion that truth is attained by accident. The short preface is a frame device, an announcement of the mythical purpose of the story, and a denial of the most overt species of allegory: "If this story is a parable, perhaps everyone takes his own meaning from it and reads his own life into it."[5] This initial frame is a necessary entry into the story.

4. "I tried to write as folklore, to give it that set-aside, raised-up feeling that all folk stories have." Steinbeck, "My Short Novels," *Wings* (October 1953), p. 8. Reprinted by permission of McIntosh and Otis, Inc.

5. *TP*, p. 2.

The Pastures of Heaven, Tortilla Flat, and *Cannery Row* open with prefaces which invite an expansion of the physical events; the same invitation is realized more powerfully in *The Pearl* because the objective details (the "is" thinking) support the parable structure and enlarge its reference, and the artful devices (framing, etc.) create the context and the narrative point of view. No one approach is so exaggerated as to exclude the others. A balanced harmony between structure and materials as well as an avoidance of the rigidity of outright allegory constitute the evident purpose of this beginning.[6]

At once, in the story proper, Steinbeck uses the group-man concept to hold various characters and events within the submerged allegory without straining the credibility of the narrative. As in *The Moon Is Down,* there are two kinds of group-man, but here they are distinguished objectively so there is no need to load the distinction. The first group-man is conceived to be an organism, while the second is an artificial growth.

The organism comprises the specific family—Kino, Juana, and Coyotito—and the entire fishing village. The family is the village in little, the microcosm, and the life of the village is represented in the common actions of the family's life in the literal and symbolic unity its Song implies:

> The Song of the Family came now from behind Kino. And the rhythm of the family song was the grinding stone where Juana worked the corn for the morning cakes. . . . Kino heard the creak of the rope when Juana took Coyotito out of his hanging box and cleaned him and hammocked him. . . . Kino could see these things without looking at them. Juana sang softly an ancient song that had only three notes and yet endless variety of interval. And this was part of the family song too. It was all part. Sometimes it rose to an aching chord that caught the throat, saying this is safety, this is warmth, this is the *Whole.*[7]

6. *In Dubious Battle* and *The Grapes of Wrath* rely on initial quotations, repeated in their titles, for this expansion, and on climactic scenes. Consult Stanley Edgar Hyman, "Some Notes on John Steinbeck," *The Antioch Review,* 2 (Summer 1942), 185–87.

7. *TP,* p. 5.

As microcosm, the family provides a typical point of view, much like the family in *The Grapes of Wrath*. As metaphor, the Song suggests the quality of the family's actions in the specific fact; because the actions are rituals, not merely duties, their value lies in what they signify—"safety . . . warmth . . . the *Whole*"—as well as in what they are. There is no discontinuity between duty and ritual; each implies the other. So the unity of the family is rooted in the metaphor, which is itself a result of daily events. And the metaphor fuses the realistic level of objective fact with the allegorical level of meaningful action. The same fusion ritualizes the family's involvement in their village and in their communal past. Again, as metaphor, "the people" help to define the family, and in turn "the people" have a part in the family's special existence:

> Now, Kino's people had sung of everything that happened or existed. They had made songs to the fishes, to the sea in anger and to the sea in calm, to the light and the dark and the sun and the moon, and the songs were all in Kino and in his people—every song that had ever been made, even the ones forgotten.[8]

The consequence of this developed metaphor, and of its long, soothing clauses, is that we tend to accept the reality of a completely natural, unified life in terms of "our Father who art in nature." The device of the Song is a nuisance that can seem precious if we bring to it only our standards.[9] But the objective narration and the close, functional view of the life of the family in the details of the Song establish a certain amount of narrative distance. We are outsiders, permitted to look for a time at a way of life that is altogether different from our own, not by reason of its quaintness (it is the natural life in its own context), but in its unity. To be sure, the family as metaphor and the use of such concepts as

8. *TP*, p. 27.

9. The distraction of a music device in *The Pearl* is heavily present in *Sweet Thursday*, lightly present in *Cannery Row* (Doc finding the drowned girl). Steinbeck must have found the device useful, not mechanical; he used it increasingly. The lack of self-criticism carries over from much of the earlier work.

"the people" and group-man derive from explicit usages in *The Grapes of Wrath*; the narrative distance in considering a primitive folk in a remote place allows Steinbeck to omit the special explanations and the occasional detached essays that are necessary in *The Grapes of Wrath*. Indeed, the way of life in *The Pearl* is communicated far more by tone, by the limpid, uncurling sentences, than by overt statement. Certainly the linguistic experiment is as ambitious and as difficult as the corresponding experiment in *The Grapes of Wrath*, and when the tone is pumped up too high (as it may be in "the *Whole*") conviction fails, as it does in several of the overly editorial interchapters in *The Grapes of Wrath*. Nevertheless, the metaphorical way of presenting the family is successful in the main, and it has an explicit narrative function. The family is so happy in its unity that it can be attacked only from "the world." That attack becomes inevitable in the development of the story.

The town is a microcosm of "the world," since it is an artificial formation of group-man. The town can *look* organic, as when Steinbeck describes it in biological terms and in his own voice:

> A town is a thing like a colonial animal. A town has a nervous system and a head and shoulders and feet. A town is a thing separate from all other towns, so that there are no two towns alike. And a town has a whole emotion.[10]

The clue that the town is only an illusion of organic life is in the phrase, "a colonial animal," which means the animal must be somewhere. The truly organic unit is everywhere, but the town is "separate." It is "a thing" while the organic unit is "a song." The distinction suggests an inert object, a kind of "death," not the ancient, always changing song that is associated with "life." Literally, the artificial quality of the town lies in its basic purpose: it exists to feed on the fishermen. The pearl buyers are especially representative of this purpose and of "the world," which is involved in its artificial values, because they can seem to be "separate" and "competitive," although in reality they are a single, para-

10. *TP*, p. 32.

sitic "thing" that cannot have any concern for dignity, justice, or life.[11] Therefore, given its nature, the town is the obvious enemy of the natural man. This truth is concealed by custom and by the teachings of the Church (the priest is a townsman). It comes into sharp focus only when Kino refuses to be handled as "a thing" by the pearl buyers, when he insists on his manhood by demanding true value for the pearl that he has found.[12] For then the town reveals itself by arranging to bring violence and murder to the family.

The corrupting power of the town is pervasive and more powerful than the organic life of the village, once it is stirred enough by Kino's find. Some of the fishermen simply fear that influence, and even Kino's supporters use a mercantile language: "From his courage we may all profit."[13] Kino cannot trust anyone but his kinsmen after the fishermen have had time to imagine the money value of the pearl. Kino's practical but narrow insight in demanding a fair price in fact measures the extent to which "the world" immediately corrupts his values.[14]

Once these factors are established, Steinbeck takes the narrative time to subtilize Kino's motives: his fierce stubbornness has a somewhat idealistic basis in pride, in his determination to remain human. Steinbeck works out the implicit, ironic changes between a stubbornness that can involve greed and a self-respect that can presume idealism, always keeping the literal and the probable fused with the moral implications at the core of the story. Thus, on the first night, when he is sure the pearl is his, Kino imagines what he will do with it; he progresses from personal and rather selfish desires—a church marriage, new clothes, a harpoon,

11. This metaphorical treatment is much more sophisticated and lends far more reality to the money-men than the more simply allegorical treatment of the owners in *In Dubious Battle* and *The Grapes of Wrath*. Compression might demand metaphor.

12. It is true that Kino is more humble to the doctor and the priest, although he refuses to give the pearl to either of them.

13. *TP*, p. 72.

14. Compare the notion of the release of the curse in *The Pastures of Heaven*. Here the curse and its results are more literal, more closely interlinked.

a rifle—to wholly selfless, idealistic thoughts of sending Coyotito to school:

> "My son will read and open books, and my son will write and will know writing. And my son will make numbers, and these things will make us free because he will know—he will know and through him we will know."[15]

Irony tenses the closely knit texture of this passage. It is the possessive "my son," and the knowledge is to be a revelation of the mystery the pearl buyers understand—words and numbers. So, indirectly and objectively, through the man's stumbling, rather mercantile thoughts, Steinbeck indicates the immediate, corrupting influence of "the world" on Kino's organic values.

This irony is deepened by the contrast between the literal pearl that Kino finds, and Coyotito, the symbolic pearl, the precious belonging of the family. Because Coyotito is stung by a scorpion, and the town doctor will not come to the Indian village unless he is paid, Kino is forced to hunt for something of value in the sea that normally provides fish. Or, on the allegorical level, Coyotito's need forces Kino to forgo the family's needs and values in nature and to obey the commands of "the world." Moreover, in keeping with the established ironic tension, Steinbeck suggests that Juana cures Coyotito with a traditional medicine, a poultice of "some brown seaweed . . . as good a remedy as any and probably better than the doctor could have done," before Kino sets out to hunt a pearl.[16] The irony is maintained and widened in reference. The greed of the doctor parallels the values of the pearl buyers, and the doctor's mumbo jumbo when he does appear, having heard of Kino's pearl, rounds our perception of the thorough corruptness of "the world" by its echo of the faked competitive system of the pearl buyers. Clearly the doctor is "a thing" in denying Coyotito's humanity, and he foreshadows the violent, inhuman response of "the world" to Kino's good fortune when he gives Coyotito a medicine to make him sick in order to create an artificial need for his services, now they can be paid for.

---

15. *TP*, p. 38.　　　　16. *TP*, p. 22.

The ironic tension increases when the nameless men try to snatch the pearl on the first night (after the scuffle, Kino calls out to Juana: "I am all right. The thing has gone."), and it continues to increase as unidentified men hunt Kino, intending to kill him for the pearl.[17] The reverse of the implicit contrast between the literal pearl and the family's pearl, Coyotito, is explored for its ironic possibilities: The scorpion that stings Coyotito is less inhuman than the doctor who makes the child sick in order to gain a fee. The scorpion is innocent of its evil function, like all nature in its various functions, but men act with reason and foreknowledge. The ultimate turn is that Kino is forced to kill in the end to keep the actual pearl, but, in the process, through an accident as casual as the scorpion's sting, Coyotito is killed by a stray bullet.

This rich development of irony demands an extensive list of paired terms, but the terms are associative, flowing out of the events in a natural sequence, not imposed on the events by the logic of an allegorical progression. Illusory needs dog real needs: the sick boy needs a doctor, doctors must be paid, pearls are worth money, Kino can buy a rifle with money, and so forth. The original "natural" need quickly involves the "artificial" cash nexus and the values of the town.[18]

This range of contrasted imagery extends into characterization, particularly Kino's, since he is the focus of attention, the man to whom things happen, and (unlike Lennie in a similar crux) he is somewhat aware of the ambiguous consequences of his actions. His complex range of responses, his subtle growth of pride after Coyotito's "natural" recovery as he realizes that the pearl is his, a symbol of his daring and strength, to own and to sell, opposes his rising fear for the future. Late on the first night, Juana asks, "Who do you fear?" Kino replies, "Everyone."[19] This admission

17. *TP*, p. 53.
18. The focus on a conflict of values prevents a reduction of the novel to social protest for its own sake. Kino clearly is exploited by the town, but that is not an isolated theme; it relates to the conflict of values.
19. *TP*, p. 52.

of fear qualifies his brave announcements to the people and suggests his developing awareness of the threat within the real situation. The subsequent events might be eliminated simply by letting Kino throw away the pearl, as Juana wishes. Although her insistence on taking Coyotito to the doctor is the cause of Kino's discovery of the pearl, she draws back fearfully from protecting and exploiting the pearl. Kino's aroused anger and pride—his character—make the story happen. His possessive defense of the pearl is an ironic amalgam of a bullish pride in his strength, in his ability to feed and to protect his family, and his increasingly tragic sense of acting out an inescapable "fate" or "curse" that can destroy the family or enrich all of them. As a man, he demands justice; thereby he endangers his family. The ambiguity is balanced and total. Kino is right and wrong. He prevails, but at a price. His heroism is disastrous and admirable, an expression of the entire man.

Kino's character justly complicates the basically simple narrative. Pride, idealism, greed, strength, despair, and horror—all are contained in the precise focus of the man's actions.

The central image is expressed as a conflict of values—the Pearl of the World and the pearl of the family, the literal pearl and Coyotito. This conflict offers Steinbeck innumerable opportunities to range universals as objective, imagistic facts, and he can do this almost at will. The dramatic structure permits a great deal of specific resonance. In short, Steinbeck makes the most of the parable's potentialities. The exact object, however complex, not its allegorical sign, its simplicity, serves to locate the story in humanly potential experience. In this way, Steinbeck drives an apparently simple narrative into the darkest areas of human awareness, and he accomplishes his purpose with full credibility.

Imaged objects define values. The pearl connotes a false standard of value. Kino's real needs are the family and his canoe, both recalling "our Father who art in nature." The canoe is explicitly an aspect of the organic life of the family:

It was at once property and the source of food, for a man with a boat can guarantee a woman that she will eat something.[20]

And it is associated with a son, as when Kino finds his canoe broken by those who want to keep him from taking the pearl to a city:

> This was an evil beyond thinking. The killing of a man was not so evil as the killing of a boat. For a boat does not have sons, and a boat cannot protect itself, and a wounded boat does not heal.[21]

The anthropomorphic thinking of a primitive man is a habit of mind which permits the association of canoe and son as a felt insight, a metaphorical depth of association in "the uncertain air that magnified some things and blotted out others."[22] But the standards of "the world" produce evil. The canoe is misused for pearl diving; this use violates its proper function as a fishing boat. The entire family is the innocent cause of the evil. Coyotito's illness occasions the pearl hunt. Juana "prays out" the pearl in response to the doctor's demand for money:

> She had not prayed directly for the recovery of the baby—she had prayed that they might find a pearl with which to hire the doctor to cure the baby.[23]

Kino finds the pearl by forcing the luck that is given "by God or the gods."[24] Finally, since Coyotito recovers, there is no organic need for the pearl; but they do not escape the pearl's evil until Kino flings it back into the sea while Juana stands "beside him, still holding her dead bundle over her shoulder."[25] This resolution does not imply a withdrawal. The differing values of organic and artificial life are set in balance again by the unconcerned sea. The act is an anthropomorphic form of penance, a ritual burial, an ejection of evil, a token of a return to the genuine life of the organism, shaded by the fact of death which no human act can

20. *TP*, p. 22.   21. *TP*, p. 86.
22. *TP*, p. 21.   23. *TP*, p. 22.
24. *TP*, pp. 24, 29.   25. *TP*, pp. 121–22.

alter. The resolution is ambiguous, then, like the rest of the parable, for it echoes our flawed humanity. Yet it is firm enough to be pointed by an ironic association of the pearl and the baby. Coyotito recovers at the moment when Kino first sees the pearl, fresh from the sea, and thinks it lovelier than anything he has seen before. After the baby's death, the pearl becomes suggestive of death: "And the pearl was ugly; it was grey, like a malignant growth."[26] The coincidences are not forced. Fresh pearls are lovely, and unpolished pearls do change color out of water. The recovered baby is lovely, but he is ugly when he is dead "with the top of his head shot away."[27] Always the visible facts are the basis for any implicit expansion into symbolic or allegorical significance. Even possibly abstract terms, such as "the Pearl of the World," derive a basic validity from events; no term exists in a vacuum.[28]

The fully rendered context, the developed characters, and a technique that eliminates overt statement in favor of objective, imagistic detail give *The Pearl* its narrative intensity and conviction. Steinbeck reproduces the form of the classic parable because he understands its secret in *The Pearl*: You must narrate objectively and let the reader discover whatever implications he can. No simple moralism is squeezed from the materials. The structural techniques serve only to embody a conception that is profound enough to reveal itself. Therefore, no sensitive reader is likely to take *The Pearl* for an anecdote, in consideration of its implications, or to take it as exotic primitivism, remote from any knowledge of himself. The parabolic form and the remote setting are not ends in themselves but means that sharpen an informed awareness of the nature of genuine and illusory values, of organic and artificial needs. The focus is sharpened, not simplified or reduced, by permitting civilized readers to examine sophisticated values from the perspective of a concentrated version of our more diffuse lives. The art that permits this critical stance is entirely and consistently self-conscious, not primitive at all. The balance of op-

26. *TP*, p. 121.
27. *TP*, p. 121.   28. *TP*, p. 34.

posites in *The Pearl* reveals lives that touch our own from the inside, within a pattern of cause and effect, and thereby discovers a harmony of structure and materials. The art is sophisticated in its completion, aware of its knowledge, but never patronizing. The materials are exact, not prettied or sentimentalized; the structure is precise, not simplified to exclude difficult truths or to point too easily at a banal "literary" pattern.

Which is to say that *The Pearl* is a triumph, a successful rendering of human experience in the round, in the most economical and intense of forms, without any surrender to the simplified or imposed patterns that mar the conclusions of such different novels as *Tortilla Flat* or *The Grapes of Wrath*.

This balance of parabolic form and infinitely suggestive meaning evokes the duality of nature, of experience; it locates that duality, by the light of imagination, in the precise fact of the Mexican setting:

> The uncertain air that magnified some things and blotted out others hung over the whole Gulf so that all sights were unreal and vision could not be trusted; so that sea and land had the sharp clarities and the vagueness of a dream. Thus it might be that the people of the Gulf trust things of the spirit and things of the imagination, but they do not trust their eyes to show them distance or clear outline or any optical exactness.[29]

The atmospheric fact encourages complexity, not pure surfaces or abstracted simplicities in apprehension; we see, but we require the vision of imagination to record what dualism "is" seen.

Duality undergirds *The Pearl*, and irony is the specific literary device that finds duality in every part of the narrative. This concept is available to Steinbeck from the beginning, in *Cup of Gold*, but its expression is usually a too-simplified distinction of good from bad—good migrants, bad owners; good natives, bad invaders; and so forth. Henry Morgan embodies both principles, but Steinbeck's technical mastery is not sufficient to do justice to the char-

29. *TP*, p. 21.

acter; we see the intention, but the treatment is not convincing. Complex but lucid characterization in *The Pearl* allows Steinbeck to express the concept masterfully.

Kino is a simple, honest fisherman and a greedy killer; he defends the family, and his action leads to Coyotito's death; Kino travels into insanity and back again as he travels into the desert and back. He is fated, identifies with the pearl; that selfishness is insane; but always he retains some kindness and he is much puzzled by his nightmare; thus he can return to sanity, to human feeling, after Coyotito's life has become the price of the pearl. The reportorial fact is also a moral insight, since Kino is Everyman, both Cain and Abel in his choice and actions. Juana is both a devoted mother and Kino's willing accomplice in the events that lead to her child's death. Her demand for a doctor is prideful and heartfelt. Juana does try to rid the family of the pearl, sensing it will bring evil and is evil in itself, but she tells Kino to open the huge oyster, she cares for Kino, she imagines the good of the new wealth, and she follows Kino obediently once she is certain that his fate is the pearl's fate. Her selfishness approximates Kino's as a trait of character; like Kino's pride, it is a fact beyond blame:

> It was this thing that made him a man, half insane and half god, and Juana had need of a man; she could not live without a man.[30]

The imagistic association of the pearl and Coyotito is at the heart of the family's shared dualities.

Dualism goes so far as to govern details in the texture of the novel. Kino's early reference to "our fortune" becomes "my misfortune," and his desire to own a rifle becomes his unfelt possession of the rifle of Coyotito's murderer.[31] The association of the fishing village and the town is a duality; both are man-made and necessary to each other. The town feeds exploitively off the village, and the villagers use the town for services they cannot render themselves. The fishermen have tried to ape the town knowledge by hiring their own pearl buyers, who ran off with the pearls; that failure

---

30. *TP*, p. 83. 31. *TP*, pp. 77, 92.

foreshadows and justifies Kino's fate. But brute nature, "the nature of things," is the prime symbol of duality's factualness. No human moralisms apply to the tide pool's cycle of breeding and feeding, birth and death. The scorpion stings Coyotito without malice, by accident; the pearl is a fact, the result of a natural process, an unknowing object which attracts human lusts; above all, the sea exists for itself, bringing death and life to the fishermen and resolving finally in its impassive objectivity all good and evil.

This organic development of a potentially abstract idea is impressive in its structural completeness, and its rich, specific contribution to the tight density of the parabolic form is remarkable in Steinbeck's fiction. The previous allegorical or semiallegorical novels are too plainly manipulated to foreshadow *The Pearl*. Many interesting ideas emerge in those earlier novels, but imagination is never as operative there as in *The Pearl*. Rather, some exterior organizing device, degenerating into allegory, is Steinbeck's usual narrative strategy. In *The Pearl*, the instrument of imagination is the technique of "is" thinking as a function of point of view.

Kino presents the main viewpoint, although an impersonal, omniscient narrator breaks in briefly at times, and there are brief shifts to the angle of vision of other characters. The image of the family's life filters through Kino's sensibility, as he rises, waits for breakfast, and eats. The short, impersonal introduction emphasizes, by contrast, this thorough shift to Kino's senses. Kino and Juana register the scorpion episode, the whole village responds to it, but Kino's mind records the astonishment of Juana's demand for the doctor.

Only to establish the doctor's greed, which Kino cannot know, the viewpoint shifts for a paragraph from Kino to the four churchyard beggars, "experts in financial analysis," whose business it is to know "every little scandal and some very big crimes."[32] They know the doctor—"his ignorance, his cruelty, his avarice, his appetites, his sins," and they join the procession to his house "to see what the fat lazy

32. *TP*, p. 14.

doctor would do about an indigent baby with a scorpion bite."[33] Their consciousness suggests, more effectively than direct information could, that Kino and Juana have come into "the world" in entering the town, in needing the town, that they expose their inner unity to the town's consciously destructive evil. Kino registers this emotion for a paragraph in the fear of the poor before authority, and the viewpoint shifts to an omniscient, scathing indictment. The objective details, however, carry the force of the distinction. The doctor's elaborate breakfast contrasts with Kino's simple meal, his discontent with Kino's joy and rage, his corrupt fat with Kino's healthy vigor. The doctor is told that an Indian baby needs care; he refuses that care when he is offered eight "almost valueless" seed pearls.[34] So a complex of greed, money, and pearls is established; violence is added when the point of view shifts back to Kino:

> Without warning, he struck the gate a crushing blow with his fist. He looked down in wonder at his split knuckles and at the blood that flowed down between his fingers.[35]

It is his public shaming, not exactly Coyotito's need, that produces Kino's rage. He merely injures himself in attempting to alter the relationship between village and town, thus prefiguring the result of his attempt to keep the huge pearl. Kino's violence is selfish in fact, noble in effect. The ambiguous image expands the narrative and climaxes the chapter.

Irony informs Chapter II, relating the context of nature, Juana's demand, Kino's violence, and the centuries of pearl diving to the objective technique of Kino's hunt on the ocean floor "in his pride and youth and strength."[36] Kino's joy in the pearl is violent, like his earlier rage:

> His emotion broke over him. He put back his head and howled. His eyes rolled up and he screamed and his body was rigid. The men . . . raced toward Kino's canoe.[37]

Coyotito is almost forgotten, except that Kino's physical acts echo some of the effects, described earlier, of a scor-

33. *TP*, p. 15.   34. *TP*, p. 18.
35. *TP*, p. 19.   36. *TP*, p. 23.
37. *TP*, p. 31.

pion bite. Through imagery, the town becomes a kind of intelligent scorpion:

> The news stirred up something infinitely black and evil in the town; the black distillate was like the scorpion, or like hunger in the smell of food, or like loneliness when love is withheld. The poison sacs of the town began to manufacture venom, and the town swelled and puffed with the pressure of it.[38]

The subsequent series of events is perceived through Kino's sensibility—the priest's humble request for a gift to the Church, the doctor's more evil machinations, the attempt of the pearl buyers to cheat Kino, punctuated by increasingly violent attacks on Kino by unknown men and broadened by Juana's increasing certainty that the pearl represents evil. The pressure of these events builds up through several days and nights, until, in Chapter V, after Kino has struck Juana and killed a man to keep the pearl, Juana is given an insight—the major instance of her point of view—which leads directly to the climax of the novel:

> Kino moved sluggishly, arms and legs stirred like those of a crushed bug, and a thick muttering came from his mouth. Now, in an instant, Juana knew that the old life was gone forever. A dead man in the path and Kino's knife, dark bladed beside him, convinced her. All of the time Juana had been trying to rescue something of the old peace, of the time before the pearl. But now it was gone, and there was no retrieving it. And knowing this, she abandoned the past instantly. There was nothing to do but to save themselves.[39]

The final, seemingly reasonable sentence involves the pervasive irony through Juana's limited point of view. She reaches this seeming reason by recognizing Kino's identity with the pearl and her identity with Kino, but she cannot know that her counsel ensures Coyotito's death. Here, indeed, Kino is willing to give up, thinking the pearl has been lost in the fight; but Juana finds it and insists they must go away. So by reason of what seems to be reason, Juana continues the "fate" they must share.

The flight is too taut with previously established sugges-

38. *TP*, pp. 34–35.   39. *TP*, p. 84.

tion to seem merely an adventure, and character is fully defined; yet the suspenseful basis in adventure holds attention as character alone could not. Steinbeck takes a craftsman's care in this, as in his fleshing the allegory.

Kino's sense of freedom lasts for about five pages, until he senses the family is being tracked. His consciousness of a continuing evil is realized in the visions of violence and illness he finds by gazing into the pearl. He is unable "to find his vision" in the pearl, but the word is picked up in an ironic shift three pages later; as Kino waits to attack the trackers if they sense him, he finds that "he had only a little vision under the fallen limb."[40] The tempo of flight cuts further into whatever vision Kino had earlier of doing good or simply of possessing power. The family had set out for the north to sell the pearl in a city, but they are forced to cut westward into more barren desert to escape death. The pursuit by the trackers firms Kino's determination to kill them or be killed by them: "There is no choice," he said. "It is the only way. They will find us in the morning."[41] In the event, since Coyotito is killed by accident, Juana's reason and Kino's "strength and his movement and his speed" operate merely to fulfill the "fate" that reason, pride, and money-lust have contrived to build from the neutral object, the enormous "Pearl of the World."

The narrator reenters the novel here, after all passion is spent. He places the story in the fairly remote past and in the common consciousness, as befits a parable, but Kino's sensibility points the family's experience as prologue to the disposal of the pearl:

> In Kino's ears the Song of the Family was as fierce as a cry. He was immune and terrible, and his song had become a battle cry.[42]

We are not allowed to remain in the comforting aura of a distant mythology, suggesting a maimed version of the Holy Family too remote in time to be very real. The remote past is forced into the present by the management of physi-

---

40. *TP*, pp. 98, 101.
41. *TP*, p. 113.
42. *TP*, p. 118.

cal distance. The narrator begins with a paragraph setting
the time; then Kino and Juana are seen by the villagers, at
a distance, the sun behind them; the next several paragraphs draw in very close as Kino and Juana walk by, not
"in single file . . . as usual, but side by side."[43] The physical
detail becomes an aspect of their inner beings:

> The sun was behind them and their long shadows stalked
> ahead, and they seemed to carry two towers of darkness
> with them.[44]

That image carries a redefinition of their unity in darkness,
the darkness Kino wakes from in Chapter I. They seem to
pass by closely, so that we see Kino's rifle and Juana's
terrible bundle in the shawl that she carries "like a sack
over her shoulder."[45] The detail becomes suddenly very
close, suggesting a view that is only inches removed:

> The shawl was crusted with dried blood, and the bundle
> swayed a little as she walked. Her face was hard and lined
> and leathery with fatigue and with the tightness with which
> she fought fatigue. And her wide eyes stared inward on her-
> self. She was as remote and as removed as Heaven. Kino's lips
> were thin and his jaws tight.[46]

The absolute objectivity, the "is" thinking technique, forces
identification with the spectators. That the event "happened to everyone" recognizes a complicity in money-lust
and murder, and it plays a change on the group-man concept
and on Kino's earlier feeling after he realizes the pearl is
his, that "he had broken through the horizons into a cold
and lonely outside."[47] Kino returns on the wave of a feeling of being "immune and terrible," proof that his manhood
has surmounted the previous "shaming."[48] The tragic irony
that the man-child's death is the price of Kino's assurance
of manhood is implicit. The spectators take note of the detachment of pain, as Kino and Juana stride "through the
city as though it were not there," and then we are placed
within Kino's sensibility:

43. *TP*, p. 119.
44. *TP*, p. 119.
45. *TP*, p. 119.
46. *TP*, pp. 119–20.
47. *TP*, p. 41.
48. *TP*, pp. 19, 89, 121.

> He looked into [the pearl's] surface and it was gray and ul-
> cerous. Evil faces peered from it into his eyes, and he saw
> the light of burning. And in the surface of the pearl he saw
> the frantic eyes of the man in the pool. And in the surface
> of the pearl he saw Coyotito lying in the little cave with the
> top of his head shot away. And the pearl was ugly; it was
> gray, like a malignant growth. And the pearl was ugly; it was
> the pearl, distorted and insane.[49]

The visual and auditory effects are on the near side of disaster as literary techniques; they are simple and allegorical
in the bad sense, much like certain of Nathaniel Hawthorne's
more excessive allegorical signs in *The Scarlet Letter*.[50] And
they are much too moralistic for "is" thinking. They succeed, not in having been "placed" with care through the
novel, but in serving (however awkwardly) to signify Kino's
state of mind. Through the suggestiveness of the pearl,
Kino's rendering of past events invokes Aristotelian pity;
as far as Kino's sense of being "immune and terrible" is altered, he returns to humanity.

This process is given in the final lines of the novel, in a
return to "is" thinking presentation, as Kino and Juana
share the point of view:

> Kino's hand shook a little, and he turned slowly to Juana and
> held the pearl out to her. She stood beside him, still holding
> her dead bundle over her shoulder. She looked at the pearl in
> his hand for a moment and then she looked into Kino's eyes
> and said softly, "No, you." And Kino drew back his arm and
> flung the pearl with all his might. Kino and Juana watched
> it go, winking and glimmering under the setting sun. They
> saw the little splash in the distance, and they stood side by
> side watching the place for a long time.[51]

Sunrise has become sunset. With all passion spent, the
family order renewed, and the ritual burial accomplished,
Kino and Juana share a common, unspoken experience of
evil; "having gone through pain and come out on the other

---

49. *TP*, p. 121.

50. Compare the "glare" attributed to the letter, the "glare" in
Chillingworth's eyes as he grows demonic, the character of Pearl,
and so forth.

51. *TP*, pp. 121–22.

side," they renounce the lure of "the world" and can reenter their former Eden, forgiven.[52]

Certainly this ending attempts "a dying fall," a resolution of Miltonic dignity. If it seems a little too easy, if something of "gazing into the golden West" is mixed into the declining rhythm, still, in the context of Steinbeck's work, this ending is not the absolute embarrassment of an imposed, superficial pattern, a failure to connect with the preceding thrust of the materials. With his weak sense of structure, Steinbeck perpetrates that kind of ending in most of the previous fiction. Here, again, *The Pearl* benefits from being built on a preexisting structure.

The ending offers an acceptance of things as they are. The extensive imagery of animal and tide-pool life may serve the function of preparing for this "primitive" moral quietness, this stoic withdrawal and acceptance. Yet the ending is human and just. Men are not animals; but Kino's manhood is more Edenic than worldly. He had striven unsuccessfully, at incalculable cost, to attain manhood in "the world," but he accepts literal and symbolic defeat on his own terms, as a rejection of the values of "the world" and a return to "Eden." As the family's idyllic, prepearl life suggests, Eden may resemble animal or tide-pool life more closely than town life, especially with an imagistic association of scorpion and town as the joint threat to Edenic life.

The culmination of this novel has an intellectual, worked-out plausibility; it is not as simply manipulative as Steinbeck endings can be; but the passage falls a bit short of being absolutely convincing, of having precisely the right image, tone, or gesture that can resolve the created situation. The ending is muted, mysterious, restrained; it does not have the click of daring perfection. Short of ending in the air, like *In Dubious Battle,* Steinbeck can do no better. The flaw in *The Pearl* is noticeable, but not a disaster.

The Pearl is a success. Its singularity is quite as important as the harmony of its parts, for extreme poles of structure dominate in the succeeding work. *The Wayward Bus* is a

52. *TP*, p. 120.

pure allegory with an extreme dramatic structure that is self-sufficient, free somewhat of an object. *East of Eden* is a species of lapsed allegory, an extreme panoramic structure which becomes chaotically free of an object in the process of its development. *The Pearl* is a rare bird in this company, especially since it shares many of Steinbeck's technical and intellectual preoccupations with other, less integrated work.

These distinctions can be specified.

8

Pure Allegory

The Wayward Bus

The Wayward Bus[1] is Steinbeck's first major novel to follow *The Grapes of Wrath*.[2] Although a few details of technique carry over, there are astonishing differences in structure, in materials, and in the degree of their harmony.[3]

The essential point is that Steinbeck applies the theory of the play-novelette to the composition of a large novel. He works out an allegorical control of the materials, which are rendered with the clarity of detail that characterizes "is" thinking. These separate novelistic elements do not fuse; the control is formal, a pure allegory without organic relation to its materials. But in the increasingly strained progression of *The Wayward Bus*, structure and materials pull against each other. The simplified formal artifice is not adequate to the realistic yet simplified materials. The consequence is that *The Wayward Bus* is both lucid and puzzling.[4]

The materials are limited by a strong thematic equation of the good life with a "natural" sexual life, on the order of

1. John Steinbeck, *The Wayward Bus* (New York: The Viking Press, Inc., 1947). Hereafter cited as *WB*.

2. It is useful to date the intervening longer fiction: *The Moon Is Down*, 1942; *Cannery Row*, 1945; *The Pearl*, 1947. Notice that the publication of *Burning Bright*, 1950, is still three years in the future.

3. "The repairs to the bus that open the book are of a piece with the burnt-out connecting rod bearing in *The Grapes of Wrath* (including the same superstition about skinned knuckles). The Chicoy lunchroom also has a prototype in the previous book." Freeman Champney, "John Steinbeck, Californian," *The Antioch Review*, 7:3 (Fall 1947), 359. Quoted by permission of The *Antioch Review*.

The Wayward Bus, not the play-novelettes, is the watershed, because it suggests *certainty*, as a major, and strictly speaking, a non-experimental effort, whereas Steinbeck is experimental in earlier, related work.

4. Here I part company with those critics who praise *The Wayward Bus* on the basis of its thought or conception. I am interested in how well thought is joined with the art of the novel.

existence in the tide pool. Steinbeck uses sexual adjustment here as it is often used in modern literature; it is a convenient and frequently employed metaphor. The tide pool is, however, a reduction of the human condition, not its metaphorical equivalent. In parallel terms, a suggestion of Edenic perfection in *The Pearl* becomes an insistent, schematic assertion of sexual realism in *The Wayward Bus*. The basis of the metaphor remains the tide pool; its nature is altered by its sharper, unqualified identity with contemporary values. The structure exhibits as drastic a reduction. There are many individually excellent panoramic scenes, but there is almost no coherent development.[5] There are many carefully planted character essays in the manner of the earliest novels, but on the whole the characters remain static; there is no strong development to involve or reveal their possible complexities. The allegory dictates the narrative events. Yet the realistic mannerisms of "is"thinking and the sexual bias of the materials assure the sense of an allegorical overlay, a form that is external rather than organic. The realized clarity of the structure is less than the range of the materials.

Steinbeck's intention and method are stated in the prefatory quotation from *Everyman*:

> I pray you all gyve audyence
> And here this mater with reverence,
> By fygure a morall playe;
> The somonynge of Everyman called it is,
> That of our lyves and endynge shewes
> How transytory we be all daye.[6]

Yet the purpose of *Everyman* is transposed by Steinbeck's intentional "mater," the nature of the good life, the contemporary sexual life, placed in a moral context and expressed

---

5. In this respect, Steinbeck returns to the primary defect of the earliest novels. I suggest, however, that a reading of any five or ten pages of *The Wayward Bus* will convince any "common reader" that here is an important novel, perhaps a masterpiece. It is the overall design that qualifies this almost certain judgment. Certainly a polished craftsmanship distinguishes *The Wayward Bus* from a novel as early as *To a God Unknown*.

6. *WB*, p. iv.

"by fygure" or method as an allegory. The transposition is arbitrary even in narrative outline.

A busload of typical, contemporary Americans—young, middle-aged, and old, drawn from every social and economic class—thrown together and then stranded for a few hours, reveal their sexual or moral health to others and to themselves, thereby providing moral instruction which relates to ourselves in the general climate of postwar America. These familiar materials approximate the grouping in such different novels as *In Dubious Battle*, *The Grapes of Wrath*, and *The Pearl*. The device of gathering people into a bus (or train, or airplane, or hotel, or ship, or country estate) is artificial, even shopworn, but what matters finally is the artist's use of the device.

The materials offer two problems in narrative. One is solved brilliantly; the other is untouched. The first problem is to realize the people in themselves and in their context. "Is" thinking contributes the brilliance to this realization. We see, feel, smell, hear, taste, and count by way of "is" thinking. Antonia Seixas (Toni Ricketts) remarks accurately:

> An apprentice writer would do well to study the way, for example, in which the character and past life of Juan Chicoy is conveyed through Steinbeck's inventory of his clothes, his scars, the contents of his pockets, the way he handles a wrench.[7]

This aspect of the novel presents Steinbeck's craft at its best. But in dealing with the second problem, the relation of details and persons to an intentional allegory, Steinbeck en-

7. On Antonia Seixas, see Ch. 5, note 2. Her views are probably Steinbeck's and, if only for that reason, important. Her article first appeared in what is in effect an unobtainable publication, *What's Doing on the Monterey Peninsula*, 1:12 (March 1947). Its successor, *Game & Gossip*, has granted permission to quote from this article. I refer consistently to the reprint: Antonia Seixas, "John Steinbeck and the Non-Teleological Bus," in E. W. Tedlock, Jr., and C. V. Wicker, eds., *Steinbeck and His Critics: A Record of Twenty-Five Years* (Albuquerque: University of New Mexico Press, 1957), pp. 277–78. Excerpts from this work are reprinted by permission of the publisher.

counters or exposes a serious difficulty. The insight that sexual adjustment equates with the good life, pure and smiling, is an end to itself, an unconscionably simplified allegorism, never symbolic or embracing or a means to an end; but it is intentional, and Steinbeck leans on it.

The association of brilliant rendering and implicational patterning is precisely Steinbeck's narrative method in *The Wayward Bus*, as when Juan Chicoy tells a story to Breed that Breed says "don't make any sense," Juan replying, "I know, that's what I like about it."[8] Evidently Steinbeck allows "is" thinking to suggest the infinite mystery of existence, to broaden out the sexual basis of the events, simply by putting down the truth. The presumed assumption is that either the truth makes you free (you gather a moral relevance from the events) or leaves you in ignorance (you do not gather, etc.). Following Steinbeck's hypothetical reasoning by his theory and practice of the play-novelette (the novel that "tells itself," that affects groups through emotion), to refrain from pointing the allegorical framework becomes necessary as well as possible. Insight remains simple because it does not expand (as it does in *The Pearl*) into human experience. The precise detail, the flow of seemingly undirected events, and the index of man's sexual nature as a moral condition, all are relaxed but puzzling ends in themselves. The least of the consequent difficulty is that *The Wayward Bus* has the rigid, purely logical structure of an allegory without the lucid, implicational quality of allegory. There is a still more severe consequence. Because the narrative does not expand in relevance, what Steinbeck presents as a moral allegory has been taken more often at face value, on its own merits, as an excuse to portray a series of tumbles in the hay. The most generous reader can make something more than pornographic sense of the novel only by reducing its characters and its events to the most rigid sort of type-allegory. Seixas, intending to praise *The Wayward Bus*, indicates as much:

> And though Steinbeck devotes pages to marvelously selective descriptions of his main characters, he doesn't tell you how

8. *WB*, pp. 183–84. The story is a small moral fable.

they got that way, or why. It isn't necessary. For they are all "type specimens"—not merely "products," but components of our civilizations. Elliott Pritchard is the type-specimen business man; his wife, Bernice, is the type-specimen "lady," sweet, gentle, and terrifyingly powerful, with the unconscious craftiness of the weak and lazy who must live by rules and force those rules on all around them. There is Horton, the traveling salesman, whose best-selling item is the "Little Wonder Artificial Sore Foot." There are the adolescents, Pimples Carson, apprentice mechanic, and Norma, the homely, pathetic waitress. The three characters most honest, most nearly in contact with their realities, are Mildred Pritchard, the college girl, Camille Oaks, the blond stripper, and Juan Chicoy.[9]

Significantly, this identification of types follows Seixas's praise of Steinbeck's careful, thorough realization of Juan Chicoy. For the fact is that Steinbeck does not realize the characters and their context so fully, through "is" thinking, that the "given" cannot decline to the simplicity of the "type-specimen." One cannot take the blood out of the Rubens nude and say, "This is not really a nude; it is a type-specimen," or still worse, "It is Truth," or Falsehood, or whatever one imagines it to be. Just so with the two Pritchards and the rest of the minor figures, and particularly so with the two major figures, Camille Oaks and Juan Chicoy. Seixas's praise is all too damning.

A severe division between structure and materials is the essential reason for the simple and puzzling impact of *The Wayward Bus*. The structure (the allegorical system) can be admired for itself, like the realized quality of the materials, but there is no way to fuse the two into a harmonious unity. E. W. Tedlock, Jr., and C. V. Wicker hit gently on this crucial point in commenting on the failure of Seixas (or, we may as well say, Steinbeck) to "discuss the possibility of an inherent philosophic contradiction between the social protest and symbolic levels and the non-teleological level" in her account of Steinbeck's four levels of meaning.[10] Steinbeck does not perceive that organic control is absolutely necessary in the practice of the novel, that otherwise

9. Seixas, p. 278.
10. Tedlock and Wicker, "Introduction," p. xxxvi.

the novel tends to fall apart or to pull apart as its basic elements line up in opposition rather than in unity.

Granting this point, it is useful to consider the management of characters and of events. Juan Chicoy and Camille Oaks, the main characters, are types of relatively healthy sexual adjustment, but they have been scarred by "the world": "Juan has an amputated finger; Camille has ugly forceps scars on her jaw."[11] The rare virtues of a self-ordered being are attributed to Juan:

> He was a fine, steady man, Juan Chicoy, part Mexican and part Irish, perhaps fifty years old, with clear black eyes, a good head of hair, and a dark and handsome face. Mrs. Chicoy was insanely in love with him and a little afraid of him too, because he was a man, and there aren't very many of them, as Alice Chicoy had found out. There aren't very many of them in the world, as everyone finds out sooner or later.[12]

The omniscient narrator and the essay method of characterization produce an intense statement, but "is" thinking enhances Juan's secular harmony. Both presentations are smooth, remote, and rounded. An early, central instance is the symbols that Juan collects near the driver's seat of the bus, for they indicate in their range that Juan has deep, richly sensed impulses which rise above logical contradictions, that he is a rounded rather than an abstracted man. Besides a "small metal Virgin of Guadalupe painted in brilliant colors" in a central position "on top of the dashboard," Juan hangs various "penates" to invoke or to ward off worldly powers. These hang "from the top of the windshield," and distract the eye when the bus is moving:

> A baby's shoe—that's for protection, for the stumbling feet of a baby require the constant caution and aid of God; and a tiny boxing glove—and that's for power, the power of the fist on the driving forearm, the drive of the piston pushing its connecting rod, the power of a person as responsible and proud individual. There hung also on the windshield a little plastic kewpie doll with a cerise and green ostrich-feather headdress and a provocative sarong. And this was for the pleasures of the flesh and of the eye, of the nose, of the ear.[13]

11. Seixas, p. 278.
12. WB, p. 6.   13. WB, pp. 19–20.

Several practical objects for defense and against injury fill "a kind of converted glove box"—a pistol, medical supplies, a pint of whiskey—"below the Virgin."[14] "With this equipment Juan felt fairly confident that he could meet most situations."[15]

These are essentially lists, enlivened by their colorful crosshatching. Juan's wide-ranging mind is given as well in the first person, as he reveals mystical propensities in talking about the almost living quality of metal and engines (he is replacing a ring gear), fusing automechanics and insight by relating the topic to Mexican superstition:

> "Metal's funny stuff," he said. "Sometimes it seems to get tired. You know, down in Mexico where I came from they used to have two or three butcher knives. They'd use one and stick the others in the ground. 'It rests the blade,' they said. I don't know if it's true, but I know those knives would take a shaving edge. I guess nobody knows about metal, even the people that make it."[16]

These three ways of presenting Juan share the thematic line that Juan lives in a thoroughly allegorical universe, in a system of vital correspondence. The precision and the realized quality of the detail produce an absolutely credible figure, and most of the novel supports Steinbeck's conception of Juan.

But there is a difficulty in fusing Juan's character with the role of "guide" to the "pilgrims," which the complete allegory requires. For one thing, Juan is too large a figure to be reduced easily to an allegorical function. Further, his relation to the events is limited to his "unconscious design" of stalling the bus in disgust and returning after an unplanned affair with Mildred Pritchard.[17] Juan may be a "guide," but it is clear that he has no ultimate concern for the "pilgrims." His function is far less certain than his striking character. Probably this uncertainty is intended; Seixas suggests as much in commenting on Steinbeck's second level of meaning, following story interest: the level of "social protest":

14. *WB*, p. 21.　　　　15. *WB*, p. 21.
16. *WB*, p. 22.　　　　17. Seixas, p. 278.

> The author seems to be saying, "Here is a typical group of *homo Americanus*. See, this is how they look, this is how they act." And though he seems to be more charmed by certain of his specimens than by others, he is like an entomologist describing the antics of a group of insects; he neither praises nor blames. He understands them, as specimens; perhaps he even loves them in a way, but he would doubtless be horrified to find any but one or two of them in his bed.[18]

Juan has much the same removed attitude toward the events and the passengers that Seixas attributes to Steinbeck-as-novelist. No doubt this distancing is influenced by "is" thinking, by the concept that accurate vision is productive of truth. Few will quarrel with that truism. The difficulty is that a pattern of organic development may not form out of a simple sum of things seen, however brilliantly, as when "is" thinking is used for structural purposes. Then any allegorical claim can be an imposed, arbitrary form. Particularly, Juan amounts to two characters: a realized, interesting example of adjustment to the good life; and an allegorical type of the good shepherd, returning at last to lead the flock to its chosen destination. These aspects of Juan remain separate because they do not occur on the same levels; one derives from character, the other from allegorical function. Therefore, a specific high point, such as Juan's affair with Mildred Pritchard, can seem to be irrelevant to the allegorical pattern—except that Juan returns to the bus at the end of the affair.

Seixas reproduces these tensions with admirable clarity, yet without the dismay I communicate, as she outlines the significance of Juan's return to the bus in relation to "is" thinking:

> We are not deserted; the Juans walk back and dig us out, and the battered old bus lumbers on. But though we go forward, it is only to more of the same. For the non-teleological position is opposed to the teleological notion of "progress." That is, it is in opposition to the idea of a predetermined design or purpose in Nature by which any phenomena can be explained. But at the same time, this "non-causal" viewpoint is a "non-

18. Seixas, p. 279.

blaming" viewpoint, since according to this, everything is simply part of a pattern. . . . It must be remembered that the bus is bound for San Juan de la Cruz—which is also the name of a mystic poet. But it must not be thought that there is any "answer" in these symbolisms, that any solutions are suggested.[19]

Probably this statement represents Steinbeck's intention, but the results are not altogether that pure. The structural use of "is" thinking has two novelistic effects. First, "is" thinking promotes a panoramic structure, a record of "something that happened," a record that acquires dramatic logic only as "a pattern of events."[20] The record is supposedly productive of a pattern; it does not remain simply a record. Hence, "is" thinking tends to assure Steinbeck that an allegorical pattern is self-evident in the truth, the report or record of events, so there can be no harm in imposing an allegorical detail (the bus's destination "happens" to be the name of a mystic poet) on the supposedly objective event. But the event is neither as objective nor as patterned as Steinbeck appears to believe it is, possibly because Juan's characterization is neither quite objective nor quite patterned.

The basic difficulty is that "is" thinking is limited to a sharply realized presentation of detail; it does not have a structural capacity of itself. As a philosophic position, it seems to imply the distancing that is familiar in Romantic poetics, in what John Keats meant by speaking of Shakespeare's "negative capability."[21] However, its practical effect in Steinbeck's usage, in this instance, is that Juan Chicoy's character appears to be unresolved, largely because Steinbeck appears to feel that a series of sharply realized

19. Seixas, p. 280.

20. Seixas, pp. 276–77. Seixas reports that *Of Mice and Men* was first titled *Something That Happened* to suggest its reliance on "is" thinking as a philosophic position.

21. *The Letters of John Keats*, ed. Maurice Buxton Forman (Toronto: Oxford University Press, 1952), No. 32, December 21, 1817. Consult, also, M. H. Abrams, *A Glossary of Literary Terms* (New York: Rinehart & Co., 1957), p. 62. Apparently Keats had in view a theory of artistic objectivity, not, as Seixas asserts for Steinbeck and as Steinbeck's practice here confirms, a principle of structure.

details do constitute a fairly rigid pattern which can be heightened further by the addition of allegorical detail. The fact seems to be otherwise: that Juan Chicoy *is* a sharply realized character, but that his allegorical function is uncertain, indeterminate, partial—an imposed, not an organic claim.

An allegory is superlatively the literary technique that can approximate the remote stance of "an entomologist describing the antics of a group of insects," providing it has no object, no causal base. This is a flat contradiction, so far as the only justification for the use of allegory is to present some moral system in the guise of a fleshed-out fiction. Steinbeck is clearly deluded, then, in presuming that "is" thinking is a literary technique that does without the value-system implicit in any use of allegory. The actual result is an allegory without an object, an imposed pattern in a functional void. *The Wayward Bus* suffers incurably from this error in critical theory—essentially, the theory of the play-novelette.

Possibly because she is less central than Juan or because she has fewer roles to fulfill, Camille Oaks is a more credible person than Juan, with a more credible function. As a naturally provocative woman, surrounded by an uneasy awareness of her mysterious sexual power over men, Camille is forced to retreat constantly from the social implications of her role as a love goddess. She is unable to live a normal life in modern American society. Her situation demonstrates that so-called civilized restraints have corrupted American life at its sexual core.

This somewhat inconclusive assertion is substantiated with considerable success. Steinbeck relies on an image to fuse what Camille is and what she can do, forced as she is to make a living by a perversion of the natural role of a love goddess:

> She tried wearing severe clothes, but that didn't help much. She couldn't keep an ordinary job. She learned to type, but offices went to pieces when she was hired. And now she had a racket. It paid well and it didn't get her in much trouble. She took off her clothes at stags. A regular agency handled her.

She didn't understand stags or what satisfaction the men got out of them, but there they were, and she made fifty dollars for taking off her clothes and that was better than having them torn off in an office.[22]

This explanatory material leads to the image. Camille sits naked in a huge wineglass before clubs of businessmen while red wine runs down "in red streams over her stomach and thighs and buttocks" and, later, is served up to the audience.[23] Often the men are accompanied by their wives. If Camille cannot understand what is amusing in her act, sufficient reasons are provided. The glass, like the occasion, is a barrier that keeps out normal responses; the wine represents blood and suggests torture; the businessmen must take part, as good fellows, in the symbolic maiming ritual. Moreover, Camille's inability to understand the image that society has evolved for her—although she senses "it isn't pretty"—is itself a kind of barrier; it keeps her innocent.[24]

Here allegory is minimal, implicit. "Is" thinking presents the objective image, the bloodied girl in the huge wineglass, and we comprehend its significance. Distancing is accomplished by the reportorial manner as a technique, as in *The Pearl*, not as a structural principle. The factual image carries its expansion naturally and successfully.

The other characters are presented rather flatly in categories, indicating varieties or representative types of sexual abnormality, inhibition, or health in relation to the "normal" standard represented by Juan Chicoy and Camille Oaks. They are placed along a continuum from health to its opposite.

Ernest Horton is a novelty salesman and a war hero. His sexual normality is certified by a frankly predatory maleness, similar to Juan Chicoy's, and by an extraordinary kindness in all circumstances. Horton's sexual normality therefore implies an excellent moral nature; the link is stated rather than justified, much as Juan's allegorical function is foisted on his essential character. Elliott Pritchard is Horton's reverse image. The contrast is the sharper because both

22. *WB*, p. 110.
23. *WB*, p. 287.   24. *WB*, p. 287.

men are "in business," although Horton sells (and lives) with "a kind of shy confidence in his manner and a wincing quality in his face, as though he protected himself from insult with studied technique," whereas Mr. Pritchard has the gray, correct, protected manner of a "president of a medium-sized corporation."[25] Pritchard's moral character derives from a dulled sexual life, dictated by his wife:

> Her husband's beginning libido she had accepted and then . . . gradually strangled, so that his impulses for her became fewer and fewer until he himself believed that he was reaching an age when such things did not matter. . . . His nerves, his bad dreams, and the acrid pain that sometimes got into his upper abdomen he put down to too much coffee and not enough exercise.[26]

His vice is timidity, enforced by an emotionally thin, business-dominated social life and by his acceptance of the controlled robbery and the perverse sexuality that a business ethic permits and encourages. His vice is acquired; his virtue is clouded but evident. He does want to *know*. Although he has acquired the convenient skill of reducing impressions to odd, easily remembered, disconnected facts, he insists on traveling through California by bus, against his wife's objection, because he wants to see for himself the country to which he may retire some day.[27] However, a canny symbol reveals that Mr. Pritchard's vices outweigh his clouded virtues. He cleans his fingernails "with a gold file" whenever experience opens vistas (during this trip, which he had desired) that tend to qualify business life and business ethics. That is, Mr. Pritchard removes the "dirt" of experience with a valuable object that identifies his certain place on the economic ladder.[28] The secondary, sexual implication of "file," a phallic note, is in ironic contradiction to the intended gesture of safe identification. Carried

---

25. *WB*, pp. 37, 39.   26. *WB*, pp. 63, 65.

27. Mr. Pritchard is not unlike Sinclair Lewis's Babbitt, even including the attractive feature, amid so much hypocrisy, of a desire for the truth, the "is" thinking attitude, which distinguishes the sympathetic characters from the others.

28. The association is clinched by repetition. *WB*, pp. 41, 148, 279, 288.

further, into the range of common experience the middle-class Pritchards reject, a file may be used to escape from a prison if it is heavier and made of common iron. Elliott Pritchard is, to be sure, unaware of being imprisoned by the defects of his sexual and moral life. The revealing, objective fact attains a symbolic range of "is" thinking, supported, as shall be seen, by the narrative events.

Louie, the bus driver who brings Camille Oaks to Rebel Corners, is a kind of Jamesian reflector of masculine sexual attitudes by way of his unwillingly comic encounter with Camille. His purely appetitive view of sexual need is cheaply vulgar and ultimately sterile. Camille easily puts him off. His function, however, is to provide a distinction between the sound views of Juan Chicoy and Ernest Horton and the inhibited, "strangled" perversity of an Elliott Pritchard. Louie's debunked performance allows Steinbeck to distinguish the concept of sexual adjustment from simple appetitiveness and to define that teleological value outside the framework of the allegory. In the end, Louie and Elliott are brothers in the flesh.

Mrs. Bernice Pritchard is frigid by nature, by biological definition, just as Camille Oaks is provocative by nature:

> She herself was handicapped by what is known as a nun's hood, which prevented her experiencing any sexual elation from her marriage; and she suffered from an acid condition which kept her from conceiving children without first artificially neutralizing her body acids.[29]

Bernice Pritchard is an antilove goddess through no fault of her own, but she compounds the natural flaws. Her "sluggish and lazy" body requires that she live by rules, not perceptions, but she is responsible for her choices because she is certain of their correctness.[30] Rejecting knowledge, she collects the items of the good life, beginning with her husband's body and mind, and such particulars as a fur coat, a greenhouse, and the trip itself. Above all, she collects the good opinion of "ladies" like herself, and the imagined letter she writes to them continually just as continually trans-

29. *WB*, p. 63.   30. *WB*, p. 64.

mutes experience into the flimflam of a happy holiday. Bernice is played off against Camille in certain particulars. The sexual flaw that shuts her out of the real world is similar to Camille's isolation in the huge wineglass, but Bernice believes that her isolation is normal, that "any variation [is] abnormal and in bad taste," while Camille knows that her job is an economic fact, not her real life, nor is it related to life as she has experienced it.[31] Because Bernice is knowingly ignorant while Camille is knowingly informed, the sexual distinction attains the level of a genuine moral difference, a conscious choice of character.

The two women represent aspects of biological determinism. To go beyond that, identifying secondary results as effective causes, intrudes an indefensible moral claim. Bernice is a comic negation—comic in her certainties and horrible in her ignorance. Ultimately, she is not responsible for what she is. At least Camille has rationalized the sexual causes of her present situation. Would a Bernice Pritchard without a nun's hood be a Camille Oaks? Not likely. The values are too manipulated to carry aesthetic conviction.

The other characters are mere sketches. Mildred Pritchard is unable to follow the examples set by her father and mother. She is curious about sex and ideas, but she knows nothing about love or thought. Pimples Carson, Juan's seventeen-year-old helper, and Norma, the waitress, are frustrated, ugly adolescents. Pimples suffers from acne and Norma suffers from hives; the physical stigmas imply an isolation that is enforced by a cultural background of the radio and the movies. Since Pimples and Norma have such vague sexual lives, their moral characters are unformed. Van Brunt and Alice Chicoy are sexually frustrated adults; they share violent emotions and find their outlets in hatred and rage. Van Brunt has had two minor strokes that have "knocked the cap off one set of his inhibitions: He was pantingly drawn toward young women, even little girls."[32] Alice Chicoy is afraid of losing Juan because she is growing old. Her bad temper and violence correspond to Van Brunt's; each shares a moral chaos that stems from a sexual

31. *WB*, p. 63. 32. *WB*, p. 295.

cause, but their warped viewpoints are as self-evident, as unquestioned, as Bernice Pritchard's. Pimples and Norma can be saved; the three driven adults cannot.

Essentially, however, all of the characters are sketches so far as an allegorized sexuality marks the limit of knowledge —what we know of them, and what they know of themselves. They seem much like "humor" types, or elements in a biological design, rather than realized personages. A "type" study need not result in an abstract or simplified humanity. But the objectivity of the "is" thinking presentation of details, admirable in itself, emphasizes Steinbeck's own purposefulness or lack of objectivity. The restriction of character to a uniform "original cause," as sexual determinism, focuses attention on the design of the novel, the succession of narrative events. "Is" thinking sharpens the presence of a selective, authorial hand, for "is" thinking allows no way to minimize the process of selection. Hence, the characters do not acquire an extensive human relevance; they are selected rather than rendered. The resulting emphasis on the narrative pattern raises the question of whether that pattern is profound enough to justify its emphasis.[33]

The events may be summarized as follows. Juan's job or duty is to transport the assorted passengers from Rebel Corners to San Juan de la Cruz, but he finds that a flooding river has washed out a bridge shoddily built by a corrupt political machine. Juan takes a vote on what to do—turn back or go ahead—and a majority decide to proceed via an old road, once used by stagecoaches, now possibly also washed out; it exists, but it is a difficult road. Due to a general weariness with life (a nagging wife, the squabbling passengers), Juan takes the chance and mires the bus; he leaves the passengers "marooned on a bare hillside with

33. I disagree with Lisca's opinion that *The Wayward Bus*, "unlike most Steinbeck novels, is more concerned with action on the level of character than on the physical level of events." Peter Lisca, *The Wide World of John Steinbeck* (New Brunswick: Rutgers University Press, 1958), p. 233. I demonstrate in the text that character is mainly an element in a design to which it contributes, that it does not exist richly in itself. Other Steinbeck novels do employ character in the proper sense—*In Dubious Battle, The Grapes of Wrath, The Pearl.* Steinbeck's most rigid novels do not.

caves for shelter and a crate of Mother Mahoney's Home Baked Pies for food."[34] The passengers confront various truths about themselves while Juan is gone for help. He returns, gets the bus out of the mud, and the trip is completed. Seixas comments:

> At the end, nothing is resolved, nothing is very much changed. . . . The bus is wayward, its passengers "are the way they are."[35]

These somewhat casual events acquire significance if they are read, like character, as elements in an allegorical pattern—a double reference involved in the formal division of good from evil along a sexual line. In the good life, sexuality is a standard of value which satisfies itself, as in the tide pool, as a drive to reproduce. An evil life lacks that awareness. The result or cause of psychic deformity, committed to the tide pool's drive to consume, the evil life is restricted to appetite, to material goods, and to worldly advantages. The narrative is fitted to this pattern of biological morality.

Juan Chicoy's role in the events is exemplary. His duty is to "guide" largely unworthy "pilgrims," but disgust overcomes him and he rejects duty to return to the happy past. He cannot find it; "a bursting, orgasmic delight of freedom" from duty is not lasting because the past is dead.[36] Mildred follows Juan and seduces him. They "can't go to Mexico," so they "go back and dig out the bus and drive to San Juan."[37] A return to the past is impossible, an affair is simply good luck, hence the real world is the moral call to duty.

With these events, even more than with character, it is difficult to fuse the sexual life and the moral life. Steinbeck assumes an inherent fusion in the materials, but that fusion does not result. Juan and Mildred's affair does not relate, in itself, to Juan's return to the bus or to a sexual standard. The events occur; they do not effectively connect.

The lesser characters are put more credibly into events that accept an allegorical dimension, a less arbitrary fusion

34. *Seixas*, p. 278.
35. Seixas, p. 279.
36. *WB*, pp. 244–45.
37. *WB*, p. 290.

of the sexual standard and the moral life. Particularly, in the aftermath of Juan's abandonment of the bus, the passengers enact a range of moral responses in accord with their established sexual drives, in a pattern of parallels and contrasts.

Bernice Pritchard's sudden quarrel with Elliott Pritchard breaks "a pattern she had been years building, the story that because of her sweetness her marriage was ideal."[38] She becomes a monster, "a tough woman," for all to see.[39] Mr. Pritchard cannot see through his wife but events force him to face himself. In succession, Ernest Horton pricks his moral certainty, and Camille reveals his submerged lust after his hypocritical try to "hire" her. Finally, he has to live with having forced sexual intercourse on his wife in reaction to Camille's revelation. Bernice is incapable of knowledge; she uses Pritchard's lust to get an orchid house for herself. The sealed enclosure, a symbol of status, a value without use, images her conscious, formal mind. Mr. Pritchard is more aware; he has learned that he must continue to please Bernice, as Juan must continue to drive the bus, but Pritchard has none of Juan's pleasure in duty. Sitting with Van Brunt, Pritchard wishes for death:

> "Why can't it be me here, dying, instead of this old man? He's never going to have to go through anything again."[40]

In the allegorical dimension, Bernice can live for appetite as Mr. Pritchard cannot (in effect, she whores—sells extorted favors, applies blackmail), and he cannot escape feeding her materialistic appetite. Van Brunt's third and probably final stroke is a neat parallel—a literal chance of death—with Mr. Pritchard's unillusioned, final insight. Throughout, Van Brunt is too neatly useful to the allegory and too fated on the level of events to be fully credible. He predicts the washed-out bridge, knowing how it was built, and he objects to any decision by the group; in Peter Lisca's phrase, "he is the Satan of this world on wheels."[41] He does not convey the terror of a Satan, however, because he is too

38. *WB*, p. 251.   39. *WB*, p. 285.
40. *WB*, p. 305.   41. Lisca, p. 244.

contrived a figure. He is not responsible for his quarrelsome character or for his lusts; both are side effects of earlier strokes. He does not compound these natural flaws with a coating of illusion, like Bernice Pritchard. He responds to events, but he is not shaped by them. Hence, it is best to read Van Brunt as a strictly allegorical type. As such, as a Satan in a moral world, he is struck down, in contrast with Juan's decision to resume the trip. Alice Chicoy's huge, destructive drunk, back at the inn, is a less contrived analogue to Van Brunt's function. Alice is an unformed Satan, reduced to self-pity in her ugly old age. Quite unlike Van Brunt, Alice is a comic figure, since her rage is drunken and finds an ultimate object in a bluebottle fly:

> Her flesh crawled with hatred. All her unhappiness, all her resentments, centered in the fly.[42]

Alice's entirely teleological drunk has the energy to exist for itself—as it does, literally, in a separate chapter. Its patterned, allegorical impact is reduced correspondingly. Pattern is similarly accidental in the events that support a positive value. Mildred leaves the bus mainly because she is disgusted by the quarrel between her parents; she searches for Juan as a second thought. Camille accepts Ernest Horton's frank, casual offer of a dinner in a frank, casual manner. Norma learns some technique from Camille, but her new face and a confession of loneliness lead Pimples to attempt a rape. This is unfortunate, but Norma is cheered by Camille, and Pimples serves Juan manfully in extricating the bus from the mud.

"Is" thinking merely presents, yet some elements of a tighter pattern are visible close under the flow of events. Mildred becomes Juan's lover, as Horton may become Camille's. Norma accepts Camille as a symbolic mother; Pimples finds in Juan a symbolic father. Norma's acceptance of Camille's instruction in makeup, Pimples's insistence that Juan call him Kit, like Norma's shaken belief in the myths of work and spiritual love and Pimples's belief in scientism, appear to be casual associations, but they imply

42. *WB*, p. 178.

that the youngsters will benefit from healthy models they can worship.[43] Horton's experience in war debunks Pritchard's position that making money is equal to service and suggests that postwar values are an improvement on prewar innocence. The pattern of contrast between Camille and Beatrice is complicated by Camille's wish to live as Beatrice seems to: "She knew as well as anything that that was not what she would ever get."[44] The tightest pattern is the contrast between the Chicoys and the Pritchards. Alice has the virtue of passion, which Bernice lacks. Juan understands his work; Elliott cannot risk understanding what he does. Alice hurts no one but herself; Bernice punishes Elliott after he rapes her. Juan knows that Alice's violence has a sexual cause, and he has the power to keep her from harming anyone; Elliott is unaware of his wife's frigidity, mistakes it for gentility, so he is unable to prevent her from imposing a "genteel" pattern on his life.

The credibility of this range of moral response depends on our consciousness of an allegorical pattern. But "is" thinking diffuses the impact of the allegory, reducing it to an intricate and schematic arrangement which seems thin and inconclusive, a matter of parallels and contrasts, either unclear in their linkage to the central event (as in the affair between Juan and Mildred) or somewhat obvious (as in most of the materials that concern the lesser characters). Therefore, and patently as Steinbeck intended, *The Wayward Bus* is in part a dramatic structure, a rigid allegory, and in part a panoramic structure, a record of things seen without comment. Our reactions fall between these structural extremes, into the void. Seixas's defense of "is" thinking in relation to *The Wayward Bus* is relevant here, as a solid, uncomplicated statement of how the novel should be read:

> If we regard it as an account, "not of what could be or should be, or might be, but rather of what actually is," the games we can play with its symbolism are endless.[45]

43. *WB*, pp. 9–12, 16, 29, 57, 120–21, 123, 159–60, 205–6, 312.
44. *WB*, p. 110.
45. Seixas, p. 280.

This statement reintroduces, at a reasoned and sophisticated pitch, Steinbeck's early and innocent idea of an "open" novel, a novel that "tells itself," like the loosely structured early novel, *The Pastures of Heaven*, or like the later, more overtly thematic novel, *Cannery Row*. But *The Wayward Bus* is not a loosely structured novel, or a thematic novel; it is an overt allegory.

This division in Steinbeck's thinking amounts to a strong pull between structure and materials—between allegory and the objective record. There is a considerable amount of allegorical detail which is difficult to reconcile with an objective record of what "is." In fact, there is no reconciliation. The two methods are separable. True, "the games we can play with its symbolism are endless," but only because the allegory-as-game is separable from the objective record of things seen. At times the allegory is firmly directive; at times the objective record is foremost, and it meanders, much like a guessing game.

A selection of details can suggest the uneven quality of reference in *The Wayward Bus*. First is the peculiarity that the bus's destination happens to be the name of a mystic poet. The bus's original name, "El Gran Poder de Jesus (the great power of Jesus)," is just visible under the name "Sweetheart," "boldly lettered on front and rear bumpers."[46] The bus is allegorical, both a means of transport and a world. Juan Chicoy's initials are significant, like Jim Casy's in *The Grapes of Wrath*.[47] The passengers see "REPENT" painted on a cliff near the place where the bus stalls. These hinting names may imply the content of an allegory in the modern shift from divine to human values and may also imply that crimes against God are no more evil than crimes against one's sexual nature. The possibly asserted fusion of theological and secular value is not altogether self-evident in other aspects of the novel, but they are lucid. This much is less true of a further detail. The bus

46. *WB*, p. 21.

47. Steinbeck wrote to Pascal Covici, after sketching out the novel in 1945, that Juan Chicoy was to be "all the god the fathers you ever saw driving a six cylinder, broken down battered world through time and space." Lisca, p. 232.

cannot pass over a jerry-built bridge that a grafting political machine is responsible for building; the journey continues along an abandoned stagecoach trail that follows an ancient footpath. The defective bridge may represent a dishonest, hypocritical modernity; the old trail may represent a return to the honest, self-sufficient, God-centered values of the pioneers. This interpretation surfaces in Juan's self-justifying thought that it would be good for the passengers to be abandoned to make their way in a wilderness:

> They'd got so used to throwing their troubles on other people they had forgotten how to take care of themselves. It would be good for them. Juan could take care of himself and he was going to start doing it too.[48]

Ernest Horton echoes this thought by doubting Mr. Pritchard's faith in the correct ordering of things:

> "Suppose you had to stay out here two weeks. Could you keep from starving to death? Or would you get pneumonia and die?" "Well," said Mr. Pritchard, "you see, people specialize now." "Could you kill a cow?" Ernest insisted. "Could you cut it up and cook it?"[49]

Mr. Pritchard is stung sharply enough to take Juan's pistol to kill a cow, but he is distracted along the way into the disastrous interview with Camille. Now, this narrative ordering is lucid. The Pritchards of this world are confused. It is less certain that the old trail is a viable detail in a coherent allegorical system. The pioneer virtues do not save even the best of the "pilgrims," nor do they connect necessarily with sexual honesty. The passengers are saved by Juan's know-how and Pimples's efforts; Camille, Norma, Mildred, and Ernest help a bit under Juan's direction, but even these mainly sympathetic characters are unable to care effectively for themselves. Only the Pritchards do not take part in the salvage (salvation?) effort. So the momentarily comic past–present comparison is simplified into narrative irrelevance, in itself and in what it seems intended to suggest. This kind of simplification reflects Steinbeck's uncertain handling of allegory in the context of "is" think-

48. *WB*, p. 234.   49. *WB*, p. 276.

ing. As a crucial instance, San Juan de la Cruz is the intentionally vague, undefined goal of the bus trip or pilgrimage.
"Is" thinking cannot make it other than vague. If the suggestiveness of the allegory is a game that provides no solution, as Seixas indicates and as the allegorical details appear
to confirm, then it is appropriate that the goal of the "pilgrims" is undefined and that "nothing is very much changed
for most of them."[50] Then, however, the moral burden of
the novel—that one's sexual life implies one's moral state
—tends to dissolve or to be a statement rather than a proven
fact. In that light, Steinbeck appears to call on "is" thinking to avoid a complex thematic development of character
and event, to drop away from moral suggestiveness within
the novel. Spots of the novel adhere rigidly to allegory, and
other spots meander; these differences occur by chance
and as a direct result of the division in Steinbeck's novelistic
method.

Within Steinbeck's shifts in method there is a certain kind
of artistic strategy—the kind that avoids earned harmony
by either planting allegorical signposts bodily in the novel
or by sidestepping the assertion of any profound commitment to a thoroughly articulated position. The novelistic result is a basic falseness, the kind of conceptual falseness
that Steinbeck practiced in *Cup of Gold* but exorcised in the
preliminary stages of his work on *The Grapes of Wrath*. The
visible, practical effect for the materials is a series of petty
details, like the JC initials, recalling the play on Elizabeth–
Ysobel in *Cup of Gold*, or a series of arbitrary implications,
like the wash-out of the bridge or the trip's goal. The structure is damaged by its internal contradictions. Violent
swings from comic situations, like the equation of cow-
killing and moral freedom, to allegorical situations, like
the equation of sexual and moral health, are simplified and
manipulated aspects of a merely implicit structure—the
events set down as they happen. The impact is not solid; it
is diffuse and uncertain.

This is apparent even in close details. For example, Ernest
Horton's rejection of Elliott Pritchard's values does not

50. Seixas, pp. 279–80.

imply the expected, moralistic connection, simply because Horton's only superiority is a greater honesty in his wish to have money—or Camille—than Mr. Pritchard can muster. Because Horton has a clearer awareness of "the world" than Mr. Pritchard, Horton is smoother and more efficient, and he suffers no qualms, ulcers, or frustrations. Really, then, Horton is the true heir of Mr. Pritchard, who calls him "son" to gain his confidence, for Horton is the type of the modern executive as Pritchard is the type of the older, cruder Babbitt.[51] Except on that basis, no solid distinction exists between the two men. Since the division of "good" from "evil" cannot occur in the absence of direct opposition, Steinbeck forces a superficially moral distinction between the two men, namely, that any need is "good," not in itself, but in the relative openness and honesty of its expression. Therefore, Horton's straightforward proposition to Camille is "good" (and rewarded), but Pritchard's hypocritical offer is "bad" (and goes unrewarded). In fact, as foreshadowing, Camille prefers the few men who "openly and honestly simply wanted to go to bed with her and told her so . . . because she could say yes or no and get it over with."[52] This early passage is predictive, but it does not provide a profound moral distinction. Horton's need is as genuine (or as selfish) as Pritchard's. The clearest conclusion is in itself ambiguous: The more predatory male, who need not be the better, wins the girl. This ambiguity meshes with Horton's willingness to join with Pritchard to make money. Superior realism and self-awareness extend "success" into sexual matters, without being a moral index in themselves.

The total structure of the novel is similarly uncertain. The predominant structure is panoramic for roughly half the novel. The characters and events are presented broadly, often in flat essay form. Yet the predominant structure is dramatic in roughly the second half of the novel, as the active consequences of the earlier blocks of essays. Steinbeck does not attempt to bridge the two methods of presentation. For example, the Virgin of Guadalupe is a sig-

51. *WB*, p. 158.   52. *WB*, p. 109.

nificant allegorical sign, Juan's "connection with eternity," his direct line to God.[53] Her significance is spelled out in Chapter II in essay form; she reappears in Chapter XIV as the force that drives Juan back to "guide" the "pilgrims." Her initial presentation is panoramic; she is planted early and visibly, but put aside for some two hundred pages. Her fictional necessity requires a strained leap from one kind of structure to another. Or it may be with a bow toward "is" thinking that Steinbeck points to a moral triumph in Juan's return to duty but refrains from fusing that suggestion with the affair between Juan and Mildred. Quite as he arranges sexual encounters between most of the characters, he suggests that the couplings happen by chance and reflect "tensions" that "come to a head." He allows "the characters [to] define their relationships to each other" so that each character must confront "a reality within himself or his world" although "at the end, nothing is resolved."[54] Seixas's phrases capture the twists in the logic of the novel—or the failure of any ultimate object in the uncertainty of Steinbeck's handling of the separate elements of "is" thinking and allegory. The actual, suggested, or attempted couplings of Juan and Mildred, Mr. Pritchard and Camille, Mr. Pritchard and Mrs. Pritchard, and Pimples and Norma, would seem to have no reference beyond the fact that they do occur. Repetition is a familiar device in comedy. Nearly anything that happens five or six times will seem comic because it is repeated. This effect results from the sexual linkings, reiterated seemingly for their own sake toward the close of *The Wayward Bus,* yet the effect of comedy is unintended given the novel's burden of a moralistic seriousness.

On the basis of these observations, *The Wayward Bus* is essentially an irresponsible work, an "open" novel that avoids being either a completed allegory (although much allegory is hinted) or a thoroughly objective record (although objectivity is much in evidence). Worse, Steinbeck does not seem to be aware of any defect. The presumption must be that he was satisfied when he finished *The Way-*

---

53. *WB*, p. 20.   54. Seixas, pp. 278–79.

ward Bus and remained satisfied with the work. In fact, this novel is the pattern of his later work in longer fiction, whether the treatment is comic or tragic.

This development is neither unlikely nor unexpected. It exists as a possibility in the earliest novels; it is present in the final third of *The Grapes of Wrath*; it is nearly the entire substance of the later play-novelettes; it mitigates against the complete rendering of such cheerfully loose novels as *Tortilla Flat* or *Cannery Row*; and it is excluded altogether only from *In Dubious Battle* and *The Pearl*. Indeed, this development seems to mark an emphatic and an apparently conscious choice by a multiple-faceted talent. If so, it is a choice Steinbeck had been leaning toward for some time.

The choice does not work fortunately in *The Wayward Bus*; it results in disaster in the succeeding, massive novel, *East of Eden*. Most of Steinbeck's contemporary reviewers took note of the polished craftsmanship of *The Wayward Bus* but expressed shock that ranged from Bernard De Voto's almost kindly adjectives, "amusing, absorbing, superficial," to Joseph Henry Jackson's flat statement of dismay: "In my opinion I'm sorry to say, the novel is not Steinbeck at his best . . . nor Steinbeck at what a good many people thought he was going to become."[55] Rather alone in praising its structure, Carlos Baker observed that the novel has "as subtle and neat a horizontal structure as Steinbeck has ever evolved."[56] A few years later, in more detailed papers, the critics remained divided in opinion. Freeman Champney, in an early paper, raged:

> When he abandons Man as Man for Man as Biological Freak he goes all the way. He jettisons not only hope and progress but cause and effect as well. Which leaves the vertebrates of *The Wayward Bus*, animated by the simpler forms of proto-

55. Bernard De Voto, "John Steinbeck's Bus Ride into the Hills," *The New York Herald Tribune Weekly Book Review*, February 16, 1947, p. 2; Joseph Henry Jackson, *San Francisco Chronicle*, February 16, 1947, p. 17.

56. Carlos Baker, "Mr. Steinbeck's Cross-Section," *The New York Times Book Review*, February 16, 1947, pp. 1, 31.

plasmic irritability, and deprived of even a biological dignity by their silly pretensions that they are up to something noble.[57]

This reaction is amusing, but does not move criticism very far. Writing in 1949, Blake Nevius sensed a division in Steinbeck's motivation but did not specify its nature:

> In his latest characters evasion has become a settled habit of mind. Juan Chicoy, longing to desert his wife and return to Mexico, shuffles off the decision onto the Virgin of Guadalupe. . . . And yet this is Steinbeck's "man of complete manness" . . . the successor to Mac in *In Dubious Battle*, Slim in *Of Mice and Men*, and Doc in *Cannery Row*, imperturbable men who can do things with their hands and are equal to every situation.[58]

In the same year, Woodburn O. Ross stated the nature of the division implicitly in a critical insight at the conclusion of a paper that proposed to define Steinbeck's values:

> The significance of Steinbeck's work may prove to lie in the curious compromise which it effects. It accepts the intuitive, nonrational method of dealing with man's relation to the universe—the method of the contemporary mystics. But, unlike them, it accepts as the universe to which man must relate himself the modern, scientifically described cosmos.[59]

Ross's insight seems to be accurate. In terms of craft, Steinbeck uses allegory, which implies an awareness of a unified pattern, and "is" thinking, which aims (like the experiments of the scientist) to capture the surface of whatever exists. These aspects of intuition and science do not fuse because Steinbeck presumes their inherent fusion in the materials of *The Wayward Bus*. Hence, "the curious compromise" fails as an expression of the art of the novel. Seixas and Peter Lisca, the most convinced defenders of the novel, divide the argument along the lines of Ross's insight. Mainly, Seixas praises the value of Steinbeck's thought as the rela-

---

57. Champney, p. 359.

58. Blake Nevius, "Steinbeck: One Aspect," *The Pacific Spectator*, 3 (Summer 1949), 310. Quoted by permission of the author.

59. Woodburn Ross, "John Steinbeck: Naturalism's Priest," *College English*, 10 (May 1949), 438. Copyright © 1949 by the National Council of Teachers of English. Reprinted with permission.

tion of "is" thinking to experience, while Lisca praises the excellence of Steinbeck's design, or the consistently allegorical characters and events.[60] These viewpoints are correct so long as they remain separated. Difficulties arise when an effort is made, as in this study, to regard the novel as a whole. Then the separation of "is" thinking from the allegory becomes all too clear as the governing reason for the aesthetic wrongness *and* the craftsmanship in *The Wayward Bus*.

Steinbeck's reputation among critics commences its irrecoverably steep decline at just this point. The cause is not a sell-out, a betrayal of social concern or analysis by the most famous novelist of the Depression, for surely *The Wayward Bus* is a trenchant, accurate portrayal of the darker side of the American dream. The overwhelming sense of a failed talent in this novel is not at all thematic. The betrayal, the failure, is almost entirely artistic. The recurring charge that Steinbeck cannot handle ideas is more accurately phrased as Steinbeck's relative inability to achieve a convincing expression of ideas—a harmony of structure and materials. No doubt the comedy of sexual mannerisms is a significant theme in America. The play-novelette form is less than ideal for the expression of that theme and of most other themes. Steinbeck's inability to comprehend this crux is apparent in his dismissal of negative criticism—and in his forging ahead to the disaster that is *East of Eden*.

60. Consult Seixas, in Tedlock and Wicker, pp. 275–80, and Lisca, pp. 231–47. I am speaking of tendencies, but they are rather strong ones.

9

Lapsed Allegory

East of Eden

The culmination of five years of determined labor, *East of Eden*[1] is clearly Steinbeck's earnest effort to attain major status as a novelist. *The Grapes of Wrath* vanishes in Steinbeck's claim for *East of Eden*:

> I think everything else I have written has been, in a sense, practice for this. . . . If *East of Eden* isn't good, then I've been wasting my time. It has in it everything I have been able to learn about my art or craft or profession in all these years.[2]

The more balanced judgment is that *East of Eden* is a strangely unblended novel, an impressive, greatly flawed work, and a major summation of the various stresses between structure and materials which abound in Steinbeck's novels.

The real importance of *East of Eden* does not lie in Steinbeck's mistaken claim to greatness, revealing as it is, but in its testimony—much like a completed blueprint—to the author's enduring difficulty in fusing structure and materials into a harmonious whole.

East of Eden (1952) is preceded by a postwar group of novels that embody various aspects of the art of fiction. *Cannery Row* (1945) is relatively a panoramic structure, a novel dependent on "is" thinking. *Burning Bright* (1950) is relatively a dramatic structure, a mythological–allegorical novel. *The Pearl* (1947) and *The Wayward Bus* (1947) lie unequally between these two structural extremes. *The Pearl* is a realized, organic structure, a brilliant resolution of an implicit pull between structure and materials, perhaps because Steinbeck has a parable structure to begin with. *The*

1. John Steinbeck, *East of Eden* (New York: The Viking Press, Inc., 1952). Hereafter cited as *EE*.
2. Bernard Kale, "The Author," *The Saturday Review of Literature*, 35 (September 20, 1952), 11.

Wayward Bus is overtly an allegorical novel; its possible harmony comes apart because Steinbeck fails to notice that "is" thinking is inappropriate (as he uses it here) to express an allegory. Each of these aspects of the art of fiction is re-iterated and exaggerated in *East of Eden* through a mytho-logical–allegorical treatment that is given in part by alle-gorizing and in part by a closely realized, episodic wealth of detail. This summation of "is" thinking and the technique of the late play-novelette is rooted in Steinbeck's artistic beginnings, although the smooth realization of the accom-plished craft is a result of maturity. In this respect, *The Wayward Bus* is a close relative to *East of Eden*.[3] Other-wise, the novels differ widely. Steinbeck intends to con-struct a major allegory in *The Wayward Bus*, but the ma-terials excite greater interest than the artificial structure— the people are more interesting than the story. In *East of Eden*, as most of the fully favorable and partially favorable reviewers noticed, the definite episodic interest and the im-pressive moral range involve a fairly implausible set of characters. This rough division suggests a major difference which surrounds a fascinating similarity. New and old, dif-ferent and the same, *East of Eden* relates suggestively, not bindingly, to Steinbeck's postwar fiction and to his earliest efforts to elevate materials into mythology within a func-tioning structural framework. He is a mature craftsman in *East of Eden*, but his grasp of the major aesthetic problem, the harmonious unity of structure and materials, remains as fumbling as ever.

3. In such Steinbeck efforts to construct allegory as the later play-novelettes, and in early efforts to create a mythology (for example, *To a God Unknown*), the scale is smaller or the technique is less formed. Scope and craft make for an essentially new work. But I cannot accept Lisca's revisionist judgment, which argues that Stein-beck's career is fractured rather than unified in that "there is very little in *East of Eden* which goes back further than *Burning Bright*." Peter Lisca, *The Wide World of John Steinbeck* (New Brunswick: Rutgers University Press, 1958), p. 275. My argument demonstrates that certain tensions in Steinbeck's work become more exaggerated in time, but I do not think *East of Eden* reflects essentially new ten-sions. Steinbeck's difficulties with the harmony of structure and ma-terials are of a piece, at greater or lesser degrees of intensity.

As its title suggests, *East of Eden* draws on Steinbeck's moral insight into the biblical story of our most remote (and perhaps mythical) ancestors, Cain and Abel, particularly on Cain's exile to "the land of Nod, on the east of Eden." Steinbeck's insight develops from the fact that we are descended from the murderer, Cain, and only through him from the good brother, Abel. Lisca's summary is convenient:

> Steinbeck sees this story in Genesis as a true account of man's condition, especially as made clear in the Lord's words to Cain after rejecting his sacrifice: "If thou doest well, shalt thou not be accepted? and if thou doest not well, sin lieth at the door. And unto thee shall be his desire, and thou shalt rule over him." Steinbeck grounds his interpretation of the story on a new translation of the Hebrew word *timshel*, which the King James version renders as "thou shalt." He proposes that the word is more meaningfully and truly rendered as "thou mayest," for this gives man responsible moral choice.[4]

So, in principle and in practice, God presents to Cain and to his heirs the free will to choose between good and evil. This insight is a mutation of Steinbeck's fairly constant interest in the nature of the good life, presented as a mythology in *East of Eden*.

Steinbeck embodies this ambitious thematic insight in the histories of two families, the Trasks and the Hamiltons. Three generations are represented in each family. The time-span extends from 1860 to 1918. Most of the action occurs in the Salinas Valley in California. The difference between East and West, or more generally the impact of the knowledge of good and evil in Eden, define the frame of reference.[5] Because the Eden incident is presumed to recur throughout time, Eden and West are identical terms; and the quasi-historical record of the two families recapitulates the original mythology.

The several generations of Trasks and Hamiltons are more

4. Lisca, pp. 261–62. The ambitious attempt "to justify the ways of God to man" places *East of Eden* in a direct line of descent with *The Divine Comedy* and *Paradise Lost* as an authorial intention.

5. Consult Henry Nash Smith, *Virgin Land: The American West as Symbol and Myth* (Cambridge, Mass.: Harvard University Press, 1950), especially Books I and III, "Passage to India" and "The Garden of the World."

complicated than the family organization in *The Grapes of Wrath,* so a genealogical chart and a supplement of important characters is a distinct help:

1. From Connecticut—three generations

Cyrus Trask (c. 1840–1894)—Mrs. Trask (c. 1840–1862)
/
        Adam (1862–1918)—Cathy Ames (1872–1918)
                Caleb (1901——)
                Aron (1901–1918)
    —Alice Trask (c. 1846–c. 1877)
/
      Charles (1863–1912), probable father
              of Caleb

2. From Ireland—three generations

Samuel Hamilton (c. 1850–1912)—Liza (c. 1850–1917)
/
      Una, Lizzie, George, Dessie,
      Will, Olive (Steinbeck's mother),
      Tom, Mollie, Joe

3. Other characters:
   a. Lee (c. 1880——), a Chinese servant to Adam Trask
   b. Abra Bacon (c. 1901——), in love with Aron Trask, later with Caleb Trask
   c. John Steinbeck (1902–1968), the third generation of the Hamilton family, the teller of the story

The essential structural presumption is the necessity of a close, working parallel between the two families. Steinbeck does not provide any structure of this kind. Certain minor, inadequate, or strained parallels occur. Samuel Hamilton's life is happy and Adam Trask's is not; Liza Hamilton has many children, unlike Cathy–Kate Trask, and in old age Liza develops a taste for alcohol, of which only a little is poison to Cathy; Tom Hamilton is "wild" and responsible for the death of Dessie, his favorite sister; Caleb Trask is "wild" and responsible for the death of Aron, his lovable brother. These limited, somewhat mechanical parallels are incapable of unifying a novel as massive as *East of Eden.* Finally, Steinbeck gives far more attention to Cathy's history outside the Trask family (as Kate) than proportion alone could warrant.[6]

6. John Steinbeck, *Journal of a Novel* (New York: The Viking Press, Inc., 1969), pp. 39, 48, 96–98, 112, 124, 146.

The lack of a structure is explained in part by the biographical record of Steinbeck's correspondence and in part by an interview Steinbeck gave to the *Saturday Review* one month before the publication of *East of Eden*.[7] Steinbeck began to compose a family saga for his two sons, but the fictional family, the Trasks, grew to be more important. The happenstance result is a revealing view (in Lisca's account) of Steinbeck's inability to deal with the necessities of structure:

> The author realized that he had a far different book on his hands from what he had originally conceived, one which centered on the Trasks and not on the Hamiltons, Steinbeck's maternal family. By this time, however, the two families were inextricably entangled, and the author decided to keep them that way, but reduced the story of his own family to its vestigial elements and struck out all the special passages written to his sons.[8]

This method created several problems. The fortunes of the two families are not really "inextricably entangled" but have a few slight parallels. Steinbeck went ahead with a seriously imbalanced novel rather than revise from the beginning. Of course, the play-novelette form in which he had been working accepts a sacrifice of the organic structure of a novel for the sake of a moralism, and in the literary application of "is" thinking, the fact—whatever "is"—must be respected even at the expense of organic form. Hence, the curious imbalance of a moral story and a factual story, the one imposed on the other to the utter destruction of organic form.

Steinbeck's disregard for structure is so thorough that it may be a "given," not a conscious choice. Certainly there is consistency in Steinbeck's narrative choice to have chronological association substitute for organic form within the two family histories. This consistency prevails in smaller details. Cathy represents evil as Adam represents good, but the pattern is broken at crucial points. Adam's rejection of

7. Laura Z. Hobson, "Tradewinds," *The Saturday Review of Literature*, 35 (August 30, 1952), 4.

8. Lisca, pp. 262–63.

Caleb's money is a cruel, rigid kind of goodness, like his inability to tell Aron who his mother is. If Adam's goodness is indistinct or confused, there is no doubt of his function. He exists to suffer, but his suffering is so passive that Steinbeck himself—though chiefly Samuel and Lee—must explain its nature. Conversely, as Adam becomes a universal father, given his name and the modern Eden he tries to establish, so Cathy might be expected to become a universal mother, but she does not. Cathy rejects her two sons when they are born, shoots Adam in order to get away from him, reenters whoredom (dyeing her hair black and changing her name to Kate); many years later, she attempts to corrupt Caleb and then Aron. Evidently Cathy–Kate got out of the author's control, thus destroying his minimal order of chronological association.[9] In the next generation, Aron's absolute good balances Cathy–Kate's pure evil, and Caleb recalls Charles's superficial tendency toward evil. Throughout, good and evil are shifting categories, notably when, midway through the novel, Lee proposes the *timshel* doctrine. The sense of improvisation cannot be put down, and strongly manipulative devices are obviously required to assert a concluding optimism. The narrative effect is similar to the last third of *The Grapes of Wrath*.

A lack of organic form is evident in particular aspects of the narrative. For example, Adam Trask's wanderings after his service in the Army relate but remotely to his later "good man" role, and an amusing episode like Olive Hamilton's plane ride has no relationship to plot or theme. Steinbeck's presence may be an intentional means of drawing together the diverse plot elements through explicitly moral essays; if so, the device is a failure.[10] Steinbeck speaks

9. Bernice Pritchard in *The Wayward Bus* seems to be a less extreme version of Cathy-Kate. The two women share an outward gentility (order, desire for nice things) that masks a consuming materialism (status symbols for Bernice, money for Kate), the visible effect of an inward moral blindness. Steinbeck's interest in this kind of woman begins with La Santa Roja in *Cup of Gold*; usually the character is an allegorical figure. Notice that Steinbeck's essential insight changes very little in time.

10. Steinbeck uses the moral essay or editorial interchapter fre-

in his own voice in ten interchapters and injects himself into events, often in the role of an interested bystander unaware of the outcome of events. The device recalls *The Grapes of Wrath*, but the familiar tone and the sense of personal involvement produce unusual strains on credibility, most notably when Steinbeck affirms his puzzlement in contemplating Cathy–Kate:

> When I said Cathy was a monster it seemed to me that it was so. Now I have bent close with a glass over the small print of her and reread the footnotes, and I wonder if it was true. The trouble is that since we cannot know what she wanted, we will never know whether or not she got it.[11]

The image of the working author involved in a direct authorial comment assumes the fiction of an inchoate "time present" in which Steinbeck discovers exactly what the reader sees at the moment. The point is not that Steinbeck is coy or disingenuous (although he is) but that he is willing to manipulate his own persona in the development of the novel.

Steinbeck's handling of Caleb Trask is especially manipulative. Caleb is the naturally evil man, his evil distinguished from that of Charles or Cathy–Kate by his being aware of man's power to choose between good and evil. Caleb's important role is qualified by its relatively minor narrative importance—about equivalent to Samuel's role. Not enough narrative time and space is allotted to him, so he is suddenly elevated into a protagonist at the novel's close; his insight and salvation are determined rather than earned; hence, the

---

quently; see *Cup of Gold, Tortilla Flat, The Grapes of Wrath,* and *Cannery Row.* The device can serve as a desperate expedient for achieving order (Steinbeck's proposal of an interlocutor in *Tortilla Flat*), as seems the case here, or in a more organic fashion as in *The Grapes of Wrath.*

11. *EE,* p. 184. The personal reference to difficulty in reading is accurate. Personal references occur on pages 3–7, 72–73, 129–32, 184, 217–20, 278–84, 292, 413–15, 484–86, 516–19. Notice that they increase and become longer as the novel proceeds, both because Steinbeck is on the scene, "placed" as a boy, and because more authorial comment seems necessary to indicate the direction of the allegory as a result of Steinbeck's avoidance of direct narration.

insight and salvation are imposed, chiefly through a speedy alteration of his character.

A similar disregard for a harmonious relationship between structure and materials is evident in the handling of quite minor characters, such as Lee, Abra Bacon, and Samuel Hamilton. Lee's central function is to convince Adam Trask that he, Adam, is a good man. For this purpose, Lee is given a split personality; he is both a servant and a sage, and he uses two languages, pidgin English and a heavily academic English (not unlike Steinbeck's "I" style) to denote his two personalities. This linguistic device removes the need for direct authorial comment, but the contrivance is so patent that Lee is convincing neither as servant nor sage. Again, when Steinbeck points out a moral difference between Caleb and Aron through their responses to love, Abra Bacon is introduced summarily, without the pretense of fitting into the scheme of the "inextricably entangled" families. Samuel Hamilton is the most striking instance of the lack of organic form in *East of Eden*. Samuel is an impressive character, despite some unfortunate language that Steinbeck gives to him. But his roles are split somewhat at random. At first, as an allegorical figure, he exemplifies moral success through economic failure, since he can make all men rich but himself; his joyous and total understanding of good and evil is an end to itself. Later on, Samuel becomes mainly a mystic. He finds water with a divining rod—a superficial gift. More profoundly, through moral insight, he identifies Adam's Edenic valley as an evil place, he doubts if Cathy is "good," he names Adam's sons when Adam cannot, and he emphasizes Adam's need to accept the Cain and Abel story as an insight into permanent human experience. In the end, Samuel is transformed into a kind of human divinity or an expression of the divine in man; his last phrase recalls God's language in the Garden of Eden after the Fall ("Here am I"), and the visual imagery is consciously mystical, an identification of man and nature. Lee confirms these impressions as a Jamesian reflector:

> Lee climbed down. "Samuel!" he said. "Here am I." The old man chuckled. "Liza hates for me to say that." "Samuel,

you've gone beyond me." "It's time, Lee." "Good-by, Samuel,"
Lee said.[12]

Unfortunately, the biblical impressiveness and even an
appeal to "our Father who art in nature" cannot hide Samuel's ultimate lack of narrative function. Rather, the variety
of his roles is evidence of Steinbeck's old fault of structuring
a series of immediate, differing effects, not the creation of a
unified character. The problem is embarrassing. Steinbeck
takes the option of killing off Samuel, his most impressive
character, before *East of Eden* is half finished.

The two family histories and the minor characters are
handled less than lucidly. Just so with the moral philosophy
—the *timshel* doctrine. Beyond question, that doctrine of
the releasing power of free will is intended to unify *East
of Eden*. At most it affects events to some extent. Lee's
explanation of the doctrine motivates Samuel to tell Adam
that Cathy is now Kate and the madam of a whorehouse in
Salinas; Adam visits Kate and thus frees himself of her influence. Adam shares with Kate in Charles's estate, according to directions; this association confirms his freedom.
Caleb acquires the same freedom by confronting Kate. At
the end of the novel, Adam grants Caleb the *timshel* sense
of free will by withdrawing the curse of Aron's death on
his own deathbed. As counterpoint, Kate's lack of free
will is indicated in some detail. Adam's reevaluation of
his relationship to his father, Cyrus, and to his brother,
Charles, promotes a novelistic unity in relation to the
timshel insight. Samuel and Lee are drawn into this unity
by their intellectual interest in the doctrine and their human
concern for Adam. Again, in counterpoint, the skeletal history of the Hamilton family sheds light on the operation of
free will.

These unities are the results of a literally associational

12. *EE*, p. 309. Samuel is similar in effect to those earlier semi-
divine nature gods or "holy men," such as Joseph Wayne in *To a
God Unknown*, Danny in *Tortilla Flat*, Jim Casy in *The Grapes of
Wrath*, Mack in *Cannery Row*, and even Juan Chicoy in *The
Wayward Bus* (the god of the machine—Samuel is an avid inventor).
The type presents a problem in narrative function in all these
instances.

unity—schematic rather than organic—not quite the same as a harmony between structure and materials; and the unity tends to collapse, once its particulars are examined in any detail. The collapse begins with the doctrine itself as Steinbeck presents it.

Steinbeck alters the Cain and Abel story to present the humanitarian notion that good and evil are intermixed in men in order to force individual choice between any specific good or evil. The original story is strained and distorted by the intrusion of an optimism that allows Steinbeck to juggle rather than explore the thematic elements of moral philosophy. A similar optimism is imposed at the conclusion of many of the earlier novels. The difference is that a juggled moral content appears sooner and is more thoroughly woven into the novel's texture in *East of Eden* than in any of the earlier novels except the immediately previous work, *The Wayward Bus* and *Burning Bright*. Obviously, the materials must be manipulated in order to take the shape that optimism requires.

The effective means to this end is *timshel*, the controlling allegorical sign, reproduced on the cover of *East of Eden*. *Timshel* suggests a new reading of the Cain and Abel story, which may be summarized as follows: Cain murders Abel because he feels unloved and rejected by God; that is, he feels that he is evil by nature. Murder is Cain's twisted "good" effort to substitute himself for Abel and perhaps to force a punishment he is certain he deserves in any event. Abel does not murder because he feels loved and accepted by God. But his serenity precludes self-knowledge; he does not have to *find* good, as Cain may, so his dramatic interest is less. By an irony, in this reading, Cain's self-equated guilt and physical ugliness are the index of his real humanity. Abel is too pure to be believably human.

This reading of the ancient story is proposed throughout *East of Eden* in particular events—Adam's relationship with Charles, Caleb's relationship with Aron (and, later, with Abra), their several relationships with Cathy–Kate, and the further evidence provided by the Hamilton subplot. These relationships are interwoven still more closely by certain marginal family events: Cyrus's relationships with Adam and Charles and the total effect of the various experiences of Adam, Charles, Caleb, and Aron with Cathy–Kate. Steinbeck's formal management is admirable. By dealing with family and interfamily matters, Steinbeck achieves a tighter, more credible development than by casual or accidental groupings as in *The Pastures of Heaven* and *The Wayward Bus*.[13] His working the *timshel* doctrine into *East of Eden* avoids a merely formal parallel that might smack of the play-novelette theory. The biblical event and the contemporary event are "placed," like the doctrine, by excited debates between Lee, Samuel, and Adam over the meaning of *timshel*; the background is filled by Lee's relatives, "ancient reverend gentlemen who are great scholars . . . thinkers in exactness," which is to say "is" thinkers; they study Hebrew for several years to ascertain the correct sense of the disputed word.[14]

Nevertheless, in proposing the *timshel* doctrine as the essential key to a harmony between structure and materials, Steinbeck ignores its possibly inherent defects. The doctrine asserts that Cain and Abel symbolize man's eternally divided moral condition. Since this division tends to polarize good and evil, each quality becomes an allegorical absolute, with evil subject to humanitarian modification. A consequent logic produces good from evil: Since evil is man's birthright (we are children of Cain), no one is responsible for personal wrongdoing; thus, free will is negated. In the narrative, this twisted logic permits Caleb's elevation—not development—at the close. Free will is also negated in the sense that Cathy–Kate is born a monster.[15] Steinbeck extends a metaphor based on physiology to explain her peculiar existence:

13. One is reminded of the credible yet myth-making Joad family. The cited examples suggest that a mythical element is likely to seem organic within a credible context, and the reverse if forced in without sufficient context, as in *To a God Unknown* or *Burning Bright*. The point is crucial, in view of Steinbeck's pronounced interest in myth-making.

14. *EE*, p. 302. The doctrine is not only "placed" but universalized through the interest of the ancient Chinese scholars.

15. Peter Lisca has noted this point. Lisca, p. 267.

> I believe there are monsters born in the world to human par-
> ents. . . . And just as there are physical monsters, can there
> not be mental or psychic monsters born? The face and body
> may be perfect, but if a twisted gene or a malformed egg can
> produce physical monsters, may not the same process produce
> a malformed soul?[16]

The nonlogical, physiological metaphor does not conceal
Steinbeck's creation of a purely allegorical figure in Cathy–
Kate. She is presented from the beginning as an allegorical
quality, a representation of pure evil; many of the good characters remark that she is not quite human.[17] However, a brilliant, sustained exercise of "is" thinking images Cathy–
Kate's personality and experiences through a series of sharply realized details that are entirely convincing. Allegory and
"is" thinking allow an enriched, two-level development of
the narrative, and the drive of the narrative removes most
of the strain of the storyless experiment, *The Wayward
Bus*. Of course, *timshel* does not apply to Cathy–Kate, to
the advantage of the narrative. For example, there is little
but an allegorical reason for such flatly reported events as
Cathy's grim marriage to Adam and her ironic will in Aron's
favor, but there is a wealth of precise detail in the presenting
of such events as Cathy's murder of her parents, Kate's
later murder of Faye, the complicated process that leads to
Kate's own suicide, and the suicide itself. "Is" thinking
has an organic function here, since the series of closely realized details tend to imply Cathy–Kate's limitation to the
material world and her complete divorce from moral claims,
humor, and imagination; the very style of "is" thinking
corresponds to what Cathy–Kate is and is not. Through this
happy use of technique, Steinbeck creates in Cathy–Kate a
female character who ranks just below Ma Joad in intensity
and conviction. Steinbeck was clearly as taken by this character as the reader is likely to be, for she has the energy
and the fascination of the totally evil—qualities that are
denied to Bernice Pritchard—and she has a fictive reality
denied to (say) La Santa Roja, although both characters are

16. *EE*, p. 72. The identification comes early.
17. Lee, Adam, Samuel, and Caleb. Charles is aware that Cathy
is evil.

earlier versions of Cathy–Kate. Nonetheless, there is considerable difficulty in defining her function in *East of Eden*. She is so fully realized that she appears more credible than her structural opposite, Adam, supported though he is by Lee and Samuel. Hence, there is a diminished clarity in the allegorical structure; for so far as Cathy–Kate is proof, within the world of the novel, that a humanitarian solution to the problem of evil is not wholly possible, the novel simply does not work. At the very least, Cathy–Kate's brilliant autonomy is a serious assault on the integrity of the novel as a whole. Her adventures can be lifted out all too easily. True, she is to some extent cut down to size. She is surrounded by enemies, and two of them unknowingly cause her death; her fear of life is suggested by her reaction to alcohol; her limitations are suggested by her aging, the onset of arthritis, her use of bromides, and the windowless shelter she builds, from a motivation that Caleb understands. Nevertheless, these facts do not qualify her durable will to do evil. She is and remains an autonomous character. Even the paralleled deaths of Kate and Adam at the close, while intended to down evil and raise good, offer further evidence of Kate's autonomy. The notion of an intermixture of good and evil is negated when her money goes to Caleb, not to Aron as intended, for she had intended as a final gesture to corrupt Aron with her gift. Death itself lends a comparative moral stature to Cathy–Kate at Adam's expense. She selects the time and manner of her death, gaining an ironic sense of free will; Adam blesses Caleb, but as directed by Lee. In short, the central statement of free will is so qualified in these paralleled events that it cannot have the intended effect of strengthening the triumph of good. Cathy–Kate gets away to that extreme degree, and *timshel* is somewhat muted in the process.

The device of the coincidence of initials, indicating moral divisions and types, is a Steinbeck favorite. Never convincing in itself, the device must be supported by a context to have any effect. Its immediacy can suggest a larger structure which is not there. Perhaps because of these dangers,

Steinbeck uses the device sparingly in most of the earlier novels, but it is worked beyond the point of absurdity in *East of Eden* and in a context that is not entirely lucid. C and A alternate as initials throughout the generations of the Trask family to emphasize the permanence of the Cain and Abel story: Cyrus–Alice, Adam–Charles, Adam–Cathy, Caleb–Aron, Caleb–Abra. The device is too trivial to bear that much repetitive weight, especially given the twists of the *timshel* doctrine and the relative lack of control of Cathy–Kate. The device is much too broad to signify much particularized difference between the varying Cain and Abel figures, and its internal incoherence produces more confusion than clarity. This result can be shown by considering the actual complexity of the characters and events.

Charles and Caleb become evil in the stress of circumstance; Cathy–Kate is born evil. Charles and Caleb strive to be loved; Cathy–Kate cannot conceive of love, as indicated by her choice of prostitution and her encouragement of sexual perversion. Alice is much like Charles in wanting to be loved. At the close, Abra shares Caleb's sense of evil. Adam is a composite figure. Despite these mixtures, character tends to solidify around a strict development of the Cain and Abel theme. So far as he loves Adam, Charles strives for the good. He expresses love indirectly and only once in a fevered letter to Adam. Charles's inability to express emotion is a moral defect, taken ironically as the virtue of blind courage. This defect cuts Charles away from humanity and permits his evil side to grow, but it stems from his sense that a beloved father loved Adam and hated him. Adam's good instincts are obscured at first by the military discipline which Cyrus imposes, but his essential goodness is as inborn as Cathy–Kate's essential evil. Rightly enough, Charles tries to kill Adam when they are children; much later, Adam recognizes that he had destroyed Charles's striving for the good by his withholding of love, an insight that defines Adam's composite nature.

Caleb's needs are still more complex and more tightly hedged by the Cain–Abel theme. Lisca observes that Caleb inherits both good and evil and therefore provides the ground for a "genuine moral struggle."[18] Caleb feels evil growing in his soul, as good develops in Aron; he submits to the growth—even protects Aron from evil—until Adam throws away the family's money in an experiment with refrigeration during World War I and rejects the money Caleb earns in speculation. That is, Adam withdraws love from Caleb as he withdrew it from Charles. Caleb's response is to hurt Aron by revealing to him (Caleb had overheard the story in a bar) that Cathy–Kate is their mother; Aron joins the Army in dismay and dies in the war. As allegory, evil can accept evil, but good is weak because it cannot. In fact, the good man, Adam, causes these disastrous events by ignoring the sense of Caleb's offer of money. Adam cannot know, in his stern goodness, that any gesture is better than the vacuum of his rejection. Charles's attack on Adam sets this pattern, which governs an intricate rather than a credible truth in the development of character: that Cains understand evil and can learn good through love, while Abels are ignorant of evil and have no defense against a knowledge of evil. The pattern tightens characterization so rigidly that Lee denies free will to Adam in his talk with Caleb after the rejection: "He couldn't help it, Cal. That's his nature. It was the only way he knew. He didn't have any choice."[19]

These events suggest that Cains and Abels are incomplete, that ideally each complements the other, as Abra complements Caleb in the end. To reach this optimistic conclusion, Steinbeck confuses still further the simple allegorical division of good and evil. At their first meeting, when they are children, Caleb insults Abra with his display of superior knowledge, while Aron charms her. In the end, recognizing an evil streak in her family, Abra finds that she loves the strong, ugly Caleb rather than the weak, pretty Aron; and Caleb wins Adam's love through the *timshel* blessing, signifying Adam's acceptance of his share of guilt in Aron's death and the cleaning of the slate for Caleb. The narrative surface of this inconclusive optimistic close is free of any redeeming irony. However, through his committing a crime,

18. Lisca, p. 268.   19. *EE*, p. 544.

Caleb gains a closer love from Adam and more than a substitute for Aron in Abra. To emphasize the belief that all
happens for the best, Cathy–Kate dies with her revenge
turned into a blessing, since her fortune goes to Caleb. No
fruitful or functional range is left to the allegorical structure and its particular element, the initial device, as a result
of these tortuous developments, for the close is a manipulation of plot and character, not a necessary fusion of the two.

Along with the *timshel* doctrine and the initial device, a
third allegorical sign is used to juggle moral philosophy. The
associational unity of the scar across the forehead (the
mark of Cain which Charles and Cathy share) and the repetition of "Am I my brother's keeper" (which Charles and
Caleb share) are merely plot mechanisms, in view of the real
differences that separate Charles, Cathy, and Caleb. A gulf
functionally divides Cathy–Kate's monstrous nature from
the need for love which Charles and Caleb share.[20] The
purely mechanical surface is evident in several examples.
Caleb has no scar; he will come to a good end. Cathy is made
pregnant by Adam and by Charles; Aron and Caleb are delivered in separate sacs to denote their separate fathers and
their presumedly different tendencies. The curiously parallel
fact that Adam and Charles have the same father but different mothers is allowed to drop out of the pattern.

These devices and parallels preclude a direct exposition of
differences in character. The substitution of mechanisms for
an organic development constitutes one of the weakest aspects of *East of Eden*. Character is flattened out; minute
particulars conflict; an external determinism prevails.

Even the main allegorical assumptions that seem intended
to control values are not always intellectually coherent in
East of Eden. For example, the allegorical meaning of Cathy–
Kate's suicide and of Aron's willed death in war must be that
pure evil and pure good cannot exist in the realized world
where good and evil are intermixed. The point is qualified
by suicides which occur for quite different reasons: Adam's
mother, James Grew, and Tom Hamilton. As another ex-

20. These materials are spaced with some care. *EE*, pp. 47, 125,
160, 270, 564.

ample, the idea that evil results from a frustration of love is repeatedly stated and acted out: Charles's gift to Cyrus, Adam's offer of "Eden" to Cathy, and Caleb's gift to Adam. Steinbeck phrases the point:

> In uncertainty I am certain that underneath their topmost layers of frailty men want to be good and want to be loved. Indeed, most of their vices are attempted short cuts to love.[21]

The point is qualified when evil rises from several other unrelated sources: Cathy–Kate's inborn hatred and greed, the sexual frustration which results in the horrible murder of Lee's mother, and Tom's ignorance which causes Dessie's death. These qualifications cannot be dismissed as the inevitable looseness of a large work, because they cut at the heart of the allegorical structure, and they could be controlled with relative ease within that structure. Hence, they may not be accidents but intentional defects, possibly devised to broaden the scope of the narrative.

This lenient view of faulty structure is less than convincing in view of the fact that a broad thematic element, the function of money, is not given a coherent development. There is no doubt of Steinbeck's intention to contrast goodness and the cash nexus. In his own voice, in a parable set in the heart of the novel, Steinbeck recalls a vulgar rich man and a clever rich man, both hated after they die, and a third man, neither rich nor hated,

> who perhaps made many errors in performance but whose effective life was devoted to making men brave and dignified and good in a time when they were poor and frightened and when ugly forces were loose in the world to utilize their fears. This man was hated by the few. When he died the people burst into tears in the streets and their minds wailed, "What can we do now? How can we go on without him?"[22]

Or, moral excellence is presented as the exact opposite of the possession of worldly wealth. This rather simple contrast is the sum of the morally accepted attitudes toward money.[23] Good characters such as Samuel, Lee, and Adam

21. *EE*, p. 414.
22. *EE*, p. 414. FDR might be the model.
23. It may be neither fanciful nor inappropriate to speculate that

are happy in relative poverty or are too rich to care about money. Cathy–Kate is the major exception which proves the rule; her lust for money is equated with her will to do evil. Quite flatly, money transactions connote guilt. The point is repeated often. Cyrus Trask leaves a fortune to Charles and Adam, leading to Charles's discovery that Cyrus had been a liar and a thief. Charles wills half of his inheritance to Cathy–Kate; she uses it for evil purposes. Adam uses his share of Cyrus's fortune to "buy" an Eden; the effort is a failure. On the other hand, a lack of business sense is the condition of moral success for Adam and for Samuel; an otherwise functionless character, Will Hamilton, is introduced into the novel to demonstrate that moral failures are likely to become wealthy businessmen; Lee is presented without qualification (unlike the more complex Samuel) as a great man because he has absolutely no interest in economic power. This moral treatment of money reaches an extreme when Caleb wins the love of Adam and Abra *after* he has failed to buy Adam's love. In the same moralistic frame, but with diminishing clarity, Steinbeck affirms that machines produce evil while human efforts to control nature are good and produce good. Adam is seduced into the unfortunate refrigeration scheme by observing a new icebox; an automobile is a status symbol and rules its owner; an airplane ride is a nightmare. In contrast, Samuel's use of a divining rod is treated seriously, and real or pretended foresight or second sight is granted to Charles, Samuel, Lee, and Ethel. Yet the sharp division between money and goodness (or moral insight) becomes incoherent when Steinbeck grants presumedly untainted wealth to Adam and especially (since it allows an optimistic ending) when the money goes to Caleb.

The general identification of wealth with evil places the focus of attention on moral excellence, but there is no gain in narrative coherence. For example, Steinbeck manipulates the Cain and Abel theme. Caleb wishes to be a farmer in order to deny his role as Cain (the hunter), but he gains a

---

Steinbeck's own painful experience with sudden wealth after the success of *Tortilla Flat* is reflected in this absolute division.

moderate fortune in wartime speculation in beans (symbolically, from a successful economic hunt; Will Hamilton tells Caleb that he is too smart to farm). But in contrast, the Cain figure in the earlier generation, Charles, remains a successful farmer all his life. Finally, Adam contradicts his "good man" role by feeling in time that he is the Cain figure. Adam's feeling denies the evidence, but it paradoxically increases his "good" identification by adding humility to his virtues.

Because a Cain-and-Abel allegory requires a Lilith figure and a serpent in Eden, Cathy–Kate is described frequently "in terms of a serpent, from the shape of her features and her flickering tongue to her dislike of the light."[24] Also, she has sharp little teeth, she bites Samuel as he delivers her sons, and she is a poisoner. These details are coherent, but only in a mechanical sense; the substitution of mechanics for organic form is the primary technique of the play-novelette. What is not mechanical in *East of Eden* tends to be incoherent.

This failure in coherence applies to the novel's broadly intellectual base, to the repeated assertion that knowledge combined with love is identical with goodness. This assertion is a developed theme throughout *East of Eden*. For example, Samuel and Lee are absolute types of good men because they love books and Adam with equal fervor. Their insights are valid; they "know" that Cathy is evil. Adam does not "know" Cathy in this sense when he marries her (but Charles, understanding evil, does); with Samuel's help, he is able to understand and forgive her. Kate's suicide is due in part to her ignorance of love. Aron is destroyed by a sudden knowledge of evil, which seems to cancel Adam's love. Caleb is saved by gaining the love of Adam and Abra. The minor characters echo this theme. Cyrus does not recognize Charles's need to be loved, and Adam's inability to love Cyrus increases Charles's isolation. Alice Trask does not know that Adam gives her presents, so she cannot love him. Cathy's parents, James Grew, and Faye are destroyed by loving Cathy–Kate in ignorance of her real nature. Mr.

24. Lisca, p. 268.

Rolf loves Cathy–Kate's soul, but he mistakes her motive in coming to church because he cannot understand her. Dessie is destroyed by Tom's medical ignorance in spite of his love for her. Samuel's love of his children does not include understanding; their tragedies in part cause his death. Like Caleb, Will Hamilton is saved from a total selfishness by his intense, unexpressed love of his family. The wise Chinese scholars combine mind and love in their study of Hebrew, and they reap joy from their work.

The moral treatment of money connects with the moral treatment of knowledge, since all of these instances demonstrate that knowledge is good and creates moral excellence. In contrast, as with the allegorical structure, the separation of knowledge and poverty from ignorance and wealth tends to negate Steinbeck's basic assumption that good and evil are intermixed. Steinbeck lets virtue triumph all too easily, as in the typical instance of Adam Trask. At first Adam is a confused rich man, but Samuel and Lee are artificially "placed" to devote their best insights to fostering Adam's growth of moral sense. Rich, stupid people, so unlucky as to lack a Samuel or a Lee, do not survive—like Faye. Luck seems to govern the pattern. This factor forces the reader to notice that details are presented for the sake of a pattern which rejects them, for the allegory tends to float above the narrative because it has no consistent base, and the narrative tends to move at random because it, too, has no firmly credible base. The abstract theme, "the never-ending contest in ourselves of good and evil," is at odds with the realistic power of the narrative.[25]

Therefore, in Cathy–Kate evil is equated with strength of will and mastery of the material world, while in Adam good is equated with moral weakness and an inability to master the material world. Cathy–Kate's life is more fascinating

25. *EE*, p. 415. There is something of the balance scale in the novel's procedure. Lee formulates this as a speculation, late in the novel, when he knows that Adam's wealth is Cyrus's stolen money and Cathy-Kate's will is in Aron's favor. "Was this some kind of joke or did things balance so that if one went too far in one direction an automatic slide moved on the scale and the balance was reestablished?" *EE*, p. 583.

than Adam's failures and partial successes. Aron and Caleb's lives repeat the pattern of Adam and Cathy–Kate in all essentials except the conclusion. Aron is physically weak and unable to live with the knowledge of imperfection, let alone with evil. Caleb is physically strong, and his knowledge of evil enables him to accept evil in others while he strives for the good. The pattern of similarity is violated only by Caleb's arbitrary and speechless salvation. Of course, good and evil are too complex to divide neatly into the extreme opposites of the allegorical pattern that Steinbeck imposes on the materials, evidently to solve the moral paradox that the evil are strong and even fascinating while the humility of the good appears to be a weak indecision. The difficulty is in part technical, since the realistic technique of "is" thinking erodes the moralistic allegory; the difficulty is also in the uncertainty of Steinbeck's hand. The structure and the materials are out of phase. The massive claims of the novel emphasize the massive seriousness of Steinbeck's defective view of harmony in longer fiction.

Still, a peculiar impressiveness survives the organizational failure of the manipulated, superficial devices and parallels. To understand this survival is to comprehend a crucial aspect of the art of fiction.

The *timshel* doctrine enables Steinbeck to broaden an autobiographical kernel into the spiritual autobiography of mankind, of life itself, since all ideas, characters, and events can suggest the vast confusion of life. This is the lasting impression of *East of Eden.*

A fiction which is purposefully a grab bag of history, which extends the manipulation and simplification of the play-novelette form into the vast range of the prose epic, and which relies on a thematic development to the exclusion of a formal harmony of structure and materials, need not be an artistic failure by definition. Certainly *East of Eden* is not simply or merely the pandering, best-selling opus that Mark Harris defines with a graceful, decisive wit in his epistolary novel, *Wake Up, Stupid!*, in this conversation between a professor and a literary agent:

What was my own field? When I replied, "The Eighteenth Century" he directed me to "name some people in that century." He asked me were the queens of that century salacious, to which I replied, "Indeed," whereupon he directed me to write a novel, without delay, of five hundred pages or more about the wickedest, sexiest queen of the century, or, if she were not wicked enough, I should combine the wickedness of several into one, rush the result to him, and we should soon be millionaires.[26]

Steinbeck's materials resist a definite structure, but they are not frivolous. Cathy–Kate's career is dangerously close to the Harris formula, except in the felt ugliness of her life. The allegorical machinery of snake imagery, moral isolation, and personified evil is too overtly lurid or too qualified to account for Cathy–Kate's "power of blackness" as a fictive creation. Her ugliness is not structured. Instead, Steinbeck creates her in fragments, "moments," even in phrases, as in the description of Adam's visit to her establishment in Salinas:

He walked quickly down the unpaved sidewalks, his eyes on the ground to avoid stepping in puddles. The row was dimly lit by the warning lantern where the railroad crossed the street and by one small carbon-filamented globe that burned on the porch of Jenny's. Adam had his instructions. He counted two houses and nearly missed the third, so high and unbridled were the dark bushes in front of it. He looked in through the gateway at the dark porch, slowly opened the gate, and went up the overgrown path. In the half-darkness he could see the sagging dilapidated porch and the shaky steps. The paint had long disappeared from the clapboard walls and no work had ever been done on the garden. If it had not been for the vein of light around the edges of the drawn shades he would have passed on, thinking the house deserted. The stair treads seemed to crumple under his weight and the porch planks squealed as he crossed them.[27]

This passage of "is" thinking is a sharp realization of detail, combined powerfully with structural elements, as in the stiffness of the remote listing from Adam's exclusive point

26. Mark Harris, *Wake Up, Stupid!* (New York: Alfred A. Knopf, Inc., 1959), p. 144. Quoted by permission of the author.

27. *EE*, pp. 314–15.

of view, to suggest his moral rigidity in approaching Kate, or in the implicit, metaphorical association of Kate's moral nature with the broken-down house and the wild grounds. In the larger frame, moral darkness is there in the dim lighting; the house is there in terms of a distant, then a close view, then specific imagery ("crumple," "squealed") which suggests ugly age. Kate's depraved helpers and her personal ugliness flow out of this sympathetic context. This account of things seen, implicitly inviting a moral evaluation, does far more to realize what Cathy–Kate *is* than all of the ponderous, sometimes uncontrolled mechanics of the allegory.

Generally, then, what remains impressive in *East of Eden* is not the theme (ideas, content, allegory), but specific, detached "moments" of sharp realization—of "is" thinking. The language is observational and precise in those moments, but it is tortured by inversion and inflation in passages where the allegory is most visible. Similarly, the grab bag nature of the novel encourages Steinbeck's skillful concentration on the creation of the sharp particulars of the moment—who the people are, what the weather is like—within an allegorical frame which is so loose it does not interpose itself on the memorable images. In brief, *East of Eden* is a triumph of "is" thinking and a vehicle for incredible or forced allegorical elements which suggest to the reader that plot need not be taken seriously. It is clear that Steinbeck intended to produce a mythological–allegorical novel, not this interesting effect. The allegorical myth is absurdly reductive, but a number of episodic, sharply realized fragments are impressive in the selection of memory. At worst, the machinery can be accepted on faith, as a fictionally necessary footing for the flashes of image, the intense passages of thereness. This much is enough to maintain a flow of narrative, but not enough to ensure a finished masterpiece, a shapely work of art.

Steinbeck's most sympathetic critics have attempted to praise the structure of *East of Eden* or even to explain it away. Mark Schorer spoke of the "audaciousness" of the structure in a review that he renounced a few years later.[28]

28. Mark Schorer, "A Dark and Violent Steinbeck Novel," *The*

At about the same time, Claude-Edmonde Magny praised the novel's mythic or parabolic quality, "which is not in the least novelistic."[29] Recently, in his study of thematic design, Lester Marks denied any structural difficulties, but he shifted his praise to Steinbeck's "thematic scheme" or "thesis."[30] These critical reactions are not false, but they mark an increasingly strong movement away from novelistic considerations to something like a pure consideration of the value of Steinbeck's content. R. W. B. Lewis turned that argument around, finding the reason for Steinbeck's failed allegory in the author's sentimental inability to contemplate tragic reality.[31]

These diverse views strike one balance, namely, that *East of Eden* really is the novel Steinbeck had been trying to write from the beginning—a novel that "has in it everything I have been able to learn about my art or craft or profession in all these years."[32] But its limited aesthetic conviction, combined with its mature certainty, point a pronounced direction in Steinbeck's career, which is pursued at a further extreme in the succeeding three novels.

This conclusion alters the frequently stated assumption that versatility is evidence of Steinbeck's lack of direction. On the contrary, *East of Eden* really is the capstone, the mature summation of Steinbeck's great abilities and failings, and thus an illustration of the art of the novel as Steinbeck sees that art in the perspective of his long career. *East of Eden* has every element that is characteristic of Steinbeck's impressive but flawed art. Consider the novel's combination of structural rigidity and narrative openness; its storytelling drive and its schematic form; its characters that "get away" and its typed, or inert, or mouthpiece characters; its

New York Times Book Review, September 21, 1952, p. 22. Lisca, p. 265.

29. Claude-Edmonde Magny, "East of Eden," *Perspectives USA*, 5 (Fall 1953), 149.

30. Lester Marks, *Thematic Design in the Novels of John Steinbeck* (The Hague: Mouton & Co., 1969), pp. 124, 128.

31. R. W. B. Lewis, "John Steinbeck: The Fitful Daemon," in *The Young Rebel in American Literature*, ed. Carl Bode (London: William Heinemann, Ltd., 1959), pp. 121–41.

32. Kale, p. 11.

artificial structural devices and its essential looseness; its precisely accurate style and its embarrassingly inflated style; its explicit thematic design and the internal contradictions which betray that design; and its optimistic, moralizing "message," embodied in intellectual and structural manipulations so extreme they drain fictive credibility. These are the elements of Steinbeck's art, and their roots are visible from the beginning of Steinbeck's career. Not surprisingly, then, the impressive aspects of *East of Eden* are its narrative power and its strong characterization, but its negative aspecst are a deadening counterweight which qualifies all but the most blindly favorable critical judgment. Indeed, *East of Eden* is utterly characteristic: an admirably massive, essentially flawed narrative. Critical judgment has an easier time with the simple extremes of the good novel or the bad novel. Steinbeck's great effort lies between these poles, and there a critical judgment must take its abode if it is to be at all accurate.

10

"Hooptedoodle"

Sweet Thursday

In 1954, at its publication, several reviewers called *Sweet Thursday*[1] "delightfully inconsequential" and "gaily inconsequential."[2] In 1960 Charles R. Metzger suggested in convincing detail that *Sweet Thursday* "appears to be a very interesting, a very serious novel—when viewed in the light of the pastoral tradition."[3] These diverse evaluations become interestingly complementary when *Sweet Thursday* is read from the perspective of the harmony between its structure and its materials.

Neither the work of an apprentice nor an experimental novel, *Sweet Thursday* exhibits the structural exaggeration of "is" thinking in its loose but sharply realized detail and the more or less rigid structure of semiallegory (parable, myth) in its plot elements. The novel develops these characteristics to their wildest extreme—a factor that sets it apart from Steinbeck's earlier efforts to combine two structural opposites.

Sweet Thursday had its origins as the scenario for a musical comedy, and it draws on the loose, episodic movement, the sentimental conventions, and the external plot which characterize that form. The materials are drawn consciously from *Cannery Row*, but the passing of time and the format of musical comedy work a considerable change on the original materials.[4]

1. John Steinbeck, *Sweet Thursday* (New York: The Viking Press, Inc., 1954). Hereafter cited as *ST*.

2. Louis Barron, *The Library Journal*, 79 (June 1, 1954), 1052; Carlos Baker, "After Lousy Wednesday," *The New York Times Book Review*, June 13, 1954, p. 4.

3. Charles R. Metzger, "Steinbeck's Version of the Pastoral," *Modern Fiction Studies*, 6 (Summer 1960), 115. Copyright © 1960, by Purdue Research Foundation, West Lafayette, Ind.

4. Peter Lisca, *The Wide World of John Steinbeck* (New Bruns-

The plot rests on Doc's inability to return to the good life of Cannery Row after six years "as a tech sergeant in a V. D. section."[5] The enforced stupidity of Army life and the stupidity of the waste of war, especially as extended into the postwar years, destroy Doc's ability to enjoy himself and his work. The desiccation of Doc's soul is framed by related events: The Monterey canneries fish out the coastal waters during the war, the shift in population to California during the war drains the subsoil water from the earth so desert will inevitably encroach on the green land, and Doc's rich friend, Old Jingleballicks, allows Western Biological to rot away through neglect. Upon this basis of universal decay, the central action of the plot concerns Doc's forced return to the good life through love. With the help of all of Cannery Row, Doc falls in love with Suzy, a prostitute at the Bear Flag who is unsuited to her profession. Suzy is blessed with the proverbial heart of gold and with an independent mind; these attributes appeal to Doc.

The novel is not ambitious in its scope; even slightly complex plot relationships are oversimplified to lead to the designedly "happy" close, where Doc and Suzy drive off—of course, into the sunset—amid the universal blessings of the inhabitants of Cannery Row. In summary, the plot line is more emphatic than the details which establish mood and tone, and the plot itself is so conventionally sentimental in its invocation of love as a healer as to simplify the frequently sharp, observational details that relate to it. The indicated novelistic reduction permits Steinbeck to work only with the most stereotyped of cause-and-effect relations, which tend to impose the rigidly limited effect of allegory in its simplest sense. As *East of Eden* opens out, even to inco-

---

wick: Rutgers University Press, 1958), pp. 276–77. Lisca indicates, from a study of Steinbeck's correspondence, that Steinbeck had in mind "a comedy . . . possibly in play form" a year prior to the completion of *East of Eden*; two years later the project had become a "musical for the sponsors of *Guys and Dolls*." In fact, the musical, *Pipe Dream*, was adapted by Rodgers and Hammerstein from *Sweet Thursday*, and had a successful Broadway run.

5. *ST*, p. 3.

herence, *Sweet Thursday* contracts to a predictable, simple cliché.[6]

Nevertheless, *Sweet Thursday* is not quite a mere surrender to popular taste or so pointlessly stereotyped as to elude critical analysis. Steinbeck is never quite a hack. There is an artistic purpose in the musical comedy conventions—an extreme kind of panoramic structure which emphasizes the artificiality, not the art, in Steinbeck's plot. Its crisply stereotyped effect is distinguished by its clarity from the heavy-handed plotting of the late play-novelettes. The result is a relative improvement, a logical plot line which can be a relief after *East of Eden*. Steinbeck's obvious relaxation permits a pleasantly breezy development that contrasts winningly with the merely formal development of *The Wayward Bus* or *Burning Bright* and with the merely paralleled development of *East of Eden*. The visible relaxation of artistic effort has the happy result, then, of permitting Steinbeck to concentrate on little more than pleasing the reader by "pure entertainment." The notable reduction in scope and relevance is matched favorably by the cheerfully lucid plot line, which is much less disturbing than the serious intentions and the ultimate confusions of the more ambitious postwar novels.

So the plot encourages a dramatic structure, a tightly eventful development, but the stereotyped development of the materials encourages a good deal of the byplay, the incidental, episodic looseness in detail, of a panoramic structure. *Sweet Thursday* is successful in this association of structures, of which little is asked, and even artful within its severe limitations.[7] Much of the success, as in *Cannery Row*, is posited on a release of considerable humor. There

6. Metzger's otherwise cogent argument is qualified by his failure to consider the artistic effect of simplification which derives from Steinbeck's self-indulgent reliance on this rigid, stereotyped, musical comedy plot.

7. For this reason, I cannot agree with Lisca's judgment (p. 278) that "it is unrewarding to subject it to those criteria of formal analysis applied to major literature." This view is too superficial and much too limiting.

is verbal humor, as in such typical chapter headings as "Whom the Gods Love They Drive Nuts" and "The Deep-Dish Set-Down," and much satiric material such as "the refusal of Whitey No. 2 to take a mass loyalty oath with some country club members for whom he caddies, Joe Elegant's struggles with his very symbolic novel, *The Pi Root of Oedipus* (in which the grandmother stands for guilt, the reality below reality), and Joseph and Mary Rivas' cultivation of marijuana in the public gardens which he tended."[8] There is also a successful novelistic firmness in the reliance on certain technical devices which Steinbeck had developed throughout his career, like the flashback (Chapter I, "What Happened in Between," the first pages of Chapter III, "Hoopetedoodle (1)," or the middle pages of Chapter XXIX, "Oh, Woe, Woe, Woe!"), the interchapter ("The Great Roque War" and "Hooptedoodle (2), or the Pacific Grove Butterfly Festival"), the inserted brief narrative (Doc's association with the seer or Hazel's effort to meet his fate of being President), the internal monologue (Doc's conversations with himself), the play on names (the Flora–Fauna pun or Joe Elegant's punning name), the ironic juxtapositioning of events which lead to Hazel's tearful attack on Doc, and, finally, a supple range of language which includes Doc's academic style, the forthright, colloquial style which Suzy and Mack frequently share, Joe Elegant's prissy style, and the seer's "iron simplicity" of expression.[9]

This association of structures and techniques is a knowingly extreme, firmly sophisticated execution of "pure entertainment," and not quite like any other Steinbeck novel in the degree of its fun and polish, although Steinbeck may have intended something similar in *Tortilla Flat*. A given, preexisting plot always seems to release Steinbeck's happier artistry.

Happily, too, Steinbeck's thematic ordering brings sophistication to the essentially simple plot. There are two familiar themes, derived most obviously from *Cannery Row*. The first theme is the inversion of social value which elevates the anarchic communal life of Mack and the boys and

8. Lisca, p. 278.   9. *ST*, p. 70.

condemns a mechanical or puritan involvement in "the world," now identified with Army life, or, in the nature of things, the exact opposite of the universe of Cannery Row.[10] The second theme assumes that everyone in Cannery Row shares a love for Doc, and this involves a communal effort, led by Mack and the boys, to restore Doc to himself. In the manner of *Cannery Row*, a variety of techniques express these themes; or, the simplification inherent in the conventions and plot of musical comedy need not be taken more seriously than fairy-tale demands. As in *East of Eden*, perhaps less by accident, the machinery of conventions and plot provides a footing for the reader; the frequent asides indicate that what really matters is the thematic development. In that perspective, the two ordering themes connect through plot to express Suzy's completely selfless embodiment of Cannery Row's love for Doc. The conventional problem in the plot is to unite Doc and Suzy—an event that is both a private affair and a public symbol of fairyland's postwar renewal of its former communal felicity.

The thematic and plot developments require a transformation of Doc's personality—he had been a confirmed bachelor, and rather aloof from people—and the introduction of Suzy, whose function is to fulfill the sentimental plot conventions. Properly, none of the attendant problems bother Steinbeck, since fairyland accepts violent shifts if they are stated frankly. The announcement of themes and plot in the first several chapters gives fair warning that *Sweet Thursday* is a sentimental novel, and that is all the reader needs.

This initial clarity of intention is more pronounced than in most Steinbeck novels, and the author's hand is expert in the best sense. The "Prologue" and the first several chapters link *Sweet Thursday* with *Cannery Row* by the device of having Mack explain to Doc how the war years had been passed on the Row. (Steinbeck remains, in these passages, limited to the essay method of presenting a character, even as exciting a character as Joseph and Mary Rivas, whose materialistic personality engulfs most of Chapter II.) The

10. Consult Steinbeck's unusually bitter "Introduction" to *Once There Was a War* (New York: The Viking Press, Inc., 1958), pp. v–xiv.

linking materials restate the fairyland quality of life in Cannery Row. War and time have removed Gay, Dora Flood, Henri, and Lee Chong, but they have been replaced by Whitey No. 2, Fauna, and Joseph and Mary Rivas, and a residue of images of Mack traveling around the country on buses, trailing a girl's radium dial watch by the clicks of a Geiger counter, and the no less fantastic image of Lee Chong waving goodby from the bridge of his ship in the sunset at the outset of a trading journey to the South Seas. At the close of this introductory matter, the second theme is announced by Doc's remark, after Mack suggests that Doc should take up things-as-they-were, "I'm afraid I've changed."[11] This theme is developed explicitly in the following pages in terms of Doc's "song," whose lowest range is the refrain, "Lonesome! Lonesome!"[12] Communal concern as well as a preparation for Suzy's entry are stated in this subsequent linking paragraph:

> Doc thought he was alone in his discontent, but he was not. Everyone on the Row observed him and worried about him. And Mack said to Fauna, "Doc acts like a guy that needs a dame."[13]

The emphasis is carefully placed. Fauna must be in the scene because Suzy will live in Fauna's whorehouse. Suzy's entrance in Chapter V is carefully highlighted by the severe objectivity of "is" thinking:

> Suzy was a pretty girl with a flat nose and a wide mouth. She had a good figure, was twenty-one, five-feet-five, hair probably brown (dyed blond), brown cloth coat, rabbit-skin collar, cotton print dress, brown calf shoes (heel taps a little runover), scuff on the right toe. She limped slightly on her right foot.[14]

Despite the directive chapter heading, which smacks of play-novelette theory ("Enter Suzy"), this listing goes on to an itemization of the contents of Suzy's pocketbook, "mirror, comb with two teeth missing, Lucky Strikes," and the like.[15] The strictly functional technique does not entail the release of metaphor (as in *Cannery Row*); clarity is its limi-

11. *ST*, p. 19.   12. *ST*, p. 25.   13. *ST*, p. 25.
14. *ST*, p. 35.   15. *ST*, p. 35.

tation. Quickly, by means of a strictly functional dialogue and narrative, Suzy is installed in Fauna's house on the advice of the local policeman, Joe Blaikey, and Suzy's join-up with Doc in all that remains to complete the plot line. The necessity for the juncture is established by a shift in Doc's point of view. He is contemplating a paper on frustration in octopi (a topic relevant to his postwar frame of mind) as a way to return to his scientific studies. Doc's first view of Suzy occurs during a thoughtful pause in his frustrating efforts to begin this paper; the passage is phrased in the manner of "is" thinking, and Doc's implicit admiration ensures the outcome of the novel:

> A girl had come out of the Bear Flag and was walking along Cannery Row toward Monterey. Doc couldn't see her face, but she had a fine walk, thigh and knee and ankle swinging free and proud, no jerk and totter the way so many women walked as they fell from step to step. No, this girl walked with her shoulders back and her chin up and her arms swinging in rhythm. It's a gay walk, Doc thought.[16]

Following this vision of physical coordination, Doc is able to work for a time—until his mind persuades him once more that the effort to write is useless.

By the end of Chapter VI, a careful development has established Doc's need, Suzy's presence, and the concern of Doc's friends in Cannery Row. The development is not merely geometric, as it can be in the play-novelettes; the people are realized too fully through sharp detail to be types. Unlike the development in Steinbeck's most ambitious novels, this is simple and precise enough to leave no doubt of its direction.

Once given this much, Steinbeck's artful concern is to bring Doc's misery to a resolution through love and to develop Suzy in more detail as a character worthy of Doc's interest. Steinbeck does all this, chiefly through parallels that pull together the otherwise detached characters and episodes. Joseph and Mary Rivas's professional estimate of Suzy's charm in Chapter VII is contrasted with Doc's warmer appreciation. Doc's chance meeting with a seer who lives

16. *ST*, p. 44.

in perfect and contented isolation provides a contrast with Doc's unhappy isolation (Chapter X) and with his increasing sense of his own lack of human warmth. He allays his uneasiness by promising himself the prospect of going to La Jolla for the spring tides to collect enough octopi to finish his study (Chapter XIII). His inability to generate much enthusiasm for a return to the prewar routine serves as a particularly effective measure of the inadequacy of prewar values in balance with the destructive memory of Army life. The narrowed conclusion is that Doc cannot burst through the immediate past by a return to a pattern of the more remote past—a collection trip. Some kind of new affirmation is required. Falling in love is presented as the most convenient affirmation.

Having developed this pattern, Steinbeck arranges to have Suzy arrive at Doc's lab with a present from Flora—a cake and some beer (Chapter XVII). The absurdity of eating cake and drinking beer leads Doc and Suzy to identical responses, foreshadowing their marriage of minds:

> Now Doc looked at Suzy and Suzy looked at Doc and they both had the same thought and they burst into laughter. . . . And the laughter was so pleasant they tried to keep it going after its momentum was spent.[17]

The bickering which follows immediately is suggestive of the less romantic relations between the sexes—an arranging of opposites to deepen the sense of human complexity, like attributing the pathos of defeat to the invaders in *The Moon Is Down.* Suzy insults Doc because she is afraid of admitting his superiority, and Doc's cruel reference to Suzy's profession is at least an outburst which has emotional roots. Sweetness survives this complete sweep of the spectrum of emotion. Doc's arid soul is refreshed by his anger; Suzy's toughness is replaced by a deep affection for Doc.

The plot line spells out these matters; nothing is left to suggestion. At the close of Chapter XVIII, after hearing Suzy's warm report of Doc, Fauna determines to promote their marriage, and Mack visits Doc to persuade him that

17. *ST*, p. 104.

marriage to a whore has definite advantages. In this way, the major and minor characters relate to the central action, the growing relationship between Doc and Suzy. The sum of these relationships widens the scope of the novel.

As counterpoint, Steinbeck interrupts this exposition to introduce materials that relate generally to the need for love. Joseph and Mary Rivas's astonished discovery that you cannot cheat at chess, in Chapter IV, proves that some relationships are absolutely "truer" than others, as love is truer than sex in the main plot. That discovery implies a rational, ordered world in contrast with the irrational confusions of war. The brief, comic history of Pacific Grove, in Chapter VIII, demonstrates the impossibility of regulating the more profound relations between people by means of the Puritan ethic. That insight lends value to the irrational emotions of love and hate. Fauna's astrological prediction that Hazel will be a President leads Hazel to take on the moral responsibility of saving Doc; the wholly unselfish affection, expressed at the cost of physical violence, contributes to Doc's need of Suzy—he cannot drive with a broken arm. Closely, Rivas's total objectivity and the seer's equally total subjectivity form a contrast which suggests that neither interpretation is complete by itself and that both resolve into a unity (love is its symbol) in the perfected, fairyland universe of an entire spectrum of responses to human experience. Significantly, Doc is given an inclusive awareness of the incompleteness of experience as a result of his private misery and as an intellectual conviction, which leaves him open to love and to hate. Joe Elegant's inability to love anything is conclusive proof that incompleteness is the price of lovelessness.

Unquestionably, these logical, external thematic developments attain lucidity at the price of simplicity. Theme does not cut deeply into character, and conversely.

However faulty, the artifice leads to the first of two Sweet Thursdays: a communal plan to marry Doc and Suzy. Two subordinate plot lines meet in this process. The first line is Fauna's request to Doc to "be nice" to Suzy (Chapter XX).[18]

18. *ST*, p. 133.

Fauna is motivated by a recognition that Suzy is a lady, not a whore.[19] The second line is Mack's idea, developed in Chapters XIV and XIX, to raffle off the Palace Flophouse, ostensibly to buy a microscope for Doc, but actually to avoid payment of rent to Joseph and Mary Rivas, the unwitting owner of the property. (As it turns out, Lee Chong has covered Mack and the boys.) Mack's motivation is a blend of affection for Doc and self-interest. The lucid plot lines and the tangled motivations suggest the complexity and the basic reasonableness of human affairs. Steinbeck sums up and restates these tensions in the central action in Chapters XXII and XXIII. In these chapters, to describe the action quite simply, love conquers all. "Is" thinking is the essential method of the narration of Suzy's preparations for Doc and her splendid dinner with Doc. The dinner succeeds in that Doc is able to say to Suzy, at its conclusion, "I'm lonely." His godhood vanishes in his humanity.

Since, in the reader's mind, there is no question of the conclusion, Steinbeck's not very difficult problem is to fill out the remaining third of the novel. He simply deepens the established theme of all-conquering love. To begin with, Fauna sends Suzy to San Francisco on an errand in the hope that her absence will increase Doc's realization of his need for love (Chapter XXIV). Then two purposes are served by the arrival of Old Jingleballicks, Doc's ancient, eccentric, and wealthy friend. First, the old man is entirely selfish. He eats Doc's dinner, takes Doc's bed, and borrows Doc's money. His selfishness contrasts favorably with Suzy's generosity. Second, at the close of the novel, and strictly as a function of plot, Old Jingleballicks endows Doc with a position at the California Institute of Technology and arranges for Doc to read a paper before the California Academy of Sciences. These fairy-tale developments contribute to the tone of the expected happy ending. Finally, in a functional shift characteristic of Steinbeck's handling of minor roles, Old Jingleballicks serves as the accurate analyst of Doc's trouble:

19. *ST*, pp. 153–54.

"You feel to me like a woman who has never had a baby but knows all the words. There's a lack of fulfillment in you. I think you have violated something or withheld something from yourself."[20]

Again, and more explicitly:

"Maybe you can't be wholly yourself because you've never given yourself wholly to someone else."[21]

The technique is familiar and embarrassing. Old Jingleballicks states explicitly (and pretentiously) what the sum of the novel has implied. The point of distinction, which avoids the gross sentimentality of (say) the final image in *The Grapes of Wrath*, is that Old Jingleballicks's insight does not inform the reader of a new truth; only Doc learns that his affection for Suzy is real. The reader has known it for some time. Steinbeck is more careful, here, than in many earlier novels to distinguish between a response designed for the character inside the novel and the reader on the outside. Old Jingleballicks's manner precludes sentiment. In any case, the novel does not require more of it. Also, the intrusion of the old man tends to shift the narrative technique from an association of dramatic and panoramic structures to a fairly exclusive panoramic method—an explanatory survey of what has been developing. This shift establishes the special quality of Old Jingleballicks, and his role is not confused in itself or in its relation to the development of the novel.

Steinbeck's attention to Suzy's self-respect is a further deepening of the established theme. Fauna has assured Suzy of her unique value by way of the transition to the dinner with Doc (Chapter XX), and this plot line serves later as Suzy's transition from whoredom to honest womanhood (Chapter XXVIII). Suzy provides a certain amount of realistic resistance to her own transformation and to the communal effort to marry her to Doc. She climaxes the fairyland of Cannery Row's masquerade party, at which she plays

20. *ST*, p. 186.   21. *ST*, p. 187.

Snow White—"a transformed Suzy in a wedding gown"—
by running away; she cannot accept the communal pressure
as Doc does.[22] She insists that Doc has to enter marriage
through his own free will.[23] In fact, Suzy's determined effort
to live alone in the boiler Mr. and Mrs. Malloy had occupied, while she works honestly as a waitress, has the expected effect of forcing Doc to declare his love in private,
dutifully, two pages before the close of the novel. Hazel acts
out a parody of the communal effort in the intervening space.
With the help of the seer's advice, a sense of duty as a coming President, and on the basis of Suzy's joking remark that
she wants nothing to do with Doc unless he breaks an arm
or leg, Hazel dutifully breaks Doc's arm with a baseball bat.
The intent of the action is as serious as Suzy's forceful expression of her worth when Doc brings her a box of candy.
Doc agrees to Suzy's estimate of herself, and she now becomes necessary to him as a driver—after Mack and the
boys give her a few hours of driving instruction—so the
lovers set off for La Jolla, the spring tides, and the enjoy-
ment of the good life.

The formal symmetry of *Sweet Thursday* is perfect. Part
answers to part. The conclusion is the result of the association of structure and materials that Steinbeck develops
carefully throughout the novel. Nothing is wasted or confused in *Sweet Thursday*. On the other hand, the mannered
development is so relaxed that an apparently random slice
of life, not an intentional construction, is the final effect.
Sweet Thursday gives the impression of having been written by an observer who looked out of his window every day
and put down what he saw until he had achieved about two
hundred pages of manuscript. Yet there is a genuine thematic
unity, as against the conventions of musical comedy, which
Steinbeck accepts only in passing. Mack defines the aimless-
ness of the narrative-as-plot in the "Prologue":

> Sometimes I want a book to break loose with a bunch of
> hooptedoodle. . . . Spin up some pretty words maybe, or sing
> a little song with language. That's nice. But I wish it was set

22. *ST*, p. 199.   23. Metzger, p. 117.

aside so I don't have to read it. I don't want hooptedoodle to get mixed up in the story.[24]

Mack's concluding hope is more pious than real, since the novel is a series of asides along the firm line of a preposterously sentimental plot. The salvation of a whore through sensitive romantic love and the transformation of the Doc of *Cannery Row* into a romantic lover are not realistic events, and they are not intended to be. The artificiality of the plot and of the conventions surrounding its events produce a thematic unity rather than a harmony between structure and materials.

A thin shadow of the language of "is" thinking is all that remains of the earlier Steinbeck's efforts to achieve a verbal art. Mack defines this reductive language in the "Preface":

> I like to know what color a thing is, how it smells and maybe how it looks, or maybe how a guy feels about it—but not too much of that. [25]

The appropriate language of "is" thinking is a hard, factual terminology of things. It is slipped in between the softer words of romantic love and loneliness. Even the sense of a group or group-man, in the united will to restore Doc to himself, to "doctor" him, is subordinated to the sentiment which resolves human nature into the happy conventions of musical comedy.

Steinbeck may be indulging in something like self-parody in this surprisingly late novel. The formally symmetrical plot and the pleasantly absurd materials transvalue *Cannery Row* by their evidence that a particular felicity from the past is available only and entirely as a pipe dream. The characters in the earlier work are not restored but altered. The novel's perfection of form matches the fantasized materials. Peter Lisca's suggestion that Steinbeck aims to destroy Doc as a serious character may be true, and it may be extended to Steinbeck's previous intellectual concerns. His awareness of technique survives most fully in the sophistication of the varied technical means he uses to achieve a

24. *ST*, p. viii.   25. *ST*, p. viii.

given end. The reductive effect of the romantic softness and the self-parody are limited to the materials. Perhaps, then, as Lisca suggests, Steinbeck is clearing away old things to make way for something new.[26] But the old things are the materials. *Sweet Thursday* is a finely accomplished structure, an extremely polished piece of work and, in this restricted sense, quite unlike as early a novel as *Tortilla Flat.*

26. Lisca, p. 282.

11

Jeu d'esprit

The Short Reign of Pippin IV

John Steinbeck was fifty-five in 1957 when *The Short Reign of Pippin IV*[1] was published. Nevertheless, the book is essentially a youthful effort, a charming miscellany of satirical and witty comment on things-as-they-are, strung out along a consciously artificial plot line. Only the easy and certain technique and the virtuosity of the technique denote the author's artistic maturity. In fact, in its miscellaneous aspect, *The Short Reign of Pippin IV* is a further extension of Steinbeck's commitment, most evident in *East of Eden*, to an exaggerated kind of panoramic structure, the result of an extreme version of "is" thinking. The firmly articulated plot line recalls *Sweet Thursday* but reaches beyond it by holding together the otherwise fragmentary episodes.

The consequences of a restoration of monarchy in France in 1957 refer to mankind at large, but the basic idea is a fantasy that invites a possibility rather than a literal fact. Fairyland becomes the fact of the political chaos of the Fourth Republic—an exaggerated mirror of fantasy which men are capable of inventing—and extends into the virtues of kingship.[2] Cannery Row can seem to be a more immediate fairyland.[3] Finally, the fantasy rests on distance; French-

1. John Steinbeck, *The Short Reign of Pippin IV: A Fabrication* (New York: The Viking Press, Inc., 1957). Hereafter cited as *SRP*.

2. Steinbeck's political instincts were accurate and wholly appropriate. The story is possible only in a country as socially civilized and as politically anarchical as France; there was something of kingship in the government of Charles de Gaulle, which came into existence on June 1, 1958, and was formalized through a somewhat royalist constitution (for example, granting an increase in the power of the executive branch, against the background of modern French politics) on September 28, 1958.

3. Ward Moore, "Cannery Row Revisited," *The Nation*, 179 (October 16, 1954), 325–27. Mr. Moore proves that Cannery Row is a real place and that many of its Steinbeckian inhabitants exist. There-

men are stranger (in Henry James's sense) than Americans. The materials of the fantasy can be entirely contemporary, the stuff of today's newspaper; and so they are.

As in *Sweet Thursday*, Steinbeck is completely aware of the impression he wishes to create and of the proper technical means to achieve his end. It is no accident that *The Short Reign of Pippin IV* is subtitled *A Fabrication*. The subtitle refers to the structure, the miscellaneous range of the episodes, as obviously as to the royal fantasy. If anything, the highly fabricated plot emphasizes the artificial quality of the dramatic structure, thus drawing attention to the entertainingly panoramic miscellany of episodes. A note on the cover of the paperback edition is an accurate measure of the range of the episodes, which exceed anything Steinbeck had attempted previously:

> John Steinbeck's hilarious and affectionate spoof on French politics, Texas millionaires, teen-age girl novelists, sex, and other human frailties.[4]

The association of an extremely panoramic structure with the rigidity of an exceedingly artificial plot line, continues and extends the novelistic formula of *East of Eden*, to the benefit of the comic spirit. The association of structures permits Steinbeck to range through any subject, in any manner, as he pleases, while the satire and wit relate to the dramatic structure, the plot line of a restoration of French monarchy. As in *Sweet Thursday*, this controlled freedom invests Steinbeck's familiar themes, techniques, and devices with a cheerful, refreshing ease.

The defect in this procedure is that, at worst, the materials are topical (the French crisis and the vogue of the girl novelist have passed or taken new forms), and the structure loses force through its inherent diffuseness, which extends to incoherence. Still, within the range of Steinbeck's work, *Sweet Thursday* and *The Short Reign of Pippin IV* are better than *Burning Bright*, at the opposite extreme. In fact, each

---

fore, as in *The Short Reign of Pippin IV*, Steinbeck begins with a basis in fact that can seem an invention.

4. John Steinbeck, *The Short Reign of Pippin IV* (New York: Bantam Books, April 1958).

of these extremes is a "fabrication," but one is charming and the other is merely rigid. The difference does not seem to lie in the extent of Steinbeck's commitment to theory, since both types are theory-ridden, but in the relative harmony (or association, as the case may be) between structure and materials that each type of novel makes possible for Steinbeck.

The plot is reductively lucid, as in *Sweet Thursday,* and it develops similarly through a series of major and minor parallels. While Pippin, an amateur astronomer, codiscoverer of the Elysée Comet, is recording an unexpected cosmic shower, the hopelessly fragmented political parties—there are forty-two—decide through their leaders to restore the monarchy. Literally, stars fall on Pippin. The detailed political squabbling includes some of Steinbeck's funniest writing. The Communists, Socialists, Christian Atheists, Christian Christians, Left and Right Centrists, and the Non-Tax-Payers' League determine to support kingship "for different reasons and for reasons beneficial to" themselves, and the ten royalist factions, after deadlocking, agree to recommend "the holy blood of Charlemagne," that is, Pippin, who alone is unaware of the fuss, lost in his delighted observation of the cosmic shower.[5]

Reactions permit a development of character. Pippin tries to find Uncle Charlie—Charles Martel, a genteel dealer in "unsigned paintings," other "art and bric-a-brac," and loans —for advice "in matters spiritual and temporal"; he turns to his daughter's touring American suitor, Tod Johnson, son of the Egg King of Petaluma, California, for advice in handling power.[6] Pippin's solidly bourgeois wife, Marie, turns for womanly consolation to her school friend, Sister Hyacinthe, a former nude dancer at the Folies Bergère, who took holy orders because her feet hurt; in due course, Sister Hyacinthe advises Pippin with deep understanding. These paralleled advisers are "placed" swiftly, but in some amusing depth. The thinnest character is Pippin's daughter, Clotilde, a twenty-year-old in revolt "against everything she could think of."[7] Clotilde is useful to the author, since the

5. *SRP,* pp. 39, 44.   6. *SRP,* pp. 19, 21.   7. *SRP,* p. 16.

theme of youthful rebellion allows Steinbeck to parody several tendencies of the time without much concern for internal consistency. Clotilde wrote a novel, *Adieu Ma Vie*, at fourteen, toured Europe and America in the wake of the novel's success as a film, introduced American teen-age clothes into France ("blue jeans, saddle oxfords, and a man's shirt"), and at sixteen and a half entered politics by joining the Communist party but encountered a priest during a strike and became inspired with religious zeal.[8] In spite of this shotgun characterization, Clotilde's function within the plot is clear. She justifies the presence of Tod Johnson, a more important and unified character.

The presentation of these characters is choreographic rather than realistic, and their balanced, lucid relationship is centered by a mutual reference to Pippin's obsessive problem of what to *do*, as a king, to promote the good life of France. The theme of the good life is familiar in Steinbeck's work, but its comic reduction conflicts with its finally serious relevance to society when Pippin attempts to alter the social order. Hence, there is a distraction in the constant humor of gratuitous juxtaposition—the astronomer become king, the nude become a nun, and the daughter become everything. *The Short Reign of Pippin IV* is more plainly a victim of its episodic humor than *Sweet Thursday* because it is ultimately a serious commentary on "a mad world, my masters," not merely a "pure entertainment." The aesthetic problem lies, not in the youthfully callow banter, but in the indeterminate intention of the fiction. Just so far as Steinbeck drops out of a tonal and thematic absurdity into seriousness, just so far the novel fails to maintain its delicate, associational structure.

The problem is uncomfortably visible in Steinbeck's handling of certain characters, where there is a recall, through an inversion of type, of earlier Steinbeckian characters. Pippin is much like the early Doc, a scientist dedicated to seeking absolute truth and to doing good; now he is the comfortable bourgeois whom Steinbeck handles roughly in the earlier work. Marie is a kind and really effi-

8. *SRP*, p. 16.

cient bourgeoise, bound to her domestic economy. Marie could be turned easily into Helen Van Deventer in *The Pastures of Heaven,* Mrs. Morales in *Tortilla Flat,* the puritanical lady in *Cannery Row,* and even Bernice Pritchard in *The Wayward Bus.* Clotilde is not unlike Steinbeck's unformed adolescents, such relatively unsympathetic characters as Rose of Sharon in *The Grapes of Wrath,* Norma in *The Wayward Bus,* and even Curley's wife in *Of Mice and Men,* but Clotilde is plainly a harmless, charming butterfly, rescued from utter futility by Tod Johnson. At least Uncle Charlie is true to type—as a sophisticated version of Mack in *Cannery Row* and (to an extent) in *Sweet Thursday*— since he knows and uses "the world" but remains uncorrupted. Sister Hyacinthe is less obvious than Uncle Charlie, but as true to type. She is the good whore or love goddess transformed into a Catholic nun; she is not unlike the clever, soft-hearted madams—Dora in *Cannery Row* and Fauna in *Sweet Thursday*—or such wise creatures of love as Camille in *The Wayward Bus* and Suzy in *Sweet Thursday,* or, even further back, the shyly pleasant and virginal mother, Lisa, of *In Dubious Battle.* Tod Johnson is the only consequential persona who is not an inverted or direct echo of an earlier Steinbeck character, perhaps because Johnson represents a class Steinbeck had not dealt with to much extent in earlier work.

Steinbeck's inversion or recall of earlier characters is not the point at issue, however, since any author must be free to do as he wishes. The point is that Steinbeck handles these characters strictly for whatever comedy can be extracted from their behavior. This use creates a comedy of inversion, which undercuts Pippin's ultimate and serious effort to refashion France so the nation may enjoy the good life.

The novel exhibits the author's considerable technical skill and range, as in the polished alternation of Pippin's private and public life, the interchapters (in effect) which concern Clotilde or the old man in charge of the statues, the inserted brief narratives of political maneuver, or the puzzlement of the city dog in the country (assuming a strange, biological determinism), the internal monologues in Steinbeck's own voice, the determined play on names, and the constant, ironic juxtapositions in large and small matters (the king's motor scooter, or the company that realizes a small fortune by selling miniature guillotines at the coronation). The range of style is also stunning, for it includes some literal French, some American slang transposed into French idiom, many epigrammatic phrases which convey the sense of ordinary French idiom, some literal American slang, and Steinbeck's relaxed, colloquial diction. Yet this talent in details does not transpose adequately from a royal fantasy into the serious proposals Pippin offers to the nation at the conclusion of the novel. Otherwise, as an end in itself, the fantasy is as delightful, as apt, and as narrowly conceived as the sentimental novel, *Sweet Thursday*, which precedes it.

The narrative sequence exemplifies these difficulties. With its focus on Pippin's adventures, the novel consists of five unnumbered sections (each introduced by a drawing), extending from thirty to fifty pages. Each section details Pippin's growing consciousness of what he is bound to attempt to accomplish through the power of kingship. This thematic development thrusts against the plot line, or the absurdity of the situation.

The first section opens with several expository pages on the theme of the felicity and privacy (equated terms) of Pippin and his family. As usual, a formal essay introduces the characters, but brevity and wit reduce the customary flatness of the introduction, and an ironic juxtaposing (always related to plot line) provides the essential momentary interest. The introduction occupies only five pages. The family lives in a converted coach house, rented from "a noble French family," which is seen only formally and by accident.[9] The irony enforces a happy anonymity. In the end, after being deposed, Pippin returns to that anonymity; no one is the wiser. Pippin is "fifty-four, lean, handsome, and healthy," his passion the "celestial hobby" of astronomy.[10] Aside from the irony of royal blood investigating

9. *SRP*, p. 12. 10. *SRP*, pp. 13, 12.

the rigid (feudal?) sequence of the heavens, Pippin's age, person, and scientific bent suggest that he is (like Juan Chicoy in *The Wayward Bus*) something of a god of the machine. (This section is prefaced by a breezy drawing of a star-studded telescope which is surrounded by tools and posed against a moving heaven—suggesting Pippin's role and its comic guise. *The Wayward Bus* has a cover drawing of Juan's gods and penates—to call attention to that novel's heavier symbolism.) Astronomy, with its overtone of a certain mysticism, is an interest that lifts Pippin above Steinbeck's Americans who know and love machines (Tom Joad, Juan Chicoy) without blurring the relationship; Pippin's budget is limited and his celestial photographs are published in *Match*. More sophisticated as well as simpler than the earlier Doc, Pippin is a broadly civilized intellect:

> He knew German, Italian, and English. He had a scholarly interest in progressive jazz, and he loved the cartoons in *Punch*. . . . He knew and liked Cole Porter, Ludwig Bemelmans, and, until a few years before, had known sixty per cent of the Harmonica Rascals. He had once shaken hands with Louis Armstrong and addressed him as Cher Maitre Satchmo, to which the master replied, "You frogs ape me."[11]

His modest, constant income from "the very best of a holding once great" in the wine country assures him the means to indulge in all of the intellectual joys, "carefully selected plays, concerts, and ballet . . . a good social club and three learned societies . . . books as he needed them," and the status of a "respected amateur" astronomer.[12] Pippin is in all ways a gentleman and one of Steinbeck's most attractive versions of the humanistic scientist. His suggestively associative name confirms Pippin's royalty and humanity.[13]

In Marie's character, Steinbeck extols French virtues that can be American vices. Marie's domestic concerns have puritanical overtones in other Steinbeck contexts; here, they are admirable, and Marie's solidity is not unlike Ma Joad's. For example, Steinbeck uses juxtaposition to alter a possibly

11. *SRP*, pp. 14–15.   12. *SRP*, p. 13.
13. Pepin the Short; and possibly, too, *piper*, to catch birds with a birdcall or to cheat; or *pipi*, to urinate; or, most likely, a combination of all.

bad quality into an excellence, sentence by sentence, in these four typical sentences:

> [Marie] was a good wife and a good manager who knew her province and stayed in it. She was buxom and pleasant and under other circumstances might have taken her place at the bar of a very good small restaurant. Like most Frenchwomen of her class, she hated waste and heretics, considering the latter a waste of good heavenly material. She admired her husband without trying to understand him and had a degree of friendship with him which is not found in those marriages where passionate love sets torch to peace of mind.[14]

If the second and fourth sentences are cut, Marie is not unlike Steinbeck's most hateful American women—middle-class and puritanical in values. But, combined with the other details, the quick, inclusive, comic portrait establishes the feel of pleasant economy combined with civilized formality which Steinbeck considers a French virtue. The portrait is an obvious contrast, then, with some unattractive elements in American life.

Similarly, Steinbeck emphasizes what is most favorable in Clotilde's character—her silliness is childish (hence, charming) rather than destructive, as in a sequence of adjectives describing her: "intense, violent, pretty, and overweight."[15] Omit the low comedy of "overweight," reverse the sequence, and one has a fearsome description of an American female, possibly of the college variety. With the details arranged as they are, the effect is disarming.

In all, the tonal control of the brief introduction sets the dominant impression of an orderly and pleasant universe, somewhat mad but most deeply rational, as expressed by the naturally witty people who inhabit it. Pippin's subsequent adventures strain the fabric of this fictional universe, but never to the breaking point. The good life, which Pippin knows, and the better life, which he can imagine out of his goodness, absorb the insane power relationships outside of Pippin's private sphere. He fails in the effort to refashion France, but his effort has its effect.

The remainder of the first section foreshadows much of

14. *SRP*, p. 14.   15. *SRP*, p. 16.

this effort and failure. Pippin's extremely formal argument with Marie suggests the extreme civilization of French manners, which permit the concurrent political crux to end, in all logic, with a restoration of the monarchy and the election of Pippin to the throne. Pippin's argument with Marie over the purchase of a better camera relates equally to the politics of the moment, for Pippin wants "to stop the fiery missiles in their flight."[16] As a further parallel, the current premier, M. Rumorgue, is really a plant expert, far more willing to work on his peculiar "feeling" thesis than at politics. Clearly, these people are more civilized than political; that is an aspect of their insane politics. Steinbeck deepens the point by a dancelike parallelism. Uncle Charlie advises Pippin to encourage Marie's guilt, just as Sister Hyacinthe advises Marie. The private wholeness of the family is restored through conflicting and somewhat cynical advice; even Clotilde's screen test has its place in that order. The private "sound and fury" which is worked out through cross-purposes is paralleled by the fantastic, formal maneuvering of the politicians, which ends in the creation of a throne and the selection of Pippin as monarch. The clutter of parties is logical; the dance movement echoes the party lists and the various reasons which convince everyone that a monarchy is necessary. The specific French context supports the political nonsense, and the classical tradition of comedy supports the designed contrivances of parallelism. The basic conception demands the slashing effect of high comedy, but many of Steinbeck's humorous touches are in the key of low comedy; the disproportion between intention and execution is a failure of artistic choice.

Pippin's will to institute the good life is a more serious matter than the bulk of the novel's comic dance of parallelism and juxtaposition can sustain. The shift is wild, as though the king of fairyland were reported to favor the fair trade law and the minimum wage. Steinbeck must not have felt that aesthetic shock, since there is no transition from the low comedy of grotesque humor to Pippin's moral earnestness.

16. *SRP*, p. 17.

This essential division deepens in the succeeding sections of the novel. Thus, Steinbeck ranges at will from satire to low comedy in the juxtapositions of Section II. Satire inspirits the comment that the coronation is "a triumph of disorder" because no American advertising agency can find the time to manage the affair:

> BBB & O was up to its ears rewriting the Constitution of the United States and at the same time marketing a new golf-mobile with pontoons. Riker, Dunlap, Hodgson, and Fellows would have taken the French job in the fall, but could not pull its key people off promotion of Nudent, the dentrifice which grows teeth.[17]

The wonderfully juxtaposed coronation march is closer to low comedy in its genial representation of past and present:

> First came the state carriages of the Great Peers, decorated with gold leaf and tumbling angels; then a battery of heavy artillery drawn by tractors; then a company of crossbowmen in slashed doublets and plumed hats; then a regiment of dragoons with burnished breastplates; then a group of heavy tanks and weapon-carriers, followed by the Noble Youth in full armor. A battalion of paratroopers followed, armed with submachine guns.[18]

As high comedy, Pippin grows bored with the procession, props up his royal robes in the carriage, and disappears in the crowd; no one detects the "prop" during the march.[19]

These several kinds of comedy are panoramic in their detail. The delightful scattering does not fuse into a whole, or with Pippin's moral earnestness. The association of structures works fairly well in *Sweet Thursday*, but the miscellaneous comedy, the series of details in the manner of "is" thinking, linked to the dramatic structure of the artificial plot, is served inadequately in this more complex novel.

17. *SRP*, p. 72. The play is evidently on Adlai Stevenson's difficulty in engaging an advertising agency during the presidential campaign of 1956.

18. *SRP*, p. 74. Obviously the May Day Parade.

19. *SRP*, p. 75. The play is on the coronation of Queen Elizabeth II. Marie observes later to Pippin, who has escaped to his telescope, "*Their* queen stood and sat, stood and sat for thirteen hours without even going to the—— Pippin, will you stop polishing that silly glass?"

Steinbeck seems to recognize and to welcome the result, since increasingly the comic detail occupies one corner of the novel and Pippin's search for effective power to institute the good life occupies another corner of the novel.

Clearly, by the third or middle section, the comic detail tends to be panoramic and the materials concerning Pippin's search for power tend to be dramatic. The detail is mainly by the side, while Pippin's adventures dovetail with the development of the plot.

Comic juxtaposition includes placing the perfect bourgeois, Marie, in "that gigantic old dustbox Versailles," among the bums who are the real nobility; and the appearance of Sister Hyacinthe, released to Versailles by her order to provide Marie with gossip "upon recognition of certain advantages which might accrue" to the order as well as "satisfaction" for a good deed.[20] These materials are framed on the one side by the "era of good feeling" of the political parties ("Christian Christians saw the churches full. Christian Atheists saw them empty."), and on the other by Tod Johnson's practical hint that titles might be sold "in Texas and Beverly Hills" to finance the retirement of the French nobility.[21] At the center, through conversations with Uncle Charlie, Tod, Clotilde, and especially Sister Hyacinthe, Pippin clarifies his basic desires for the nation on the principle that "people are good—just as long as they can be."[22] Sister Hyacinthe is the primary catalyst of the elements in Pippin's developing idea of kingship. She recognizes the danger of mere pride, yet concludes earthily, "You are a good man, Sire, and a good man draws women as cheese draws mice."[23] Pippin's primary adviser is Tod Johnson (through his father's questions), the pragmatic businessman. Tod observes that a government must have something to sell; Pippin suggests "perhaps peace, order—perhaps progress, happiness," or the good life.[24] Tod recommends a corporate organization, the socialism of business, and a firm grip on authority. In short, Tod understands power and

---

20. *SRP*, pp. 92, 94.   21. *SRP*, pp. 90, 122.
22. *SRP*, p. 101. Notice the echo from *East of Eden*.
23. *SRP*, p. 111.   24. *SRP*, p. 121.

Pippin's compulsion to do good, but he shows Pippin a course of action that no Frenchman can envisage in a context of Uncle Charlie's fearful cynicism, Clotilde's anger, and Sister Hyacinthe's resignation.

The division between comic detail and plot is intensely continued in Section IV. Comedy is mostly restricted to the opening frame of juxtaposed hits. The "little cloud," like a similar device in *Cannery Row*, introduces mainly serious matters.[25] The parable of a city dog recovering a sense of the past, once free in the country, illuminates Pippin's awareness of a role to play. Several visits to a Wordsworthian old man clarify his resolve. Sister Hyacinthe's mysterious faith in love sets off Uncle Charlie's brutal realism. The smoothly lucid progression, joining the parabolic freedom, the old man's sense of duty, and Sister Hyacinthe's faith that only love is the source of goodness and good deeds, puts down Uncle Charlie's worldly realism. As an association, Pippin *acts* for the first time, on his second visit to the old man, by entering the fight with the toughs. That private, releasing act moves Pippin to determine to act as a public figure for the good of the entire country: "——by God, I'll do it!"[26] Pippin determines to play the sacrificial Christ role, and Sister Hyacinthe confirms the rightness of that choice by praising it:

> I have read your remarks to the convention. They were bold remarks, Sire. Yes, I imagine that you have failed, you personally, but I wonder whether your words have failed. I remember another who failed—whose words we live by.[27]

Steinbeck identifies other men with Christ in other novels (Jim Casy, Juan Chicoy) in part through initials. Here, the frank identification requires proof through action, not through a device. Steinbeck gains clarity through directness—at some cost, it should be noted, to the novel's structural integrity.

A final event pulls together the plot, since the comedy has been lost. Still wet from the fight (he had been tossed into the moat) and hot with a conviction to act, Pippin re-

25. *SRP*, p. 129.
26. *SRP*, p. 179.   27. *SRP*, p. 179.

turns to the palace, bursts in on Marie, and makes love to her. This event recalls Mr. Pritchard's gesture, but it is more fortunate. Marie does not show Mrs. Pritchard's bitchy reactions. Pippin's lovemaking is his second positive act, denoting his willingness to perform in accord with his conscience.

Some absurd or comic detail is scattered about, such as Pippin's habit of going into the country on a motor scooter, his crown replaced by a crash helmet, or the "elderly nobleman who spoke earnestly and loudly in Gothic type into Charles's ear," but this kind of detail tends to be associated with the development of the plot more consistently here than in the earlier sections.[28] A formal pattern of opposites governs the comic touches. Pippin is told, for example, that his speech to the convention that will adopt the Code Pippin must be restricted to patriotic generalizations, but he nevertheless orders the convention to undertake a program of economic reform. A low comedy detail is fitted carefully into this pattern of opposites, for as Pippin turns away from the convention, which is in a state of shock, he is revealed as a silly figure, to the relief of the audience:

> An open-mouthed page was standing on the edge of his purple and ermine-collared cape. It ripped from his shoulders and fell to the floor, exposing the row of safety pins up the back of his tunic, and the baggy crotch of the trousers flopping between his knees. Strain in children and adults opens two avenues of relief—laughter or tears—and either is equally accessible. The safety pins did it. Beginning with a snigger in the front benches, it spread to giggles, and then to hysteric laughter. . . . Thus they channeled the shock the king's message had given them, the shock and the terror and their own deep sense of guilt.[29]

The twelve final words indicate Steinbeck's purpose and reveal the rationale for the completely appropriate comic strategy. After all, Pippin is not in fact a Christ, nor is his message a religious insight. He is a modern saint, perhaps, in the sense that he has an orderly, humanistic, scientific mind. He had studied the problems thoroughly; his evident interest in the truth is the cause of the cloud that prefigures

28. *SRP*, p. 139.   29. *SRP*, p. 175.

the ultimate horror in the audience. So, in not being a Christ, a heroic persona of sacrificial dignity, Pippin must be the fool. His sad calm and his safe, anonymous return to the converted coach house (where Marie has preceded him) is a metaphor of the acceptance of merely human limitations, of the best one can do in an imperfect universe.

So these comic details are structural in their support of the satiric plot. The governing principle is that Pippin's humiliating public display—his speech as well as the accident that follows it—is really the only way in which Pippin can act. As a framing detail before the speech, the convention committee insists on wearing court dress and forces Pippin to wear an especially badly fitting costume. The old Socialist, "Honnete Jean Veauvache, now Comte des Quatre Chats," explains why in an essay speech which concludes on this key point:

> "And if to this assembly should come the king, dressed in a two-button suit and a Sulka tie, carrying his papers in a briefcase, I shudder to think of the reaction. Indeed I feel that such a king would be laughed out of office."[30]

"A venerable Academician" underlines the suggested threat: "The king may not permit himself to be ridiculous."[31] Again, as another framing detail, Pippin consults with Uncle Charlie, who is ready to fly the country in expectation of the address and who repeats the point in somewhat racier language:

> "When a pawn tries to do the work of government—then the pawn is a fool."[32]

In a sense, Pippin is laughed out of office, since he does permit himself to *seem* (but not to *be*) ridiculous, and he plays the fool by intent as well as by accident. If he is somewhat a victim—of birth as of accident—assuredly he wills the speech of reason and goodness which is his true downfall. His comic exit assumes that he will not be harmed for truthfulness, essentially because the nation is mindlessly forgetful and rational in equal parts. Hence, after the con-

30. *SRP*, p. 159.
31. *SRP*, p. 160.   32. *SRP*, p. 164.

frontations which clarify these points, Pippin simply goes home to become again (even to the gendarme called out by the rioting) no more than the private citizen. Of course, with French prudence, Pippin takes the precaution beforehand of secreting his motor scooter; he does not need it for flight, only for a return to the converted coach house; and it runs out of gas. The conclusion is that the clown is allowed everything and forgiven everything.

Several conclusions are in order. First, *The Short Reign of Pippin IV* is in genre a *roman à clef*, whose parts separate into superficial comic hits and serious essays on the good life. The aesthetic result is a novelistic wabble—a delightful comedy of the times and a serious tract for the times. Second, because the two intentions do not fuse, the novel lacks structural unity. As comedy, the novel accepts the condemnation that Steinbeck applied to *L'Affaire Lettuceburg*: "And this book is fairly clever, has skillful passages, but tricks and jokes."[33] As a serious work, the novel depends heavily on the essay, the set speech, the authorial comment. The sharp detail of "is" thinking degenerates into relatively isolated hits; an externalized plot provides an otherwise unobtainable narrative lucidity; instead of a dramatic structure conceived as a sequence of actions, as in Steinbeck's most impressive work, pure statement carries the burden of the events, recalling the play-novelette theory and the allegorical signs that crop up repeatedly in the ambitious longer fiction which Steinbeck produced in the period after 1940. Third, the mix of these various tendencies and devices does not seem to cause Steinbeck misgivings. Completely relaxed, he indulges what he knows. The consequent aesthetic mess is clearly intentional. No further development seems possible along the line of misguided novelistic theory as exemplified by *The Short Reign of Pippin IV*.

33. Lewis Gannett, "Introduction: John Steinbeck's Way of Writing," *The Viking Portable Steinbeck* (New York: The Viking Press, Inc., 1946), p. xxii.

12

The End of the Road

The Winter of Our Discontent

Steinbeck's valedictory novel, *The Winter of Our Discontent*,[1] is a bitter examination of a narrowed America. The bleak fifties reveal to Steinbeck a morally weakened people, a people who are enduring the irreversibly corruptive effects of material affluence. The comic mood has passed. The result is a major novel, a heavy and direct consideration of the decayed times.

In an altered setting, *The Winter of Our Discontent* recalls the materials of *The Grapes of Wrath*. Much seems to be changed, and is; but a close, sympathetic reading suggests that much remains as it was, seen in a darker light. The Okies have been replaced by Easterners, the farm by the small city on the fringes of a metropolis, and literal survival has become the doubtful relevance of moral rectitude (that is to say, the classical American past). The climate comprises such contemporary facts as ethnic prejudice, kickbacks, real estate promotion, political manipulation, sexual blackmail, rigged quiz shows and essay contests, loss leaders, and general sharp dealing. These details have their equivalent parallels in *The Grapes of Wrath*—in the sophisticated "townie" treatment, the economic exploitation of "rural" innocents, as when the Okies sell off their goods, buy automobiles, and head for a falsified West: oversold, exploited, or simply cheated. Their literal wasteland, the Dust Bowl, has become the contemporary, internalized wasteland of spoiled or irrelevant idealism. Their search for survival and their reach for human dignity in work have become an increasingly hopeless search for a minimum of domestic self-respect, modulating into an intelligent sell-out.

1. John Steinbeck, *The Winter of Our Discontent* (New York: The Viking Press, Inc., 1961). Hereafter cited as *WOD*.

To object to Steinbeck's particular evidence of American corruption in the fifties on grounds that such human flaws are trivia or have always been with us in one form or another, is to miss Steinbeck's point. The darkness in *The Winter of Our Discontent* is almost total, whereas a sustained idealism lifts *The Grapes of Wrath* to a conclusion (however forced) that promises a brighter future.

As the ultimate similarity to *The Grapes of Wrath, The Winter of Our Discontent* is a major effort; it is not, for Steinbeck, a merely journalistic exposé of temporary conditions.[2] Its probable genesis is Steinbeck's 1956 short story, "How Mr. Hogan Robbed a Bank." Steinbeck's personal discontent is recorded in several essays during the period.[3]

Despite its excellences, *The Winter of Our Discontent* does not jell as a novel. The expansion of the crisply objective short story produces a sermonic platform, an essayish, mechanical, finally incoherent parable. The novel's failure is due, in part, to the point of view and in part to a lack of conviction in the materials—which are petty in detail, querulous in tone, and thoroughly ambiguous in their fictive embodiment. Perhaps the failure is the revenge of actuality on the author's overly bleak selection of particular details. More immediately, the failure is a direct consequence of Steinbeck's mature practice as a novelist.

The Winter of Our Discontent, in fact, recapitulates the novelistic strategies in Steinbeck's immediately preceding novels. The plot is "busy" and fully articulated, while the thematic material is diffuse and self-contradictory.[4] The

2. Few people could have imagined, in the late thirties, that the needs of the Okies would be accommodated by wartime jobs and later by Cold War jobs. There is no reason to think that Steinbeck's vision of the fifties is intended to be any less permanent than his view of the thirties. His sense of history may be at fault, but not his intended realism as a novelist. Similarly, there is no reason to doubt the intended seriousness of his moralistic analysis of American social-economic conditions, or the symbolic tendencies of American life, in the fifties.

3. For an excellent analysis of the "is" thinking short story in relation to the seriously flawed novel, consult Warren French, "Steinbeck's Winter Tale," *Modern Fiction Studies,* 11 (Spring 1965), 66–74.

4. So much so that James Woodress has read *The Winter of Our Discontent* as "an imaginative grappling with the author's own sur-

characters are hardly more than sketches of persons at the mercy of the plot line. Steinbeck's association of panoramic materials, of miscellaneous details rendered in the objective, lucid manner of "is" thinking that are linked to the dramatic structure of an external, artificial plot, is not an intolerable strain in a comic novel, with its artifice and its need for a lucid narrative surface. This fictional method does, however, prevent the profound, analytical probing of cause and effect which is the *raison d'être* of a novel with realistic, social pretensions. The main character, Ethan Allen Hawley, is delineated in his various actions. Steinbeck records his moral disgust, and he can report but he cannot explain Hawley's reactions by supplying motivation beyond the given surface of a particular event. To be sure, plot mechanisms are necessarily unrelated to the development or analysis of character. Once Hawley is in limbo as an understandable character, the plot machinery produces a series of isolated, seemingly arbitrary climaxes, as the events occur within a design that is free of internal necessity. In this respect, events evolve through the localized plot twisting of a melodrama. The absence of organic form is especially visible because of Steinbeck's effort to deal with a large social theme, which forces comparison with the predominately organic form of *The Grapes of Wrath*. What had been epic, pastoral, and naive in the earlier novel has become narrowly playlike or theatrical in form, and the materials have become correspondingly urbanized to agree with an ironic or cynical point of view.[5]

---

render to prosperity during the years of his literary decline in the Fifties." Consult James Woodress, "John Steinbeck: Hostage to Fortune," *South Atlantic Quarterly*, 63 (Summer 1964), 395–96. Quoted by permission of the author. The dedication to the novel and the prefatory statement leave no doubt of Steinbeck's overt intention to attack American materialism and the cash nexus as manifested in the fifties. Steinbeck's control of the novel's materials is less than successful.

5. Warren French notes that "the University of Texas has also acquired a manuscript of a work entitled 'How Mr. Hogan Robbed a Bank or The American Dream,' described by the author on the cover as 'an unpublished, unproduced, unconsidered play in one act.'" Consult Warren French, *John Steinbeck* (New York: Twayne Publishers, Inc., 1961), p. 174. Quoted by permission of Twayne Pub-

Very probably Steinbeck intended these differences between the earlier and the later novel. There is no point, after all, in rewriting *The Grapes of Wrath*. On the other hand, the given materials of the later novel would seem to demand an organic form.

Steinbeck's unwillingness or inability to elucidate Ethan Allen Hawley approximates, in unearned mystery, the conception of character-making in his first novel, *Cup of Gold*. Henry Morgan is entirely unknowing, the victim of an unfathomed symbol; Hawley is marked by a similar opacity because his motivation is less than secure.[6] Hawley's denial of the New England ethic in his maturity (he is just under forty), to gain wealth and power in the world, occurs for the apparent reason that he wishes to please his wife and his children.[7] But Mary Hawley is a sexual toy, not unlike Henry Morgan's mulatto; Hawley despises his crude son and at best tolerates his strange daughter.[8] These ugly impressions, recorded by Hawley's sensibility, do not square with his view of himself as an inheritor of integrity, a living representative of the better old days, although they have failed to motivate his "metamorphosis."[9] Even the integrity

---

lishers, Inc. Whether the play version was an afterthought or the basis of the short story cum novel is unknown, but there is considerable interest (given my argument) in the fact that Steinbeck did think of the work on some level in terms of theatre.

6. Particularly, the "I" is evasive. Ellen sees that Hawley is opaque, and Mary is aware of this characteristic at times. Margie Young-Hunt recognizes Hawley's ruthlessness. Whether these qualities are flaws remains unclear. The narrative voice never directly engages that aspect of Hawley's character. Instead, the objective narrative method excludes us from Hawley's mind, on the surface of the unfolding events. This device may be an intended irony of discontinuity; in practice the result is baffling. The effect that emerges is the absolute isolation of each character from the other within the family. Hawley does not use Mary's name; she is often asleep. Hawley sees no good at all in his son, and his remarks to Allen are consistently shocking—truly ugly; Hawley is never conscious of this tonal ugliness. Mary is. Hawley sees Ellen as little more than a scheming female. The three of them regard him as a failure. Suddenly, at the end, Ellen demonstrates an intense love for her father. This mixture of responses and attitudes does little to clarify Hawley's character.

7. *WOD*, pp. 18, 39, 52–53, 114–15.

8. *WOD*, pp. 7, 83–86, 114, 128–29.

9. *WOD*, p. 140.

of the old days is qualified by the great symbolic event in the past, the burning of the whaling ship, the *Belle-Adair*, which Capt'n Hawley and Capt'n Baker owned jointly; Hawley believes that Capt'n Baker may have set the fire to collect insurance money.[10] Against this ambiguous background, we may gather that Hawley can embark on an apparently uncharacteristic career of polite crime because the willingness is already there, latent in Hawley's view of himself and his family, posed against the long view of the continuity of evil in the social, moral, political, and economic orders. In this sense, Hawley may be a passive victim of the age, which is like all ages, as he determines at last to avenge his felt injustices by playing the clever scoundrel. Or he may be acting cheerfully and successfully in a role the social order expects and approves, out of inner capabilities he does not know he possesses until he begins to exercise them. Or he may be acting playfully, at first, but with an increasing self-loathing and with an all-encompassing disgust at contemporary manners and morals. The novel supports all of these possible readings. The consequent uncertainty of Hawley's motivation provides immediate and localized gains in suspense, in the turns of the plot, at the cost of blunting any persuasive analysis of a specific character, or of a given time, or of a particular coherence in the parable.

Steinbeck's technical innovation is a first-person narration. This device intensifies the internalized quality of the times and reinforces the uncertainties of Hawley's motivation. Hawley reports his actions as ends in themselves, events on the surface of the narrative, along with his twinges of remorse and disgust. His narration is a report, however, and so it lacks the self-analysis or illumination that could delineate a particular motivation.

Perhaps there is some clue to Steinbeck's best intention in his choice of dividing the novel into two parts. Each part is preceded by two chapters of third-person narration; then follow eight and ten chapters of first-person narrative. Aside from the awkwardness of shifting the narrative voice

10. *WOD*, pp. 19, 283.

without apparent cause, the third-person narration under-scores Hawley's moral passivity. He is acted on by others, especially at the opening of the novel, where a processional device increases his distanced passivity, for there, on the early morning of Good Friday, 1960, with the commemoration of the Crucifixion yielding to family and business concerns, Hawley enters the novel by getting "a couple of shocks" during spaced encounters with various personages: Mary, his wife, discontented with his superior joking and economic failure; Red Baker, an unconcerned red setter; Joey Morphy, a clever bank teller with a casual theory of how to rob a bank, and (as he closes out the chapter) a sense of moral relativity about kickbacks; Mr. Baker, the local banker, Capt'n Baker's descendant, who encourages Hawley to make money ("You've got to scrape up some courage, some daring."); Alfio Marullo, the owner of the grocery store Hawley had owned and in which he now clerks, who shows Hawley how to profit by tricks ("You got to learn the tricks, kid, or you go broke."); and Mr. Biggers, a grocery salesman, who proposes a kickback in return for custom and who gives Hawley a concealed bribe to begin with.[11] These overwhelming encounters firmly establish a thematic line: Hawley is a failure by the measure of his inability to take either a legal or illegal profit.

This moral assault continues into the later part of the same day in Chapter II, still in the third person. Hawley's teenage son Allen is in pursuit of the main chance; he is writing an essay on "Why you love America" for a Hearst promotional contest. Hawley stigmatizes the contest and all it implies by judging his son with incredible harsh-ness: "Do you really love America or do you love prizes?"[12] Still, the usable past is shelved in Hawley's attic; great-grandfather's library is available to Allen's pragmatic use. The cash value of patriotism, of the rhetoric of history, is the effective usefulness of the past for Allen as for the Hearst organization. The immediate present is Mary's nag-ging. She wishes Hawley would make some money to sat-isfy her pride and the pride of her two children. Hawley is

11. *WOD*, pp. 32, 19, 25. 12. *WOD*, p. 35.

never very serious with Mary, and she does not take seriously his offer to rob a bank, but that is precisely the idea Joey Morphy has dropped into Hawley's consciousness, or conscience. The potential crime is an elegant test of intellect and restraint, an individual test of disciplined courage, an act that suits Hawley's submerged but innate moral and intellectual distinction. It is both a realistically symbolic flouting of a corrupt society and a measure of acquiescence in the values of that society. Further, Margie Young-Hunt, the descendant of a witch, has predicted (for Mary) that Hawley will "get money and lots of money."[13] The convergence of these active forces sets off Hawley's passive quest.

Hawley's mixture of desire and disgust, of acquiescence and self-loathing, determines Steinbeck's formal arrangement of the novel: Hawley must act, but he must hate his actions; his luck must turn, but he must hate its turning. Above all, he must seem to remain passive, and therefore innocent. These appositions mean that Hawley cannot know himself, nor can the reader know him. Evidently Steinbeck accepted the resulting uncertainty in Hawley's characterization as the acceptable price of delineating a good man's bemused, almost playful acceptance of the main chance, the cash nexus. The "is" thinking device of the sharply rendered, objective detail, combined with the distancing effect of third-person narration and the procession of external "shocks," are the triumphantly proper techniques for rendering Hawley's unwilling immersion in the ways (and values and expectations) of the world. In short, Hawley's resistance to this process is stylistic and formal; his actions amount to an overreaction, a more than complete acquiescence in the various evil roles that his family and would-be friends force on him.

Also, by a remarkable *tour de force* (through first-person narration), Chapters III through X of Part One preserve the initial third-person impression of Hawley's passivity. Thus, for example, his musing alters New Baytown's past; what had been an emblem of familial pride becomes a more realis-

13. WOD, p. 39.

tic contemplation, forced (as it were) into Hawley's consciousness:

> Its first settlers, and my ancestors, I believe, were sons of those restless, treacherous, quarrelsome, avaricious seafaring men who were a headache to Europe under Elizabeth. . . . They successfully combined piracy and puritanism, which aren't so unalike when you come right down to it.[14]

Hawley has become poor, like his dreamy father, and he is akin in failure to his alter ago, Danny Taylor. He has used history to create a false superiority, a prideful name, to keep from the necessary and traditional family task of feathering his nest. Hawley's musings on these ambiguities of history, on his own atavistic propensity for evil, and on the contemporary hanky-panky in New Baystown, occupy a leisurely three chapters; by Chaper VI Hawley has persuaded himself to "get ahead," not as a Good Man, but by actions that confirm Margie's vision of his inner being—a rattlesnake.[15] He has no real wish to prosper; he distrusts wealth, but he feels propelled by the pressures and revelations of past and present.

A marked lack of movement, a grinding away within a limited space, is apparent at about this point in the novel. Clearly, that effect is intentional. Because Hawley's inner motives are withheld, because he acts as others wish while preserving his rooted innocence (as in the rereading of the past), his character takes on an ambiguity which also informs the novel's materials; he, and Steinbeck, have it both ways. In a strange passage in Chapter VII, Hawley strikes Mary as a terrible man—apparently his normal impression —and as a terror.[16] There is no corresponding flavor of this persona in Hawley's winsome, rather blarney style—in his way of seeing himself. The impression of the style is that Hawley is, for the most part, a charming man, especially in his musings, yet most of his actions deny this impression.

---

14. *WOD*, p. 44. Hawley recalls a variety of Steinbeck characters —Junius Maltby, the *paisanos*, the early Tom Joad, Mack and the boys, and others—in this determination "to avoid the trap."

15. *WOD*, pp. 95, 101.   16. *WOD*, pp. 114–16.

Thus, the first-person narration preserves Hawley's passivity and contributes a further range of ambiguity to his character.

For example, the rabbit kill, at the beginning of Chapter VIII, sickens Hawley. A few pages later, he warns Danny Taylor in explicit detail that Danny's property has become valuable; it is to be the site of an airport, a site that Mr. Baker is trying to buy (dishonestly) from Danny. Hawley insists that Danny must sell the property at a good price, finance a cure, and begin a new life. Hawley's consciousness fuses these several facts. The rabbit kill seems to him a symbol of what he is capable of doing; Danny succeeds in forcing Hawley to loan him a thousand dollars (Mary's money) for an unwanted alcoholic cure, and leaves Hawley a willed transfer of the property. Does Hawley hunt down Danny with money to assure the transfer? Hawley thinks that is the case. An image at the close of Chapter IX fuses the rabbit kill and Danny's doom.[17] The text supports the probability that Danny reads Hawley's motive as self-interest.[18] At the close of the novel, Danny's corpse is found on the property, in the ruined basement the two men as youths had made into a secret place. The intangibles of friendship and sorrow are replaced by the fact that Hawley has the property.

In this indirect fashion, but with much less soul-searching, Hawley develops other main chances. He is direct, in a sense, in reporting to the Immigration and Naturalization Service Alfio Marullo's probably illegal entry into the States. Even so, the damning probability of the illegal entry is given to Hawley by Morphy as an educated guess, and Hawley's betrayal by telephone is anonymous.[19] There are two ironic consequences in the moral twilight of Hawley's new world. First, in his belief that Hawley is the ideal American type, "a monument to something he believed in once," Marullo leaves the grocery store to Hawley.[20] Second, the government man arrives at the grocery store just in time

---

17. *WOD*, p. 173.   18. *WOD*, p. 177.

19. *WOD*, pp. 148–49, 188.

20. *WOD*, p. 255. Marullo sells the store to Hawley for the giveaway price of $3,000. In effect, he gives Hawley the store.

to unwittingly prevent Hawley's attempt to hold up the local bank; and Morphy has intuited a holdup. These extreme, externally plotted turnabouts exceed the needs of irony; they embrace melodrama.

A further series of discoveries close out the novel in a blaze of irony at the extreme, for each public or semipublic disclosure of a moral wrong reflects on Hawley's similar (but secret) action. Allen's plagiarism is found out; Ellen informs on him: "I didn't want him to go to jail."[21] The city administration is exposed in its time-honored dishonesty, as part of Mr. Baker's scheme to manipulate some land deals. Now that Hawley is economically respectable, Mr. Baker proposes that Hawley should stand (in an obviously rigged election) for town manager.[22] In turn, Hawley confronts Baker and beats him at every move, emerging as a free agent; he even transfers the onus of reporting Marullo to Baker.[23] Hawley goes further by extorting a larger discount from Mr. Biggers, as a sort of preparation for dealing with Mr. Baker. In short, the bad guys are caught out at various kinds of stealing, the tables are turned on them, and the time (just after the Fourth of July) proclaims Hawley's triumphant, successful independence, his disarming public integrity. Moreover, while he takes pleasure in demonstrating to Biggers that he is not "a country boy" and to Baker that "I am not a pleasant fool," he misses any sense, in his rage at his son's lazy arrogance, that father and son are not dissimilar.[24] Margie Young-Hunt sees the similarity by applying blackmail, not to an overt crime of Hawley's, but to his private sense of a vanished integrity; she proposes to become his friend, for a price.

These sudden and violent developments are focused and extended by certain technical devices. Animals serve a symbolic purpose: Red Baker and the store cat lead truly independent lives, in contrast with the involved obligations of human beings, but animals are easy victims, as in Hawley's

---

21. *WOD*, p. 307.

22. *WOD*, p. 282. Baker's politics are identified by his expressed wish to keep out "the egghead fringe," p. 281.

23. *WOD*, pp. 290–91.   24. *WOD*, pp. 284, 291, 294.

rabbit kill. Mary Hawley is seen often in sleep (in Hawley's narration) to emphasize her real distance from her husband; Hawley's constant teasing during Mary's waking hours continues that overtone. There is a good deal of formal and developed mysticism: Ellen is a sleepwalker, and in that state she has a mysterious, somewhat sexual attraction to the family's snake talisman; Margie Young-Hunt is a witch, or at least a highly perceptive soothsayer in her prediction or intuition of Hawley's change, which she claims to have caused as the novel closes because she wants to have Hawley as one of her protectors.[25] Hawley himself has a foreshadowing dream of Danny Taylor's death.[26] Among these devices, familiar in Steinbeck's repertory, there is a detached essay, almost a short story, about Margie Young-Hunt (Chapter XII), distanced by third-person narration; a considerable use of flashback as an instrument of Hawley's memory; and a tight patterning that will support an allegorical reading, or a typified fable of American life, as in the heavy use of the processional. Above all, characters are split, paired, and doubled. Danny Taylor is Hawley's double or alter ego, but other characters take that role in ironic counterpoint as the novel develops. Marullo sees Hawley (falsely) as his idealized double. Allen and Mr. Baker seem to Hawley to be his opposites. He hates and rejects both of them, but, in fact, as the novel concludes, he knows they are his secret doubles. The government man is an experienced grocery clerk, and he takes on Hawley's former role for a short time when he brings the good news of Marullo's esteem for Hawley. Mary Hawley and Margie Young-Hunt are paired, much like Hawley and Morphy. The language is rich, as in *Cup of Gold* (Hawley is a Harvard man), observational, and sometimes strained as in the epithets for Mary. The language approximates Hawley's mental processes.

These several devices are finely crafted in themselves, but they do not reduce the effect of an overly swift, twisted plot as the novel concludes, and they stand by the side (as it were) of the novel's real impact. This novel's ultimate

25. *WOD*, pp. 301–2.   26. *WOD*, pp. 278–79.

frisson is the closely patterned demonstration of how far a seeming passivity can carry a man on the seemingly wayward current of success, when in fact the passivity is a mask for intelligent, entirely self-interested maneuver. This disproportion between ends and means is Steinbeck's theme, and it informs the materials—the wider evidence of an absolute falsity in American life in the fifties—with a pervasive irony. For example, the leading detail of the title provides the paradox that spring is false in its promise; because it is a hopelessly corrupted period in an essentially forgotten religious calendar, spring is truly a winter of moral discontent. This ironic turnabout is substantiated in every nuance of Hawley's destructive resurrection. His three-month rise from a numbed poverty into economic respectability is a humanly fearful process. The power of the novel lies in this theme and in its associated materials.

Interestingly, the intensely schematic plot vitiates the powerful theme and the displayed materials by its melodramatic twists and turns. Emphatic coincidence, sudden revelation, and unexpected irony reduce the potentially tragic (perhaps intended) impact of the novel to something closer to stage comedy. To some extent, this reduction underlines Hawley's real and pretended passivity. To a much greater extent it drains the significance of the theme and the materials.

If Steinbeck's probable intention is to display the ironic terror of a false passivity, surely the intention is inadequately served by the novelist's structural technique. The strictly formal, manipulated pattern, the use of suspense for immediately mysterious effects which are blunted or reversed in the end, and the lack of insight into Hawley's deepest motivation produce a novel that is skin deep—a contrivance, a simplified pattern of plot gymnastics, a manipulation of theatrical situations and theatrical characters. This judgment may account for the novel's incredible conclusion, as a species of formal resolution.

Hawley's self-hatred is the discovered sum of what he has done so easily and so precisely and of his accumulated evidence that evil is tawdry and ever present. Humanistic or spiritual values are not practical; family, decency, and love are mere words. Nevertheless, those values motivate Marullo and Ellen. While Hawley's occasional remorse does not affect his action, remorse invokes a pattern that requires his self-sacrifice as an affirmation of good and a denial of evil. In fact, he intends to cut his wrists in the mystical Place, the cavelike hole in the remains of the stone foundation of the old Hawley wharf or dock. That is the Place where he can think, where he is truest to himself and to the idealized past. The harbor lights carry Hawley into a contemplation of "the light," and as he reaches into his pocket for the razor blades he grasps the family talisman, "the light-bearer."[27] So he determines to live, "to return the talisman to its new owner"—presumably the honest Ellen —"else another light might go out," a phrase that echoes the novel's dedication.[28]

Here, the rise of suspense and the turnabout into hopefulness is plainly the stuff of melodrama. With one stroke, Hawley's experience of wickedness becomes its opposite. The snake talisman, the image of circularity, of things becoming their opposite, is intruded to justify a purely formal resolution, an upbeat of idealism which is not an aspect of the novel's development of character and theme. Certainly this ending is a *coup de théâtre*, a victory of plot over substance.

Given its characteristics, then, *The Winter of Our Discontent* does not mark a development in Steinbeck's career. Instead, this last novel recapitulates Steinbeck's particular, mature conception of what a novel is, of how it is put together. The resulting strengths and weaknesses are typical rather than unique in Steinbeck's late fiction.

27. *WOD*, p. 311.   28. *WOD*, p. 311.

Epilogue

John Steinbeck's difficulty in fusing structure with materials is remarkably self-sustaining.

What does this say? Surely not that Steinbeck is a failed novelist—more fairly, that his longer fiction is flawed in one aspect. This is knowledge, and knowledge permits a better level of judgment. Its relative absence presented earlier critics with an enigma. Look, they said, this or that novel is masterful, but somehow these other novels are much less accomplished. The fragmented perspective is often implicit, unquestioned. At most, its support is the "decline and fall" presupposition; namely, that Steinbeck was a splendid writer at one point, but the changing times, a shift in residence, the death of a friend, and so on, caused a precipitate decline in the quality of his work. I do not deny that Steinbeck was affected, personally as well as in his writing, by these and other external factors. Cause is always difficult to assign, since it can comprise many factors, but one factor may be predominant. In fact, the famous decline is oddly ever present, except where structure and materials are fused. What, then, shall we make of these representative facts: that *Cup of Gold* is closely related structurally to *The Winter of Our Discontent*; that "is" thinking exaggerates (without denying or changing) the "open" structure of some of the earliest novels; that the device of the interchapter is a ubiquitous element in most of the novels? In short, what shall we make of the truth this study demonstrates from the fact that Steinbeck uses and reuses a limited set of structures and structural devices and evidences rather persistent trouble in fusing them with particular materials? At the least, some certainty that Steinbeck's *modus operandi* is of a piece would appear to eliminate a simple or total reliance on the presumption of a "decline and fall." Precisely that presumption may be the rationale for the plainly mistaken conclusion that Steinbeck's longer fiction is not of a piece. The novels are either better or worse. They are, however, recognizably the work of a single, unique intelligence.

Steinbeck's weakness has been the focus of this study. In spite of this concentration on his failings, the focus is positive, not negative. To know in substantial detail what a characteristic weakness is permits a more compelling, a less defensive praise of what is best in the longer fiction. Thus, I have been enabled to praise Steinbeck's work, not *en passant*, but as an integral part of this study. We can best praise the best when we know why it is the best.

I do not hesitate to claim that this study will enhance, not harm, Steinbeck's reputation, for the candid reader may draw from it a sensible knowledge of Steinbeck's art and appreciate the essential unity of that art and its relevance to all of Steinbeck's longer fiction. Such knowledge is the necessary basis for perceiving the justice of evaluative judgments that rest on the accuracy, the soundness, the completeness of the evidence. Genuine distinctions of value need to claim that solid basis. I have made the claim; I trust the result is worthy.

Selected Works by John Steinbeck

Books

Cup of Gold: A Life of Sir Henry Morgan, with Occasional Reference to History (New York: Robert M. McBride Co., Inc., 1929.

The Pastures of Heaven (New York: Brewer, Warren & Putnam, 1932).

To a God Unknown (New York: Robert O. Ballou, 1933).

Tortilla Flat (New York: Covici, Friede, Inc., 1935). Reprinted by The Modern Library, with a Foreword by Steinbeck, 1937.

In Dubious Battle (New York: Covici, Friede, Inc., 1936).

Of Mice and Men (New York: Covici, Friede, Inc., 1937).

The Long Valley (New York: The Viking Press, Inc., 1938).

The Grapes of Wrath (New York: The Viking Press, Inc., 1939).

Sea of Cortez (New York: The Viking Press, Inc., 1941). Written in collaboration with Edward F. Ricketts.

Bombs Away (New York: The Viking Press, Inc., 1942).

The Moon Is Down (New York: The Viking Press, Inc., 1942).

Cannery Row (New York: The Viking Press, Inc., 1945).

The Viking Portable Steinbeck (New York: The Viking Press, Inc., 1946).

The Pearl (New York: The Viking Press, Inc., 1947). First publication: "The Pearl of the World," *Woman's Home Companion*, 72 (December 1945), 17ff.

The Wayward Bus (New York: The Viking Press, Inc., 1947).

A Russian Journal (New York: The Viking Press, Inc., 1948).

Burning Bright (New York: The Viking Press, Inc., 1950).

The Log from the Sea of Cortez (New York: The Viking Press, Inc., 1951).

East of Eden (New York: The Viking Press, Inc., 1952).

The Short Novels of John Steinbeck (New York: The Viking Press, Inc., 1953).

Sweet Thursday (New York: The Viking Press, Inc., 1954).

The Short Reign of Pippin IV: A Fabrication (New York: The Viking Press, Inc., 1957).

Once There Was a War (New York: The Viking Press, Inc., 1958).

The Winter of Our Discontent (New York: The Viking Press, Inc., 1961).

Travels with Charley (New York: Curtis Publishing Co., 1961).

America and Americans (New York: The Viking Press, Inc., 1966).

Journal of a Novel: The "East of Eden" Letters (New York: The Viking Press, Inc., 1969).

Articles and Essays

"Dubious Battle in California," *The Nation*, 143 (September 12, 1936), 302–4.

"The Harvest Gypsies," *San Francisco News*, October 5–12, 1936.

"... the novel might benefit by the discipline, the terseness ... ," *Stage*, 15 (January 1938), 50–51.

Their Blood Is Strong (San Francisco: Simon J. Lubin Society of California, Inc., April 1938). A pamphlet reprint of the *San Francisco News* articles "The Harvest Gypsies," with an appended epilogue. Reprinted in *A Companion to "The Grapes of Wrath*," ed. Warren French (New York: The Viking Press, Inc., 1963), pp. 53–92.

"Critics, Critics Burning Bright," *The Saturday Review of Literature*, 33 (November 11, 1950), 20–21.

"The Secret Weapon We Were Afraid to Use," *Collier's*, 131 (January 10, 1953), 9–13.

"My Short Novels," *Wings* (October 1953), pp. 1–8.

"How to Tell Good Guys from Bad Guys," *The Reporter*, 12 (March 10, 1955), 42–44.

"How Mr. Hogan Robbed a Bank," *The Atlantic Monthly*, 197 (March 1956), 58–61.